TOP CAREERS FOR

Communications Graduates

Checkmark Books®

An imprint of Facts On File, Inc.

Checkmark Books
An imprint of Facts On File, Inc.
132 West 31st Street
New York NY 10001

Top careers for communications graduates.
    p. cm.—(Top careers)
  Includes bibliographical references and index.
  ISBN 0-8160-5487-8 (pbk. : alk. paper)
    1. Communication—Vocational guidance. I. Facts on File, Inc. II. Series

  P91.6.T67 2003
  302.23'73—dc21   2003055153

Checkmark Books are available at special discounts when purchased in bulk quantities for businesses, associations, institutions, or sales promotions. Please call our Special Sales Department in New York at (212) 967-8800 or (800) 322-8755.

You can find Facts On File on the World Wide Web at http://www.factsonfile.com

Text design by David Strelecky

Cover design by Cathy Rincon

Printed in the United States of America

MP FOF 10 9 8 7 6 5 4 3 2 1

This book is printed on acid-free paper.

CONTENTS

SECTION I

Why Do You Need a College Degree? 3

Introduction: Meet the Communications Major 7

Chapter 1: Your High School Years 10

Chapter 2: Making the Most of Your Experience
as a Communications Major 21

Chapter 3: Taking Your Communications Degree
to Work 33

SECTION II—CAREERS

Advertising Account Executives 49

Advertising Workers 56

Announcers 68

Book Editors 79

College Administrators 87

Columnists 95

Disc Jockeys 101

Event Planners 110

Executive Recruiters 119

Foreign Correspondents 126

Fund-Raisers 134

Health Advocates 142

Literary Agents 149

Lobbyists 154

Magazine Editors 162

Media Planners and Buyers 169

Media Relations Specialists 181

Newspaper Editors 188

Press Secretaries 196

Public Relations Specialists 204

Radio Producers 212

Radio Program Directors 220

Reporters 226

Research Assistants 236

Science and Medical Writers 246

Speech Teachers 256

Sports Broadcasters and Announcers 264

Sports Publicists 275

Sportswriters 280

Technical Writers and Editors 289

Television Directors 301

Television Editors 311

Television Producers 319

Television Program Directors 329

Travel Agents 335

Weather Forecasters 346

Writers 355

Communications Glossary 366

Further Reading 370

Index 371

SECTION I

Why Do You Need a College Degree?

More people are receiving college degrees than ever before. In 2000, more than 1 million students earned their bachelor's degree. By 2001, 58 percent of all individuals between the ages of 25 and 29 had completed some amount of college education. The National Center for Education Statistics reports that 29 percent of this same age group held at least a bachelor's degree.

Since more college graduates are entering the workforce, many employers now require a college degree for jobs that previously had lower educational requirements. This "educational upgrading" has occurred primarily in occupations that are considered desirable and are high paying. Employers want workers with good communication, teamwork, and problem-solving skills. They want workers who are able to learn quickly, who can adapt and adjust to workplace challenges, and who have the desire to excel and achieve. Above all, they want college graduates.

In this book you will read about more than the importance of a college degree. You will also find information on how to define and evaluate your skills and interests, how to choose a college major, how to make the most of your college program, and how to turn your college degree into a satisfying job. This book, in particular, focuses on students interested in studying communications.

Communication—the transfer of a message through signs, symbols, and language—is a fundamental element of any society. Given its importance, the communications field includes careers that are as varied as the means through which people interact. Whether your interests include writing, politics, or even meteorology, this book will help you turn your interests into a promising communications career. Below are brief descriptions of the contents.

SECTION I

Introduction: Meet the Communications Major provides an overview of college majors typically associated with a communications education. It also provides basic information on colleges and universities, suggested courses, skills, potential employers, starting salaries, and further avenues for exploration.

Chapter 1: Your High School Years will help you select a major and prepare for college study while you are still in high school. You will read about suggested courses, self-assessment tests, methods of exploring and choosing a major, and how to choose a college.

Chapter 2: Making the Most of Your College Experience as a Communications Major will help you make the best of your college years—even if you are not sure of a major. Topics include typical communications curricula, the benefits of a minor, methods of exploring careers, and preparing for the workforce.

Chapter 3: Taking Your Communications Degree to Work offers tips on finding your life direction after graduation, job searching, improving your resume, applying for jobs online, and successful interviewing, in addition to advice on whether a graduate degree is right for you.

Section I also includes informative interviews with college professors, administrators, and workers in the field who provide further insight on the communications major and its career options. In this section and throughout the book you will also find helpful sidebars with further information about issues in the field, salary statistics, a list of accredited communications programs, and top cities and employers for the field.

SECTION II

The second half of the book features profiles of 37 careers in the communications field. Each article discusses the occupation in detail.

The **Quick Facts** section provides a brief summary of the career, including recommended school subjects, personal skills, work environment, minimum educational requirements, salary ranges, certification or licensing requirements, and employment outlook. This section also provides acronyms and identification numbers for the following government classification indexes: the Dictionary of Occupational Titles (DOT), the Guide to Occupational Exploration (GOE), the National Occupational Classification (NOC) Index, and the Occupational Information Network (O*NET)-Standard Occupational Classification System (SOC) index. The DOT, GOE, and O*NET-SOC indexes have been created by the U.S. government; the NOC index is Canada's career-classification system. Readers can use the identification numbers listed in the Quick Facts section to access further information on a career. Print editions of the DOT (*Dictionary of Occupational Titles*. Indianapolis, Ind.: JIST Works, 1991) and GOE (*The Complete Guide for Occupational Exploration*. Indianapolis, Ind.: JIST Works, 1993) are available from libraries, and electronic versions of the NOC (http://www23.hrdc-drhc.gc.ca/2001/e/generic/welcome.shtml) and O*NET-SOC (http://online.onetcenter.org) are available on the World Wide Web. When no DOT, GOE, NOC, or O*NET-SOC numbers are present, this means that the U.S. Department of Labor or the Human Resources Development Canada have not created a numerical designation for this career. In this instance, you will see the acronym "N/A," or not available.

The **Overview** section is a brief introductory description of the duties and responsibilities involved in this career. A career may often have a variety of job titles. When this is the case, alternative career titles are presented.

The **History** section describes the history of the particular job as it relates to the overall development of its industry or field.

The Job describes in detail the primary and secondary duties of the job.

Requirements discusses high school and postsecondary education and training requirements, certification or licensing, if necessary, and any other personal requirements for success in the job. The majority of the careers in *Top Careers for Communications Graduates* require a minimum of a bachelor's degree, but we have also included a few careers that may have a minimum educational requirement of a graduate degree. For example, the career of college speech teacher requires a master's or doctorate degree, but individuals with a bachelor's degree may be able to work at a community college.

Conversely, the book includes a few careers that do not require a college degree; however, some college-level communications courses are highly recommended for these positions. Examples include the job of customer sales representative, disc jockey, tour guide, and travel agent.

Exploring offers suggestions on how to gain some experience in or knowledge of the particular job before making a firm educational and financial commitment. While in high school or the early years of college, you can learn about clubs and other activities, for example, that will give you a better understanding of the job.

The **Employers** section gives an overview of typical places of employment for the job and may also include specific employment numbers from the U.S. Department of Labor.

Starting Out discusses the best ways to land your first job, such as through a college placement office, newspaper ads, or personal contacts.

The **Advancement** section describes what kind of career path to expect from the job and how to get there.

Earnings lists salary ranges and describes the typical fringe benefits.

The **Work Environment** section describes the typical surroundings and conditions of employment—whether indoors or outdoors, noisy or quiet, social or independent, and so on. This section also discusses typical hours worked, any seasonal fluctuations, and the stresses and strains of the job.

The **Outlook** section summarizes the job in terms of the general economy and industry projections. For the most part, Outlook information is obtained from the Bureau of Labor Statistics and is supplemented by information taken from professional associations. Job growth terms follow those used in the *Occupational Outlook Handbook:*

- Growth described as "much faster than the average" means an increase of 36 percent or more.
- Growth described as "faster than the average" means an increase of 21 to 35 percent.
- Growth described as "about as fast as the average" means an increase of 10 to 20 percent.
- Growth described as "little change or more slowly than the average" means an increase of 0 to 9 percent.
- "Decline" means a decrease of 1 percent or more.

Each career article concludes with **For More Information,** which lists organizations that can provide career information on training, education, internships, scholarships, and job placement.

At the end of the book there is a glossary of the terms most often associated with the communications field, as well as a list of books that provide more information on communications careers, college preparation, and job seeking.

Whether you are a high school student unsure of a college major, a college student interested in learning more about careers, or an adult thinking of returning to school, this book will help you learn more about the communications major and the career options available to those who pursue it.

MEET THE COMMUNICATIONS MAJOR

WHAT IS COMMUNICATIONS?

Communications refers to the ways in which we exchange and interpret information with one another. Communications students learn the manners and methods that individuals, businesses, and societies use to communicate ideas through outlets such as print media, radio and television broadcasts, the Internet, and public events. Communications studies help us to speed up the exchange of news and information worldwide and make subsequent advances in business and technology.

According to the U.S. Department of Labor, 55,760 communications bachelor's degrees were awarded in 2000. In addition, 5,169 master's degrees were granted that year, and 347 students earned doctorates. To view a list of colleges offering bachelor's degree communications programs in the United States, visit Universities.com (http://www.universities.com). Schools offering master's degrees and Ph.D.'s in communications are listed at Gradschools.com (http://www.gradschools.com).

WHAT COURSES WILL I TAKE?

Because a communications major is applicable in so many arenas, courses will cover many disciplines. Typical course loads include classes in English, journalism, speech, business, and creative writing. Public relations, advertising, marketing, and media studies courses will also likely be required. In addition, government, history, and film courses are an integral part of many communications course loads. General education credits in a variety of areas, such as sociology, psychology, foreign languages, and statistics, are also required for communications majors.

WHAT WILL I LEARN?

The skills that you will develop as a communications major include the ability to write and speak clearly and effectively and to work well both in teams and independently. Communications majors should also be able to analyze and apply information gathered from research and be able to meet deadlines. Staying up to date on changes in technology is also critical in this field. Communications graduates will be expected to have a working knowledge of several computer software programs, including Microsoft Word, Excel, Access, and PowerPoint, as well as QuarkXPress and Adobe Photoshop, among others.

WHERE WILL I WORK AND HOW MUCH WILL I EARN?

A major in communications can be used in a variety of industries, from the media to politics and business. With a bachelor's degree, you can become a journalist, television or radio broadcaster, public relations specialist, or editor. Communications majors also become lobbyists, foreign correspondents, and media planners and buyers, and they work in a variety of other occupations.

Large cities provide the most opportunities for work in this field. The majority of magazines are based in New York City, and publishing companies are based largely in New York and Chicago. Newspapers and radio and television stations are located in thousands of large cities and small towns throughout the United States and around the world. If you hope to write or edit for a website, you will find that many of them are based in California and New York.

The largest employers of communications majors include advertising firms, publishing houses, schools, hospitals, large corporations, government agencies, radio and television stations, newspapers and magazines, and public relations firms. According to the *Winter 2003 Salary Survey* by the National Association of Colleges and Employers, the average starting salary offer for communications majors was $33,267.

FOR MORE INFORMATION

The Internet is is full of information about communications, from college programs to media organizations and job opportunities. The following are a few good sites to explore as you get to know this field.

Advertising Age
http://www.adage.com

American Society of Journalists and Authors
http://www.asja.org

Communications Roundtable
http://www.roundtable.org

Council of Public Relations Firms
http://www.prfirms.org

MediaLine
http://www.medialine.com

Society for Technical Communication
http://www.stc.org

Writers Write
http://www.writerswrite.com

CHAPTER 1

YOUR HIGH SCHOOL YEARS

So you're approaching the end of your high school career and aren't sure what to do with your life yet? Decisions about your future, such as choosing a college, a major, and eventually a career, can be intimidating, but don't panic. Whether you realize it or not, your high school experience has already provided you with valuable experience to help you tackle these decisions. Over the past couple of years you have learned much about your interests and strengths and, in turn, you have already begun to narrow down your career choices.

SUGGESTED COURSES

If you are interested in communications as a possible college major and career path, there are several high school classes you can take to prepare you for work in this field. English and speech classes are the most important among these. If your favorite classes involve writing and public speaking, there is a good chance that communications is the right field for you. Some high schools offer journalism courses, which strengthen writing skills and may give you a chance to learn layout programs and broadcasting techniques. Take creative writing and business writing classes if they are available. College application essays and lengthy term papers are just around the corner, and high school is the time to boost your writing skills.

Gaining a solid background in history, government, and current events is also important, as you will be dealing with the public, possibly writing speeches for a prominent politician, or delivering newscasts to millions of viewers. If you think a career in broadcasting may be in your future, take theatre classes to learn how to build and project your voice.

In general, you should take a well balanced college preparatory course load in high school, including science, mathematics, social studies, and foreign language classes. Meet with your guidance counselor to make sure that your courses will adequately prepare you for college admissions and a communications major.

ASSESSMENT TESTS

Test-taking doesn't always have to be a stressful trial to get good grades. Certain tests are available to help you decide what major and careers are right for you. Many of these tests, called self-assessment tests, are best done while you're in high school so you can choose a college and plan your courses accordingly. Typical test questions help you evaluate your college and career options by focusing on your values, interests, academic strengths, and personality. The following are some of the more popular tests available. While some of these, like the SAT, are mandatory for college admissions, others are simply valuable tools that will help you envision your goals. (Note that some of the following require prior registration and a fee. Check the related websites for details.)

- Scholastic Aptitude Test (SAT): The SAT is a three-hour test measuring verbal and mathematical reasoning skills. Many colleges and universities use the SAT as an indicator of academic performance (in addition to grades, class rank, extracurricular activities, the personal essay, and teacher recommendations). Visit http://www.collegeboard.com for more information.

- American College Testing Program (ACT): Similar to the SAT, the ACT is designed to assess high school students' academic abilities and estimate their college performance. The test covers four basic areas: English, math, reading comprehension, and scientific reasoning. For details, visit http://www.act.org.

- Kuder Career Planning System: The Kuder test helps individuals evaluate their interests, skills, and values. Suggested college majors and careers are ranked based on survey responses. For sample tests and more information, visit http://www.kuder.com.

- Myers-Briggs Type Indicator: This assessment test identifies an individual's personality type using four general, but opposite, dispositions: extraversion/introversion, sensate/intuitive, thinking/feeling, and judging/perceiving. Based on responses to test questions, the individual is characterized as one of 16 personality types. Although most organizations charge a fee for this test, you can visit http://www.humanmetrics.com/cgi-win/JTypes1.htm for a free test based on the Myers-Briggs Type Indicator.

- Armed Services Vocational Aptitude Battery (ASVAB): The ASVAB, administered by the U.S. Department of Defense, is a multi-aptitude test available at over 14,000 high schools nationwide. The tests evaluate students' vocabulary skills, reading comprehension, math skills, math reasoning, general science knowledge, shop and technical skills, mechanical knowledge, and knowledge of electronics. Scores are combined to reveal three general scores for verbal, math, and academic ability. See http://asvabprogram.com for more information.

INTERVIEW: Jennifer Follis

Jennifer Follis is a Journalism Lecturer in the College of Communications at the University of Illinois at Urbana-Champaign. Within this communications program are several specific majors: news-editorial journalism, broadcast journalism, advertising, and media studies. Follis spoke with the editors of Top Careers for Communications Graduates *about her program and the journalism major in particular.*

Q. What do you think are the most important personal and professional qualities for communications majors?

A. Clear writing. Integrity. Interest in public affairs.

Q. When the average student enters your communications program, what are their expectations? Are these expectations realistic or unrealistic?

A. Students who enter our program wanting to produce TV entertainment or to be "personalities" are disappointed in our broadcast program because we constantly push news reporting and writing. Our program is public affairs journalism, regardless of the medium.

Likewise, news-editorial majors who really want to work in public relations are disappointed when professors keep steering them to journalism instead. Students should know what they are signing up for when they pick a school. Wishful thinking doesn't work too well. Educational institutions change slowly. You usually can figure out what the programs will be like based on what they currently are.

Q. What is one thing that you don't like about this field (i.e., any misconceptions that students have about the field or other issues)?

A. The blurring of entertainment and journalism is troublesome. Students should understand that being a journalist is not the same as being an on-air personality. Journalism carries a component of public interest that is not the same as curiosity about people's private lives. Students interested in careers in journalism should have an interest in facts and verification and a notion of the public good.

Q. How do you suggest that students find jobs and volunteer opportunities in the field of communications during college so that they have some related experience to put on their resumes?

A. As one alumnus told journalism students at our recent career night, people like to be helpful. Students who have work and volunteer experience are students who asked to be admitted into newsrooms. Knocking on doors and asking for information is vital to success in this field, and is necessary for finding work experience.

Q. Are careers in the communications field stressful?

A. Stress is relative. Deadlines bring stress, but meeting deadlines brings the relief and satisfaction of accomplishment. Students well suited to journalism should see the adventure of asking questions, working as a team, and wanting to get a message out to the public.

Q. Are there any changes in this job market that students should expect?

A. It's hard to say. The market for strong writing and editing skills doesn't seem to diminish, despite the changes in technology.

Q. What is the most important piece of advice that you have to offer communications majors as they graduate and look for jobs?

A. Personal relationships and networks matter in journalism. The best bosses don't hire "job descriptions"; they hire people. That matters a lot in this business.

EXPLORE AND GET YOUR FOOT IN THE DOOR

You can participate in the field of communications long before you decide to major in it. The hands-on aspect of communications (i.e., seeing your writing published or hearing your voice on the radio) is what initially attracts many students to this field of study.

By taking part in some of the following activities, you should get a sense of whether or not the communications field is for you.

- To get a sense of the work skills and talents that this field requires, join your school's newspaper staff as a writer or editor. This will teach you how to conduct interviews with sources, meet deadlines, and write pieces that are polished enough to be published.

- You will gain similar experience by joining the yearbook staff. Yearbooks often include longer, more developed articles than newspapers do, which will allow you to try a different writing style.

- Join the staff of you high school's literary magazine, or consider starting your own if one doesn't already exist. The focus of your writing is up to you (e.g., politics, short stories, current events, etc.), but the important thing is to get experience with writing and having your work published.

- To get a taste of a career in broadcasting, get involved with a television or radio station, either through your school or a local professional station. You may be able to do on-air work at a student-run station, and professional station employees may let you assist with off-air duties.

- Competing on your school's speech and debate team will build your broadcasting voice and strengthen your communication skills.

- Participate in theatre performances through your school and your community to become comfortable speaking in front of others. This is a key skill for communications majors.

- Pursuing leadership positions, such as a student council position, is also very beneficial. This shows college admissions workers that you are a strong communicator and a leader.

- If you have an interest in public affairs, attend school board and city council meetings (and write about them) to become more familiar with politics and government.

- Volunteer to help a local politician with his or her campaign. Your duties may be few, but any sort of experience with public relations that you can get will be helpful.

- Write all that you can, even if it's in a personal journal.

- You may also want to consider attending a summer journalism program. To view a list of programs for high school students, visit the High School Journalism Web page (http://www.highschooljournalism.org/Students/student-programs.htm).

In addition to the above activities, there are several books that can help you decide if a communications career is right for you. *Great Jobs for Communications Majors* (New York: McGraw-Hill Trade, 2001) and *Creating Your Career in Communications and Entertainment* (Sewickley, Pa.: Graphic Arts Technical Foundation, 2001) are two good books on the topic. Additional books are listed in the "Further Reading" section at the end of this book.

Reading communications-related publications will also give you good exposure to this field. Check out *Advertising Age* (http://www.adage.com), *The Public Relations Strategist* (http://www.prsa.org), and, if you hope to become a sports journalist, *Sports Illustrated* (http://www.si.com).

Visit websites such as Creative Writing for Teens (http://www.teenwriting.about.com), High School Journalism (http://www.highschooljournalism.org), and Journalism.org (http://www.journalism.org) to get writing tips and ideas. Also visit the Youth Forum at Writing.com (http://www.writing.com), where you can create an online portfolio of your writing. Broadcast-live.com (http://www.broadcast-live.com) has live radio and television reports from around the world, which will enable you to investigate different forms of broadcast journalism.

THE ROAD TO BECOMING A FRESHMAN—AGAIN

Once your junior year of high school arrives, there's no avoiding it: you must start to narrow down your college choices and tackle the college application process. If this process has your stomach in knots, take a minute to relax and remember that there are many resources to help with your decision. This is the beginning of a very exciting time in your life, so be sure to solicit as much advice and information as possible to help you make informed choices.

Choosing a College

As you begin a new phase of your life after high school, what sorts of things do you hope are in store? Have you always dreamed of going to college far away from home, or would you prefer a school that's close to your current stomping grounds? Is a small, quiet school more your style, or would you feel more at home in a larger, bustling environment?

The right college will provide you with the tools for academic and career success. It will also introduce you to excellent instructors and friends who will make a lasting impression on your life. Picking the wrong college for you is not the end of the world, but it might delay your education or simply make you frustrated or unhappy. In order to make the best decision possible about your future college, be sure to take advantage of the following sources early in your college-exploration process.

Guidance Counselors

Your high school guidance counselor is a great resource for information on colleges and universities, including application deadlines, financial aid, and academic programs. When deciding on a college, some important characteristics to consider are academic programs offered, reputation or ranking, atmosphere (small, intimate college or large, active university), location, costs, and clubs or other student activities.

Sit down with your guidance counselor and make a list of what you're looking for in a school. Save the list and refer back to it often as you learn more about different schools. Keep all your college information organized in a folder or binder so that you can find the appropriate information when you need it.

If college seems out of reach financially, talk to your guidance counselor about financial aid packages. There are a multitude of scholarships, grants, and loans that you may qualify for.

INTERVIEW: Susan Carlson

Susan Carlson is a traffic anchor and general assignment reporter for the CBS2 morning television news in Chicago, Illinois. She spoke with the editors of Top Careers for Communications Graduates *about the communications major and her career.*

Q. What are your primary and secondary job duties?

A. I am the traffic anchor on the CBS2 morning news show and a general assignment reporter. I monitor traffic conditions and report on them frequently throughout the two-hour show. I also work as a general assignment reporter, covering hard news or feature stories for the later newscasts.

Q. How did you train for this job? What was your college major?

A. I majored in communications, with a double concentration of journalism and radio/TV/film and minored in English. My real training came from on-the-job experience provided by internships and an entry-level news position at a small radio station.

Q. Did this major prepare you for your career?

A. I was satisfied with my major. All reporters have to be able to write well, but a journalism degree is not required to get a job in this field.

Q. Did you participate in any internships while you were in college?

A. Yes. I interned both at FOX-TV in Chicago and here at CBS, where I'm working 13 years later!

Q. What are the most important personal and professional qualities for people in your career?

A. To be a reporter, listening and writing skills are most important. To be on TV, you also have to be able to communicate through how you look and speak—facial expression and inflections determine how the story is told.

Q. What is the most important piece of advice that you have to offer college students as they graduate and look for jobs in this field?

A. Don't give up! It's very hard to find a job in broadcast journalism. The opportunities are slim and the candidates are abundant. The people who get those coveted jobs never stopped trying to land one.

Q. What is the future employment outlook for your career?

A. I wish it were better. It's a very tough field to succeed in, with jobs being few and far between. Some people say television news will dwindle in the future as we continue to see growth in the availability of news/information on the Internet. However, I don't necessarily agree. I believe most people would prefer to get their news from a person than a computer. There's a connection there, with viewers tending to feel like they "know" people on television news programs. There will always be a need for good TV journalists/personalities, and there will always be an overabundance of candidates vying for those few jobs.

College Recruiters

Throughout the school year your high school will probably host recruiters from colleges and universities. These recruiters will give presentations on their colleges, providing information on everything from admissions and academic offerings to student housing and extracurricular activities. Recruiters will also provide information on location, cost, and many other important topics. Sign up for all the recruiter visits that you are interested in—you will learn valuable information at these presentations, which should help you narrow your list of schools. Prepare a list of questions to ask the recruiter. This is your chance to gather the information you need to narrow down your college choices, so be sure to address all of the factors that will help you make your decision.

College Fairs

Another helpful way to learn about colleges is to attend college fairs. Representatives from colleges and universities all across the country attend college fairs to provide information and recruit students. Each school's representatives usually set up an information booth, where they hand out information packets and answer students' questions.

The atmosphere at a college fair is fairly relaxed—you should feel comfortable walking up to representatives from all sorts of schools and asking many questions. However, it is a formal gathering, so dress appropriately (don't wear jeans and a T-shirt). College fairs vary in size—there may be 25 school representatives at one college fair and 200 at the next. Your guidance counselor should have information about fairs; also be sure to watch the newspaper for announcements about upcoming fairs.

Before going to a college fair, make a list of the qualities you are looking for in a school. In addition, prepare a list of questions to ask representatives, who should be able to inform you about financial aid, first-year classes, computer facilities, student housing facilities, extracurricular activities, etc.

There are also some questions you should ask that pertain particularly to the communications field, such as:

- What sorts of media opportunities are offered inside and outside of class at your school?
- What sort of alumni contact should I expect here?
- Does your school help students find internships?
- What is your school's job placement rate (particularly for communications majors)?

Be sure to bring a pen and paper to the college fair so that you can keep track of everything you learn. You may also find it helpful to bring a backpack to hold all the college pamphlets you'll pick up. For a list of college fairs, visit http://www.nacac.com/fairs_ncf.html.

Contact Colleges Yourself

Contact college admissions offices directly to obtain their catalogs. You can also view catalogs and other information on colleges at their websites. Visit CollegeSource Online (http://www.college-source.org) to view over 22,000 college catalogs in their entirety.

Campus Visits:
Giving Schools a Test Drive

You probably wouldn't consider buying a car without at least sitting in it and taking it for a test drive. This same philosophy applies to picking a college, since you'll also be investing lots of money and time in your decision. Thus, it is important to schedule a campus visit.

Touring a campus will tell you much more than a college's brochure will. For instance, seeing a school's layout, facilities, and student body firsthand will have a much larger impact on you than a few random pictures ever could. Almost all schools look appealing in their brochures, so only by covering some ground on the campus will you get a true feel for what the school is like.

It is important to schedule a guided campus tour in advance; you won't learn nearly as much if you just show up and wander around the school. Contact the school's admissions department to arrange this appointment. If possible, try to spend at least a full day on campus, and take your tour when classes are in session. Visiting a school when no one is around can drastically alter its atmosphere and your impression of it.

Most schools give you the option of staying overnight in a college dorm, which is a good learning experience. A dorm stay will give you a preview of what your living quarters may be like, as well as a chance to try the meals, check out the laundry facilities, and meet a few people. Once the formal tour is over, feel free to check out any other areas of interest that you haven't seen yet, such as the soccer fields, the churches, a different dorm, or a lecture hall that is used for communications classes.

Have a pen and paper with you throughout your stay so you can take notes. Ask lots of questions, and try to chat with some students besides your tour guide; this will give you a variety of viewpoints on life at that school.

If a college visit is not an option for you, check out Campus-Tours.com (http://www.campustours.com). This website provides virtual campus tours of more than 850 colleges and universities.

LAST, BUT NOT LEAST

Parents, guardians, and teachers will also be willing to help and provide input on your college decision. Listen to everyone's advice, but be sure that your ultimate decision is yours alone.

For more information on choosing the right college, visit:

Adventures in Education (see the "Choosing the Right College" section)
http://www.adventuresineducation.org

College Board
http://www.collegeboard.com

CollegeNet
http://www.collegenet.com

Colleges.com
http://www.colleges.com

College Is Possible
http://www.collegeispossible.org

CollegeLink
http://www.collegelink.com

CollegeNews
http://www.collegenews.org

Princeton Review
http://www.princetonreview.com

CHAPTER 2

MAKING THE MOST OF YOUR EXPERIENCE AS A COMMUNICATIONS MAJOR

Once you've decided on a college, there are a few things to keep in mind to ensure that you have a great experience there. As a communications major, you should be active both inside and outside the classroom. Employers in this field look for candidates who have learned the basics and have gained some real-world experience. Communications majors are becoming increasingly sought after in this age of fast-paced information exchange. According to a study by the National Communication Association, estimates indicate that the average person spends 75 percent of each day communicating in some way. In addition, society relies on media employees more than ever before to deliver fast, accurate news. Given these trends, communications majors have important and demanding jobs ahead of them. The following suggestions should help you prepare for this type of work and truly make the most of your college experience.

SUGGESTED COURSES

College offers many exciting opportunities, both social and academic, and you should take advantage of as many of them as possible. One of the first and most important choices you must make is determining your course schedule. Before you start school, talk to an admissions counselor or member of the communications department about which courses are recommended or required for your major. The course load for communications majors usually contains classes in English, journalism, speech communications, communication theory, media studies, public relations, advertising, and marketing. Courses in political science, economics, history, and business will likely be required, as well. As a communications major, you may also be required to take other specialized courses such as pop culture, creative writing, telecommunications, and media history.

In addition, most colleges require completion of a core curriculum, or general education credits, which covers a wide variety of fields, including foreign languages, psychology, sociology, philosophy, theatre, mathematics, and statistics.

Computer courses are very important in this field, so communications majors must stay current on changes in technology. Classes vary depending on your major. For example, broadcasting majors should become familiar with radio scriptwriting programs, such as EZNews, and editing software, such as Software Audio Workshop. Print journalism majors should learn layout and design software programs, including QuarkXPress, Adobe Photoshop, and Macromedia FreeHand.

All communications majors should be familiar with word processing software (such as Microsoft Word), database and spreadsheet programs (including Microsoft Access and Excel), and presentation programs, such as Microsoft PowerPoint.

Staying on top of current events is very important for communications majors. Since their jobs involve communicating with others and with the public as a whole, communications workers cannot afford to ignore the news.

If you enter college as a general curriculum major and hope to be accepted or transfer into the communications department (some communications programs do not accept students before their junior year), talk with an academic advisor about which specific classes will increase your chances of acceptance. At some schools, students are coded as pre-journalism by academic advisors, and this coding may help (and certainly will not hurt) their chances of being accepted.

DON'T FORGET A MINOR

If you know exactly what you'd like to do after you graduate, consider choosing a more specific minor to supplement your communications degree. For example, if you are set on becoming a foreign correspondent, think about minoring in a foreign language. Even if you're unsure of what to do after college, a minor will make you a more marketable job candidate, as it shows that you have varied interests and experience.

Two things to keep in mind when selecting a minor are the following: how will the minor affect your existing communications workload (be careful not to overload your schedule), and how might the minor be viewed as an asset to future employers?

EXPLORE AND
GET YOUR FOOT IN THE DOOR

Although attending classes and hanging out with friends are important parts of the college experience, you should also accomplish some important career-related tasks. When you graduate and enter the world of work, employers will expect that you've already gotten some work experience in the communications field. Here are a few ways to gain this valuable experience:

- Write or edit for a college or local newspaper. Save clips of your published work; employers may ask for several writing samples.

- Work or volunteer for a politician (if possible, writing speeches or press releases).

- Work for a newsletter or a literary magazine. For example, write stories for your college's alumni newsletter or magazine, or start your own newsletter on a topic that interests you. You may even try asking different academic departments of your school if they need help with brochures and pamphlets, or if the sports department needs help with its media guides and roster booklets. Religious groups may also offer opportunities to help with newsletters.

- If your specialization is broadcast communications, get any job that you can at a radio or television station (college and/or local). Make tapes of your audio, as most broadcasting jobs require audition tapes. Learn how to operate microphones and other equipment.

- Take all kinds of elective writing classes, such as poetry and creative writing.

- Design fliers or pamphlets for an upcoming event, such as a band's performance.

- Enter pieces of your writing in contests (which are held by companies such as Hearst Publications).

- Apply for as many scholarships, internships, and fellowships as you can. For example, if you are offered a Dow Jones Newspaper Fund internship but could not accept it for one reason or another, employers will still be very impressed with the fact that you qualified.

- Tour newspapers, radio stations, and TV stations.

- Design a website.
- Read several newspapers daily and all kinds of books.
- Read other related publications, such as *Publishers Weekly* (http://www.publishersweekly.com), *Journalism and Mass Communication Quarterly* (http://www.gwu.edu/~jmcq), *Advertising Age* (http://www.adage.com), and *The Public Relations Strategist* (http://www.prsa.org).
- Join professional communications organizations that offer opportunities for you to attend conferences and develop professionally. A few to try are The Association for Women in Communications (http://www.womcom.org), The Society of Environmental Journalists (http://www.sej.org), and The National Press Club (http://npc.press.org).
- Pay close attention to all types of media: radio program formats, television newscasts, and website designs, to name a few.
- Attend a summer publishing institute.
- Intern at a market research firm.
- Compile a portfolio containing samples of your published writing, graphics, audio, and ideas for the creative department.

For More Information

Communications Roundtable
http://www.roundtable.org

Dow Jones Newspaper Fund
http://djnewspaperfund.dowjones.com

PR.com
http://www.pr.com

INTERVIEW: Erin Quinn

Erin Quinn is a police/public safety reporter for the San Angelo Standard-Times *in San Angelo, Texas, a town in the western part of the state with a population of 90,000. She has worked there for one-and-a-half years. The* Times *is owned by Scripps-Howard and has a circu-*

lation of 36,000. Quinn spoke with the editors of Top Careers for Communications Graduates *about her experience and about the communications major in general.*

Q. Please briefly describe your primary and secondary job duties.

A. My primary job is developing and maintaining sources within the city police department, sheriff's office, and within the Texas Department of Public Safety. With those sources and the help of a paging service and a police scanner, I am able to always be out at the scene of any major crimes. My secondary job duties are time management and writing the stories. Communication is also key in the newsroom. Because I work nights, I have to be in constant communication with the copy desk when there are late-night major crimes.

Q. How did you train for this job? What was your college major?

A. I majored in editorial journalism at the University of Illinois at Urbana-Champaign. Editorial journalism was really the perfect major: I apply most everything I learned in college to my job.

Working at the *Daily Illini*, the independent college newspaper of the university, was the best training for my job. There, I was able to experience beat-reporting and also deadline-writing. While I had summer internships and attended the journalism classes, I think the daily writing and reporting was the most beneficial.

Q. Did you participate in any internships while you were in college?

A. Yes. I interned at an 8,000-circulation weekly in Ogden, Illinois. I was able to copy edit, take photos, lay out pages, and write everything from obituaries to news, sports, and features. I also interned at a TV station and a radio station because I wanted to understand all aspects of the media, and I wasn't quite sure in college of what facet of the media I wanted to work in.

Q. What are the most important personal and professional qualities for people in your career?

A. Personally, I think you have to be outgoing and have a positive attitude. More than that, you have to be sympathetic and understand that there are real people affected by what you do. I think reporters often get an arrogance about them that disconnects them from the people on which they are reporting. You need to put yourself in their shoes and remember the golden rule. If a reporter does that, I think you will get a mutual respect from the source. Professionally, I think you have to respect your co-workers and their jobs, and realize a newspaper doesn't come together with the work of just one person. Also, I think you need to be organized and always be on top of things. When someone emails or calls with a reaction to your story, don't blow it off. They could become a valuable source or connection to the community with the right response from you.

Also, be nice to everyone. I've gotten some of my best interviews by being friends with the secretary. And, also, it makes you feel better about yourself and enjoy your job more.

Q. What is the most important piece of advice that you have to offer college students as they graduate and look for jobs in this field?

A. Have a positive attitude. Don't get swept up in worrying about the length of your skirt and color of your resume paper. Just go into an interview and be yourself. Remember that human resources people and editors are people too. Don't get intimidated—everyone was once in your spot. The most important thing is to just be real. Also, have confidence in your training and in who you are. Confidence and attitude are everything, and people can see that right when you walk in the door.

Q. What is the future employment outlook for your career?

A. I think there will always be a need for people who give a voice to people with none and have time to investigate questions in government or businesses. I don't know how much longer it will be needed in the form of a newspaper, but I think there will always be a need for journalists.

PREPARING FOR THE WORKFORCE

Soon after you've completely settled into the college lifestyle, it will be time to start preparing for your next step. You've worked hard all during your college career, and it is just as important to complete these years with a strong finish. The tasks ahead—keeping your grades up in advanced classes while starting your job search, preparing for graduation, deciding where you want to live—can seem daunting. However, if you stay organized, make new and valuable contacts, and start working early on clearly defined goals, the process of wrapping up school and securing a job can be a smooth one.

Using Your Connections

While in college you should make as many contacts in the communications department as possible. Through the wisdom of their experiences, these faculty members can offer you advice on your job search; you may also need them to provide recommendations for job interviews or graduate school applications. Most educators are glad to write recommendation letters, but only if you've made a point to get to know them and proven that you are dedicated, talented, and a hard worker. Try to obtain two or three general letters of recommendation before your graduate. Some schools will even allow you to keep them on file in the career placement office.

Internships/Job Training

Internships are key to obtaining work in the communications field. If a hiring decision comes down to two applicants with similar education and work experiences on their resumes one candidate's internship may be the deciding factor between the two. Students studying communications can inquire directly with the organization (e.g., radio station, television station, newspaper, website, magazine, or government agency) at which they hope to intern, check postings at their school's career-placement center, contact alumni for ideas, and search the Internet for internship listings (see websites listed at the end of this section).

You and your family should prepare for the reality that many internships in the communications field are unpaid or pay very little. To make the most of your internship, ask to sit in on as many meetings as possible. Your responsibilities as an intern may range from filing papers and getting coffee to reporting and writing stories. Some companies offer competitive salaries and let their interns assist with special events, media list development, media contact, and research.

Serving an internship does not guarantee you will be offered a full-time position with the company or organization, but it is good experience that shows potential employers you are familiar with handling the pressures of a communications job.

For More Information

Internship programs.com
http://www.internshipprograms.com

Internships.com
http://www.internships.com

TV Jobs.com
http://www.tvjobs.com

Workinpr.com
http://www.workinpr.com

INTERVIEW: Andrew King

Andrew King is the chair of the communications studies department at Louisiana State University, one of the oldest speech communication departments in the nation. The Department offers both undergraduate and graduate degrees. King spoke with the editors of Top Careers for Communications Graduates *about his program and the communications major in general.*

Q. What types of jobs do communications majors find after college?

A. We've have had great success in the advertising industry—many ad agencies prefer our students because of their grounding in persuasion and applied communication. We have placed a good many students in ad agencies and in public relations. Our students do not learn mere technical strategies, but how to frame a situation, develop problem-solving scenarios, and then shape them for a particular constituency.

We also place a lot of people in publishing, tourism, and in consulting. In developing executive coaches, we have gotten in on the ground floor. Very early on we began to dominate political communication consulting. We do so because we work at the place where marketing, media, textual, and visual analysis all intersect.

Q. What do you think are the most important personal and professional qualities for communications majors?

A. Imagination, a delight in the power and majesty of language, and the ability to find patterns (linguistic, visual, and behavioral). They should also have the ability to move back and forth between high culture and popular culture.

Q. When the average student enters your program, what are their expectations? Are these expectations realistic or unrealistic?

A. Students who come to us are often confused. Frequently they are refugees from other disciplines. They seldom understand the distinction between training and education.

Q. What is the most important piece of advice that you have to offer communications majors as they graduate and look for jobs?

A. Learn as much as you can from each job. Do not make quick judgments, and listen to the stories other employees tell you. Listen to your inner voice. You can't live wholly in dreams, but you cannot live outside of them either.

Q. Are there any misconceptions about this major that you'd like to clear up?

A. [Work in this career] is not about rolling your hat down your arm or doing a bit of the old stockade shuffle to amuse and insinuate yourself upon others. It is about building and maintaining human community through responsible discourse.

Q. Are there any changes in this job market that students should expect?

A. My advice is simple: Things look good for us in a world in which communication is the central human act, but it is always utterly vain to make predictions. Almost all the futurists are wrong. Read the predictions of 20, 30, 40, or 50 years ago. They are completely off the mark. For example, we may be able to predict some of the new technologies that will be developed, but no one knows how we will use them. I recall listening to a speech by Watson about the future of IBM in 1960. "Ever larger communal computers," he said. Thus, they missed the personal computer revolution utterly. In 1820, Josiah Moreland spoke of the ever-growing commerce on British canals. Canals were the future. In 1825, another British invention, the train, was born and by 1850, canals were a small commercial niche. [With that said], become a learner and roll with the punches.

Job Fairs and Corporate Recruiters

Job fairs provide you with an opportunity to make contacts in the communications field. The atmosphere at a job fair is formal yet generally relaxed; you should feel comfortable walking up to a recruiter and asking specific questions about job duties or general questions about working in the industry. You won't necessarily get an interview each time you go to a job fair. In fact, you may never get an interview from a job fair; sometimes companies just send representatives to collect good resumes to keep on file for a later date when positions open up. Regardless, it is a good way to get your name out there. Here are a few tips for success at job fairs:

- Bring 15–20 copies of your resume (printed on quality paper) and pass them out to companies that interest you. If you have multiple job objectives, bring multiple versions of your resume (more on this in Chapter 3).

- Bring letters of recommendation from your professors, employers, or internship supervisor to pass out to recruiters. This extra step will show recruiters that you are serious and prepared; the more information recruiters have about you, the better your chances of getting noticed.

- Make an effort to project a friendly and enthusiastic persona; depending on the size and turnout of the job fair, you may get only a minute or two to make an impression on a recruiter.

- When you speak to a corporate recruiter, ask for his or her business card if it seems appropriate. If your conversation was especially promising, make a note to stay in touch with the recruiter and pursue the company further.

- If you set up an interview with a recruiter, send him or her a note to say thank you, and be sure to include a sentence about how interested and excited you are about the company.

For More Information

American Job Fairs
http://www.americanjobfairs.com

CareerFairs.com
http://careerfairs.com

CollegeGrad.com
http://www.collegegrad.com

JobWeb Online Career Fair
http://www.jobweb.com/employ/fairs

The Job Fair, Inc.
http://www.thejobfair.com

Information Interviewing

As you narrow down your career possibilities in college, you will come across questions that may be best answered by communications professionals. A good way to get the facts firsthand is to go straight to the source, that is, the business that interests you, and conducting an information interview.

Information interviewing is a job search tool that is growing in popularity. An information interview is a planned meeting with a professional that a student attends strictly for the purpose of gaining knowledge about the field or a particular position. It is different from a job interview in that you are asking the professional for job advice, but not for a job.

You will want to first do some research and locate several professionals that you would like to interview. When you call to try to set up an interview, make it clear that you are not looking for a job. Prepare for an information interview by learning all you can about the position and the company beforehand. Use the information interview as a chance to learn about a position and a company, not to push your resume onto a professional. Here are some recommended questions:

- I have done some research on this position, and _____ is what I've found. Can you tell me more about what sort of work is done here?
- What is a typical day like at this job?
- What sort of advancement potential does this career have?
- What do you think is most rewarding about your position? Most challenging?
- Why did you decide to work for XYZ organization?
- Who are your major clients? Major competitors?
- How do you suggest that students find jobs in this field?

- When you hire new employees, what do you look for in candidates?
- What additional training or education should I pursue to enhance my potential for finding a position within this field?
- How have you been able to balance the demands of the office with your personal life? Do you often find yourself bringing home additional work that you didn't finish at the office?
- How stressful is this career?
- What is your least favorite aspect of this career?

For More Information

About.com: Informational Interviewing
http://jobsearch.about.com/cs/infointerviews

Career Key: Information Interviewing
http://www.careerkey.org/english/you/information_interviewing.html

Quintessential Careers: Informational Interviewing Tutorial
http://www.quintcareers.com/informational_interviewing.html

CHAPTER 3

TAKING YOUR COMMUNICATIONS DEGREE TO WORK

As college graduation approaches, you may be experiencing some anxiety about entering "the real world," where people go to bed before 2 A.M. and where pizza is only an occasional part of one's diet. Take heart, however, because you're not alone. Many new graduates feel that same sense of confusion and anxiety once they've stepped off the stage with diplomas in hand, because now everyone faces the same tough questions: Where should I go from here? What kind of job will I be able to find?

Before you try to answer these questions, you should do a self-assessment. You've probably taken the tests before (see Chapter 1), whether it was the Myers-Briggs or some other formal assessment. As you take the test this time, your career should be the primary focus. Write down your interests and skills, and then think about particular jobs that might suit your strengths and preferences. Are your writing skills strong, or are you more confident in public speaking and oral communication? Or is it a combination of both?

After writing down and evaluating your skills and interests, consider some of the following questions:

- Do you enjoy working independently, or do you prefer a team-oriented work environment? Do you work best in a silent setting where you set your own pace, or do you thrive with more interaction and supervision?

- Are you good at motivating yourself to get work done in a timely manner? Does a very deadline-oriented position, such as a newspaper or TV spot, thrill you or intimidate you?

- How important is a flexible schedule to you? Would you mind the irregular hours that many media employees work, or would you prefer the 9-to-5 schedule that is more common in public relations firms?

- Are financial rewards (i.e., higher salary) important to you—either out of necessity or desire? You may fantasize about getting your first job at a radio station in a large city, but you'll need to carefully assess whether such a position will provide you with enough money to pay the rent.
- Is personal fulfillment your primary career goal, regardless of the size of your paycheck?

Continue to think of more narrowly focused questions. These answers should lead you to answer the biggest question of all: What type of communication career would suit me best? The key is to keep in mind your given strengths and interests—and be true to them.

JUMP-START YOUR JOB SEARCH

Once you've narrowed your list of job possibilities, you are ready to start your job search. Begin with researching job sites on the Internet, newspaper classifieds, and by calling company human resources departments to inquire about available positions. Your focus here should be on finding companies that are hiring. You should keep track of all of your job-search activities, such as sending resumes, attending interviews, making calls, sending thank-you notes, etc., because you never know how long and involved your job search might become. Update your notes when employers call you back and when you learn that positions have been filled; this will help you narrow down your options and focus on available positions.

NETWORKING

Once you decide on a communications career path, contact the network of contacts you've made over the last few years. Networking is a great way to find out about credible job openings. Spreading the word, and occasionally reminding people, about your job search is the best way to ensure that your communications contacts will keep you in mind when they hear of opportunities in your field.

Start by speaking with family, friends, and professors. Contact old supervisors from summer jobs and internships to touch base and let them know you are now looking for a job. Other alumni in the communications field may also have tips or job leads. Most colleges keep track of alumni activity and can likely offer you information about where communications students have found positions in the past. Your school's office of alumni relations can provide you with alumni contact information, which will enable you to speak with graduates who have been in the workforce for a couple of years. Ask them how they went about finding their first jobs, and if they have any information or tips for you. These alumni may be established professionals in the communications field, and they might recommend you for an available position if one is available in their workplace.

CREATING A RESUME THAT GETS NOTICED

Before you follow up with your contacts, you need to create and fine-tune your resume. Along with your cover letter, the resume serves as your one chance to grab an employer's attention, so be sure that it shines.

The Content

A resume is a one-page document that lists your contact information, educational and work experiences, and the skills and activities that will make you an attractive candidate in the eyes of a prospective employer. Recording your contact information, educational background, and extracurricular activities is the easy part. The challenge is summing up your work experience and job skills to make yourself stand out from the other candidates. The following list offers tips for tackling this crucial part of your resume.

- Write down a list of all the jobs or positions you've held (paid or unpaid) that have fostered your current career goals. Unless you were a manager, leave out your freshman year job at McDonald's.
- Record your job responsibilities. Don't worry about using fancy language to describe your jobs just yet; just be sure to list all the tasks you handled.
- List the skills that you learned from handling these job duties, such as specific computer programs or particular organizational skills. For example, if you worked as an editor on your college newspaper and handled submissions from other columnists, you've gained valuable writing, managerial, and technical experience. Be sure to examine each experience from every possible angle.
- Take a trip to the library or bookstore and pick up a resume guide. These resources should have examples of quality resumes. Look over the job descriptions that are used, and see if any could be applied to your own experience.

■ Return to your list of job duties, and write short sentences using some of the active-language examples found in the resume guide's job descriptions. "Action" words include short, definitive sentence starters like "managed," "organized," and "coordinated." The point here is to be as succinct and effective as possible. Just don't copy verbatim from your resume guide.

The Format

Resumes are usually organized in one of two ways: chronologically or functionally. Look at your resume books and choose the format that you think would work best for you, but note that most employers favor a chronological format. Don't worry about making your resume look stylish or ornate; this will only distract employers from what is really important: your skills.

Keep the layout as clean and uncluttered as possible, and be sure that the type is easy to read (12pt is a standard). Employers sometimes have hundreds of resumes to review for one position, so they won't waste their time trying to decipher a page of small text and long paragraphs. Short bulleted lists offer a concise and easy-to-read format for your work and educational experiences.

Last but not least, feel free to increase the type size on the element you want the employer to remember most: your name!

Share It with Others

Once you're through with this first draft (notice the word "draft"; this should not be your final version), show it to family members, friends, and other connections and ask for suggestions. Write and rewrite until it is the best representation of what you have to offer a company.

Create Several Versions

Before sending out your winning resume, take note: The most successful resumes are the ones that are tailor-made to fit a particular position. That means that every time you apply for a job, you should review your resume and adjust skills and experiences that can apply directly to the position. You are much more likely to be considered for a job if you highlight specific ways in which your past education and experiences can be an asset to the hiring employer. Thus it's a good idea to keep several drafts of your resume on hand, each of which is tailored for a certain type of position.

For example, if you are applying for entry-level editorial positions at a large newspaper and at a small art magazine, you may want to accentuate different aspects of your experience. The newspaper would be interested in your editing and layout work on the campus newspaper, while the arts magazine might want to read more about your minor in art history and the online literary journal you've created and managed. In this job-seeking example, it is a good idea to have two separate resumes that accentuate different skills and experiences.

The Cover Letter

Always include a cover letter with your resume. As with your resume, the letter must be polished and tailored to the job for which you are applying. Address the cover letter to the individual in charge of hiring. If a name is not included in a job listing, call the company to inquire, or visit the company's website and check the staff listings. If you still can't find what you're looking for, addressing the letter to "Human Resources" should get it into the hands of the right person. The heading of the letter should include your name, address, and phone number, as well as the same for the person to whom you're sending it.

Your cover letter should also be concise. The body of the letter should contain three short paragraphs, as follows:

- The first paragraph should mention the position for which you are applying and where you saw the job listing. Employers like to keep track of how and where their applicants learn about positions. For example, a good first paragraph might simply state, "I am applying for the position of Advertising Assistant, which I saw advertised in *The Daily Bugle* on 22 March 2003." If a friend or associate recommended you for the job, you can mention that here, but only if that person gives you permission to do so.

- In the second paragraph, state briefly why the job interests you and why you will be a valuable addition to the company. Do not restate the contents of your resume here: simply touch on one or two of your strongest skills and what you can bring to the position. Most importantly, write with confidence. Avoid phrases like "I think I would be . . ." or "I feel that I . . . ." Rather, state simply, "I will be . . ." and "I am . . . ." Clear and definitive language, as opposed to cluttered equivocation, is more likely to grab the attention of the person reading your cover letter and resume.

- In the third paragraph, encourage the employer to review your resume and provide any additional information that may have been requested in the job listing, such as salary requirements, ability to travel or relocate, etc. Here you can also state that you will follow up on your resume submission, but do this only if you honestly plan to do so by phone or letter. Do not include such a statement if the job listing states that only suitable candidates will be contacted. This is the employer's way of saying, "Don't call us, we'll call you."

Resume Advice from Those Who Trash Them

Companies receive resumes by the handful, by the pile, and occasionally by the ton. The number of resumes that come across a typical hiring manager's desk can be overwhelming, especially during times of slow economic growth. Fortunately for them (but not for the job seekers), many applicants commit glaring errors that send their resume right into the trash bin. The following is the monster.com top-10 list of resume mistakes, reported by the recruiters and hiring managers who see them every workday.

1. Spelling errors, typos, and bad writing

   Fix: Read your resume carefully, use spell check, and have friends and family members look it over for mistakes you might have missed.

2. Too many duties, not enough explanation

   Fix: Instead of simply listing your previous job descriptions, describe your accomplishments. Employers don't need to know exactly what you did at your last job, but instead, they want to hear about the direct results of your efforts. For example, list any improvements you brought to your previous job or department.

3. Employment dates are wrong or missing completely

   Fix: Include time ranges in months or years for all work positions. Explain any gaps in your work history in your cover letter. Employers need dates to verify your experience and gain a sense of your overall work history.

(continues)

Resume Advice from Those Who Trash Them
(continued)

4. You don't seem to know your name and address

   Fix: Double-check your contact information each and every time you update your resume. The whole point of the resume is to get a phone call asking for an interview. Employers will not look you up to contact you.

5. Converted or scanned resume shows formatting errors

   Fix: If you are emailing your resume, save and send it in plain-text (ASCII) format. Even if you send your resume by fax or mail, use plain text because some employers scan resumes for easy browsing. Fancy fonts, boxes, or colors are unnecessary on a professional resume and will only cause problems.

6. Resume organized by function

   Fix: Most employers prefer a chronological resume, where work and school experience is listed by date, over a functional one, where experience is listed by skills or functions performed. Month- or even year-long gaps in employment (which become obvious in chronological resumes) are more common now than in previous years and can be filled with volunteer work or continued education.

7. Too long

   Fix: Highlight only the work and educational experience relevant to the job at hand. Recruiters don't have the time to read long resumes.

8. Too wordy

   Fix: Similar to #7, pare down your work, school, and other descriptions to include just the most important highlights.

9. Unqualified

   Fix: Apply only to jobs for which you are qualified. You're not only wasting the employer's time, you're wasting your own when you apply for positions that require higher degrees or more work experience than you have.

10. Too personal

    Fix: Include your fondness for stamp collecting if you are applying to work in a hobby shop. Otherwise, leave it off your resume. In other words, list only information that is pertinent to the employer and the open position. Listed activities and interests should be included only if they are related to the job.

For More Information

Career-Resumes
http://www.career-resumes.com

CollegeGrad.com
http://www.collegegrad.com/resumes

JobStar: Resumes
http://jobstar.org/tools/resume

JobWeb Guide to Resumes and Interviews
http://www.jobweb.com/Resumes_Interviews

Resume.com
http://www.resume.com

The Resume Place, Inc.
http://www.resume-place.com

APPLYING FOR JOBS ONLINE: SERIOUS INTERNET SURFING

The Internet has revolutionized the way employers and employees find their right match. Not only can you browse jobs online, but you can also apply for them through email. In fact, many employers prefer, if not require, that applicants submit resumes by email. According to a survey by the National Association of Colleges and Employers, 90 percent of employers prefer applicants to respond to job listings online. While it seems resume advice is available in nearly endless quantities, many career-seekers have questions about how to prepare their resumes for email responses to online job postings. Here's a quick list of the things to consider before you hit the Send button:

1. If submitting your resume online, save it as "Text Only" to convert it into ASCII format. This is the only way to guarantee that the recipient of your resume will read it in the manner and format in which you intended. Fonts and automatic formatting that you may have used in a word processing program may not be converted correctly when the resume reaches the desk of an employer. Sending your resume in text-only format also ensures that employers receive your information free from possible attachment viruses. Only send your resume as another type of attachment, such as Microsoft Word, if the ad explicitly states that you should do so.

2. Once you save your resume as text, clean up the body of the email, watching out for new line and section breaks. If you used bullets, use asterisks (*) instead. If you used formatted section breaks, use dashes (—-) to separate sections.

3. When you prepare your email to send to the employer, write your cover letter in the body of the email, then attach the text-only version of your resume. When the employer reads your email, your resume will actually be viewed in the body of the email instead of as a separate attachment.

4. Make sure this text-only resume is as clean and error-free as your original. As one recruiter on the monster.com website puts it, "Do you know what we call people who submit electronic resumes with typos? We call them unemployed."

5. Be sure to mention the name of the position, any job codes that may have been mentioned in the ad, and the words resume and cover letter in the Subject line of the email. The latter is just in case the employer automatically looks for an attachment and overlooks your cover letter in the body of the email.

Some employers enable you to apply for jobs directly from their company websites. If this is the case, follow the directions on the site very closely, and have your cover letter and resume in plain-text format at the ready.

THE PRESCRIPTION FOR A PERFECT INTERVIEW

If all goes well, your well-crafted resume and cover letter will score you a few interviews. These one-on-one encounters with employers can be intimidating, but there is much you can do to prepare before stepping into an employer's office and shaking the hand that may one day feed you. Follow these tips for a successful interview:

1. **Do your homework.** Research the company before your interview so you can better understand the job for which you are applying. With the growth and popularity of the Internet, almost all companies have an online presence. Check out the company's website and explore its departments, services, locations, and other open positions. This research will not only help you to understand the job, but it will enable you to ask more intelligent questions. Be sure to take notes.

2. **Be punctual.** If you can't make it to an interview on time, how is the interviewer going to think you'll be able to make it in to the office on time every morning?

3. **Listen hard . . . then speak up.** When asked a question, carefully consider what the interviewer asked, think a moment, then answer. This sounds simple, but it is often hard to do when under pressure.

4. **Ask away.** Certainly you will want to be attentive to all the interviewer has to say about the company's structure, work environment, and the specifics of the job. But when the tables are turned and it's your time to ask questions, be sure to do so. Have a list of questions made up beforehand covering issues that might not be touched on by the employer. For example: What sort of training will I receive on the job? Who will I be reporting to? How many people will I be working with? This will show that you are truly interested in the job and in getting to know more about the employer.

5. **Be ready to write.** For many communications positions at publishing houses and public relations firms, you may be required to take a writing or editing test. These tests vary in length and depth, and you may be asked to complete one or more as part of your first interview or at a subsequent interview. Some media companies may give you a take-home writing test, and magazines and other employers may give you a design assignment to complete. It might also be useful to bring a few writing samples with you (published articles, pieces from a literary magazine, etc.), but present them only if the employer asks for them or if doing so fits into the flow of the interview. In addition, some companies administer basic tests of computer programs, such as Microsoft Excel, at interviews.

6. **Dress appropriately.** A dark blue or black suit is recommended for most interviews. While what you wear shouldn't score you points with an employer, poor, sloppy dress and overdressing can definitely work against you. Try to get a feel for the atmosphere of the company before your interview by reading their website and by speaking to any people you know who might work there or who know someone who does.

7. **Say thanks.** Your mother was right: Be polite. Always thank the interviewer for his or her time, and follow up with a

handwritten or emailed note that reiterates your gratitude and (when appropriate) your continued interest in the job.

INTERVIEW: Anna Rzewnicki

Anna Rzewnicki is the associate news director at Ohio State University's Fisher College of Business. She has worked at the University for five years. Rzewnicki spoke with the editors of Top Careers for Communications Graduates *about her career.*

Q. What are your job duties?

A. As associate news director, I help reporters make contact with faculty experts who might provide insight for business stories. I also identify, develop, and write stories about the college; this includes faculty and student accomplishments, research results, new initiatives and programs, and outreach and engagement activities. I develop distribution lists based on the appropriate media contact for each story, and send the stories to local, regional, and national media, including trade publications. The stories that I write appear on the college's website, are used in college and university communications materials, and often are incorporated into stories written by reporters about the college or on specific business-related topics.

Q. What was your college major? Did this major prepare you for your career or, in retrospect, would you pursue another major?

A. I have a bachelor of science degree in journalism from Northern Illinois University. My degree provided great preparation for my career, which has included news reporting, photography, freelance writing, feature writing, and media relations/public relations.

Q. Did you participate in any internships while you were in college?

A. Northern Illinois' journalism program included a news service: students managed a beat, including developing story ideas and writing for the news service that was used by area newspapers. I also was a member of several communications-related professional organizations (including the Public Relations Student Society of America) that also provided practical learning opportunities. As a professional, I belong to the National Federation of Press Women.

Q. What are the most important personal and professional qualities for people in your career?

A. Professionals in this field should:

- have a genuine interest in people and a desire to tell their stories

- respect individuals and their uniqueness

- be creative—be able to look at things from several perspectives and connect the right perspective to the target audience

- have a commitment to accuracy, honesty and integrity, and doing the research before going in for the interview

Q. What advice can you give to college students who are about to enter the workplace?

A. They should be prepared to learn from each situation, each interview, and carry that knowledge with them to each new job along their career track. However, preparation begins in their junior and senior year. Students should take every opportunity to write stories—as a freelancer, a volunteer for community organizations, or in any other way that they can gain experience and begin building a file of clips.

THE SITUATIONAL INTERVIEW

When most people think of a job interview, a question-and-answer session between a job seeker and a hiring manager usually comes to mind. However, a new trend in applicant evaluation has emerged. Some employers now look at an individual's ethical makeup as much as his or her education and job experience. In light of recent developments in the working world, with many powerful companies being scrutinized for unethical business practices, employers want to hire good people as much as they want to hire skilled people.

In these situational, or behavioral, interviews, applicants are put through real-life job situations (such as being verbally harassed by an upset customer) and then are analyzed based on their gut instincts, actions, words, and even body language. According to the *Handbook of Industrial and Organizational Psychology,* while the traditional sit-down interview is reported to be approximately seven percent effective in predicting job performance, the situational interview is approximately 54 percent accurate.

Unlike standard interviews, these character evaluations are tough to prepare for. The only thing to do is be yourself, think before you speak and act, and ensure that your responses reflect your years of education and training.

For More Information

Ask the Interview Coach
http://www.asktheinterviewcoach.com

Collegegrad.com: Interviewing Information
http://www.collegegrad.com/intv

Job-interview.net
http://www.job-interview.net

Monster Interview Center
http://interview.monster.com

YOU'VE GOT THE JOB . . . NOW WHAT?

Once you've found that first job, it will take some time to settle in and learn the ropes. Employers won't expect you to know everything on your first day, so don't be too overwhelmed. Remind yourself that your employer hired you because of your abilities and potential.

As you get further into your new career, you will eventually take on more responsibilities and may be allowed to work at a more independent level. As this begins to happen, you should start to think of opportunities for advancement and growth within your field.

There are two main ways to advance in the communications field: by moving laterally, either within your company or by taking a similar, better paying job at another company, and by moving vertically to a more authoritative, higher paying position. In most jobs you will have an annual review with your immediate supervisor. Take this opportunity to discuss your achievements, what your future with the company might entail, and any advice he or she might have to help you grow in your career. Factor the outcome of this conversation into your decisions about where and how to advance your career.

THE GRADUATE FACTOR

Depending on the type of job you hope to get, additional education may be required; for some positions, employers may not even consider applicants who have only a bachelor's degree. Graduate school is not for everyone, but it may be something to think about if you're seeking an advanced position.

A graduate education school for communications majors is not always required or even recommended: It depends entirely on the specific area of communications that you want to specialize in. If you have any interest in graduate school, talk to academic advisors, teachers, and your parents. A graduate degree is more heavily emphasized in certain areas of the field. For example, if you hope to be a lobbyist, you should further your education as much as you can. A communications major who hopes to be a radio broadcaster, however, might not necessarily find that graduate school will lead to career advancement.

You may also find it helpful to get a graduate degree in a complementary field, such as business. According to an article on the Council of Public Relations Firms' website (http://www.prfirms.org/career), public relations firms are increasingly hiring candidates who have their master's in business administration (M.B.A.) degree, as these individuals have experience in business management and communications.

If you are considering pursuing a graduate degree in communications, take the Graduate Record Examination (GRE). This exam is composed of verbal, quantitative, and analytical writing sections on various subjects. Your score on this exam is one of the determining factors as to whether you'll be admitted to graduate school, and it is required by most schools. Visit http://www.gre.org to learn more.

Most schools that award the M.B.A. degree require that you take the Graduate Management Admissions Test (GMAT) before you apply for admission. The GMAT evaluates verbal, mathematical, and analytical writing skills, not business or management skills. For more information on this test and on pursuing the M.B.A. degree, visit http://www.mba.com.

For More Information

Graduate School Guide
http://www.graduateguide.com

Graduate School Directory of Communications Studies: Gradschools.com
http://www.gradschools.com/listings/menus/
   CommStudies_menu.html

Peterson's Graduate Schools and Programs
http://www.petersons.com/GradChannel

CAREERS

ADVERTISING ACCOUNT EXECUTIVES

QUICK FACTS

School Subjects
Business
English
Speech

Personal Skills
Communication/ideas
Helping/teaching

Work Environment
Primarily indoors
Primarily one location

Minimum Education Level
Bachelor's degree

Salary Range
$20,000 to $55,940 to
$150,000+

Certification or Licensing
None available

Outlook
Faster than the
average

DOT
164

GOE
08.01.02

NOC
1122

O*NET-SOC
11-2011.00

OVERVIEW

The *advertising account executive* coordinates and oversees everything related to a client's advertising account and acts as the primary liaison between the agency and the client. Account executives are also responsible for building and maintaining professional relationships among clients and coworkers to ensure the successful completion of major ad campaigns and the assurance of continued business with clients. Advertising account executives and related workers hold 707,000 jobs in the United States.

HISTORY

When the advertising industry formally developed in the late 1800s, advertisers themselves were usually the ones who handled the promotion of their products and services, placing ads in newspapers and magazines in order to reach their customers. As the number of newspapers increased and print advertising became more widespread, however, these advertisers called on specialists who knew how to create and coordinate effective advertisements. One such specialist, the advertising account executive, emerged to produce and handle the ad campaigns for businesses.

Advertising agencies were commonly used by companies by the 1920s, and account executives worked for such agencies. Together with a staff of creative professionals, the account executive was able to develop an advertising "package," including slogans, jingles, and images, as well as a general campaign strategy. In addition, account executives did basic market research, oversaw the elements that went into a campaign, and worked hand-in-hand with writers and artists to develop effective ads for their client companies.

Today, account executives handle all aspects of their clients' ad campaigns. As a result, they bring to the job a broad base of knowledge, including account management, marketing, sales promotion, merchandising, client accounting, print production, public relations, and the creative arts.

THE JOB

Account executives track the day-to-day progress of the overall advertising campaigns of their clients. Together with a staff commonly consisting of a creative director, an art director, a copywriter, researchers, and production specialists, the account executive monitors all client accounts from beginning to end.

Before an advertising campaign is actually launched, a lot of preparatory work is needed. Account executives must familiarize themselves with their clients' products and services, target markets, goals, competitors, and preferred media. Together with the agency team, the account executive conducts research and holds initial meetings with clients. Then the team, coordinated by the account executive, uses this information to analyze market potential and presents recommendations to the client.

After an advertising strategy has been determined and all terms have been agreed upon, the agency's creative staff goes to work, developing ideas and producing various ads to present to the client. During this time, the account executive works with *media buyers* (who purchase radio and television time and publication space for advertising) in order to develop a schedule for the project and make sure that the costs involved are within the client's budget.

When the ad campaign has been approved by the client, production can begin. In addition to supervising and coordinating the work of copywriters, editors, graphic artists, production specialists, and other employees on the agency team, the account executive must also write reports and draft business correspondence, follow up on all client meetings, interact with outside vendors, and ensure that all pieces of the advertising campaign clearly communicate the desired message. In sum, the account executive is responsible for making sure that the client is satisfied. This may require making modifications to the campaign, revising cost estimates and events schedules, and redirecting the efforts of the creative staff.

In addition to their daily responsibilities of tracking and handling clients' advertising campaigns, account executives must also develop and bring in new business, keep up to date on current advertising trends, evaluate the effectiveness of advertising programs, and track sales figures.

REQUIREMENTS
High School

You can prepare for a career as an advertising account executive by taking a variety of courses at the high school level. Basic courses in English, journalism, communication, economics, psychology, business, social science, and mathematics are important for aspiring advertising account executives.

Postsecondary Training

Most advertising agencies hire college graduates whose degrees can vary widely, from English, journalism, or marketing to business administration, speech communications, or fine arts. Courses in psychology, sociology, business, economics, and any art medium are helpful. Some positions require a graduate degree in advertising, art, or marketing. Others may call for experience in a particular field, such as health care, insurance, or retail.

While most employers prefer a broad liberal arts background with courses in marketing, market research, sales, consumer behavior, communication, and technology, many also seek employees who already have some work experience. Those candidates who have completed on-the-job internships at agencies or have developed portfolios will have a competitive edge.

Other Requirements

While account executives do not need to have the same degree of artistic skill or knowledge as art directors or graphic designers, they must be imaginative and understand the communication of art and photography in order to direct the overall progress of an ad campaign. They should also be able to work under pressure, motivate employees, solve problems, and demonstrate flexibility, good judgment, decisiveness, and patience.

Account executives must be aware of trends and be interested in the business climate and the psychology of making purchases. In addition, they should be able to write clearly, make effective presentations, and communicate persuasively. It is also helpful to stay abreast of the various computer programs used in advertising design and management.

EXPLORING

Read publications like *Advertising Age* (http://www.adage.com), *Adweek* (http://www.adweek.com), and *Brandweek* (http://www.brandweek.com) to become familiar with advertising issues, trends, successes, and failures. Visit the Clio Awards website (http://www.clioawards.com). Clios are awards for advertising excellence and given each year in the categories of TV, print, outdoor, radio, integrated media, design, Internet, and student work. The site also has information about advertising and art schools, trade associations, and links to some of the trade magazines of the industry.

To gain practical business experience, become involved with advertising or promotion activities at your school for social events, sports events, political issues, or fund-raising events. If your school newspaper or yearbook has paid advertising, offer to work in ad sales.

EMPLOYERS

More than 700,000 advertising, marketing, promotions, public relations, and sales managers work in the United States. Advertising agencies all across the country and abroad employ advertising account executives. Of the 22,000 agencies in the United States, the large firms located in New York, Chicago, and Los Angeles tend to dominate the advertising industry. However, four out of five organizations employ fewer than 10 people. These "small shops" offer employment opportunities for account executives with experience, talent, and flexibility.

STARTING OUT

Many people aspiring to the job of account executive participate in internships or begin as assistant executives, allowing them to work with clients, study the market, and follow up on client service. This work gives students a good sense of the rhythm of the job and the type of work required of account executives.

College graduates with or without experience can start their job searches in their schools' career placement offices. Staff there can set up interviews and help polish resumes.

The advertising arena is rich with opportunities. When looking for employment, you don't have to target agencies. Instead, search for jobs with large businesses that may employ advertising staff. If you want to work at an agency, you'll find the competition for jobs intense. Once hired, account executives often participate in special training programs that both initiate them and help them to succeed.

ADVANCEMENT

Since practical experience and a broad base of knowledge are often required of advertising account executives, many employees work their way up through the company, from assistant to account executive to account manager and finally to department head. In smaller agencies, where promotions depend on experience and leadership, advancement may occur slowly. In larger firms, management-training programs are often required for advancement. Continuing education is occasionally offered to account executives in these firms, often through local colleges or special seminars provided by professional societies.

EARNINGS

According to the U.S. Department of Labor, advertising account executives earned between $29,210 to $125,880 annually in 2001, with median annual earnings of approximately $55,940. In smaller agencies, the salary may be much lower ($20,000 or less), and in larger firms, it is often much higher (over $150,000). Salary bonuses are common for account executives. Benefits typically include vacation and sick leave, health and life insurance, and a retirement plan.

WORK ENVIRONMENT

It is not uncommon for advertising account executives to work long hours, including evenings and weekends. Informal meetings with clients, for example, frequently take place after normal business hours. In addition, some travel may be required when clients are based in other cities or states or when account executives must attend industry conferences.

Advertising agencies are usually highly charged with energy and are both physically and psychologically exciting places to work. The account executive works with others as a team in a creative environment where a lot of ideas are exchanged among colleagues.

As deadlines are critical in advertising, it is important that account executives possess the ability to handle pressure and stress effectively. Patience and flexibility are also essential, as are organization and time-management skills.

OUTLOOK

The growth of the advertising industry depends on the health of the economy. In a thriving economy in which many new products and services are developed and consumer spending is up, advertising budgets are large. Although the economy has been weaker as of late, the U.S. Department of Labor still predicts that employment for advertising account executives will grow faster than the average for all occupations through the next decade.

Most opportunities for advertising account executives will be in larger cities such as Chicago, New York, and Los Angeles, which enjoy a high concentration of business. Competition for these jobs, however, will be intense. The successful candidate will be a college graduate with a lot of creativity, strong communications skills, and extensive experience in the advertising industry. Those able to speak another language will have an edge because of the increasing supply of products and services offered in foreign markets.

FOR MORE INFORMATION

The AAF combines the mutual interests of corporate advertisers, agencies, media companies, suppliers, and academia. Visit its website to learn more about internships, scholarships, and awards.
American Advertising Federation (AAF)
1101 Vermont Avenue, NW, Suite 500
Washington, DC 20005-6306
Tel: 202-898-0089
Email: aaf@aaf.org
http://www.aaf.org

For industry information, contact:
American Association of Advertising Agencies
405 Lexington Avenue, 18th Floor
New York, NY 10174-1801

Tel: 212-682-2500
http://www.aaaa.org

For information on the practice, study, and teaching of marketing, contact:
American Marketing Association
311 South Wacker Drive, Suite 5800
Chicago, IL 60606
Tel: 800-AMA-1150
http://www.marketingpower.com

ADVERTISING WORKERS

QUICK FACTS

School Subjects
English
Psychology
Speech

Personal Skills
Artistic
Communication/ideas

Work Environment
Primarily indoors
Primarily one location

Minimum Education Level
Bachelor's degree

Salary Range
$18,960 to $44,000 to
$750,000

Certification or Licensing
None available

Outlook
Faster than the
average

DOT
131

GOE
01.01.02

NOC
1122, 5121

O*NET-SOC
41-3011.00

OVERVIEW

Advertising is defined as mass communication paid for by an advertiser to persuade a particular segment of the public to adopt ideas or take actions of benefit to the advertiser. *Advertising workers* perform the various creative and business activities needed to take an advertisement from the research stage, to creative concept, through production, and finally to its intended audience. There are 155,000 advertising sales agents and 100,000 advertising and promotions managers employed in the United States.

HISTORY

Advertising has been around as long as people have been exchanging goods and services. While a number of innovations spurred the development of advertising, it wasn't until the invention of the printing press in the 15th century that merchants began posting handbills in order to advertise their goods and services. By the 19th century, newspapers became an important means of advertising, followed by magazines in the late 1800s.

One of the problems confronting merchants in the early days of advertising was where to place their ads to generate the most business. In response, a number of people emerged who specialized in the area of advertising, accepting ads and posting them conspicuously. These agents were the first advertising workers. As competition among merchants increased, many of these agents offered to compose ads, as well as post them, for their clients.

Today, with intense competition among both new and existing businesses, advertising has become a necessity in the marketing of goods and services alike. At the same time, the advertising worker's job has grown more demanding and complex than ever. With a wide variety of media from which advertisers can choose—including newspapers, magazines, billboards, radio, television, film and video, and the World Wide Web—today's advertising worker must not only develop and create ads and campaigns but keep abreast of current buying and technology trends, as well.

THE JOB

Approximately seven out of every 10 advertising organizations in the United States are full-service operations, offering their clients a broad range of services, including copywriting, graphics and other art-related work, production, media placement, and tracking and follow-up. These advertising agencies may have hundreds of people working in a dozen different departments, while smaller companies often employ just a handful of employees. Most agencies, however, have at least five departments: contact, research, media, creative, and production.

Contact department personnel are responsible for attracting new customers and maintaining relationships with existing ones. Heading the contact department, *advertising agency managers* are concerned with the overall activities of the company. They formulate plans to generate business, by either soliciting new accounts or getting additional business from established clients. In addition, they meet with department heads to coordinate their operations and to create policies and procedures.

Advertising account executives are the contact department employees responsible for maintaining good relations between their clients and the agency. Acting as liaisons, they represent the agency to its clients and must therefore be able to communicate clearly and effectively. After examining the advertising objectives of their clients, account executives develop campaigns or strategies and then work with others from the various agency departments to target specific audiences, create advertising communications, and execute the campaigns. Presenting concepts, as well as the ad campaign at various stages of completion, to clients for their feedback and approval, account executives must have some knowledge of overall marketing strategies and be able to sell ideas.

Working with account executives, employees in the research department gather, analyze, and interpret the information needed to make a client's advertising campaign successful. By determining who the potential buyers of a product or service will be, *research workers* predict which theme will have the most impact, what kind of packaging and price will have the most appeal, and which media will be the most effective.

Guided by a *research director,* research workers conduct local, regional, and national surveys in order to examine consumer preferences and then determine potential sales for the targeted product or service based on those preferences. Researchers also gather information about competitors' products, prices, sales, and advertising methods. To learn what the buying public prefers in a client's product over a competitor's, research workers often distribute samples and then ask the users of these samples for their opinions of the product. This information can then be used as testimonials about the product or as a means of identifying the most persuasive selling message in an ad.

Although research workers often recommend which media to use for an advertising campaign, *media planners* are the specialists who determine which print or broadcast media will be the most effective. Ultimately, they are responsible for choosing the combination of media that will reach the greatest number of potential buyers for the least amount of money, based on their clients' advertising strategies. Accordingly, planners must be familiar with the markets that each medium reaches, as well as the advantages and disadvantages of advertising in each.

Media buyers, often referred to as *space buyers* (for newspapers and magazines), or *time buyers* (for radio and television), do the actual purchasing of space and time according to a general plan formulated by the *media director.* In addition to ensuring that ads appear when and where they should, buyers negotiate costs for ad placement and maintain contact and extensive correspondence with clients and media representatives alike.

While the contact, research, and media departments handle the business side of a client's advertising campaign, the creative staff takes care of the artistic aspects. *Creative directors* oversee the activities of artists and writers and work with clients and account executives to determine the best advertising approaches, gain approval on concepts, and establish budgets and schedules.

Copywriters take the ideas submitted by creative directors and account executives and write descriptive text in the form of headlines, jingles, slogans, and other copy designed to attract the attention of potential buyers. In addition to being able to express themselves clearly and persuasively, copywriters must know what motivates people to buy. They must also be able to describe a product's features in a captivating and appealing way and be familiar with various advertising media. In large agencies, copywriters may be supervised by a copy chief.

Copywriters work closely with art directors to make sure that text and artwork create a unified, eye-catching arrangement. Planning the visual presentation of the client's message, from concept formulation to final artwork, the *art director* plays an important role in every stage of the creation of an advertising campaign. Art directors who work on filmed commercials and videos combine film techniques, music, and sound, as well as actors or animation, to communicate an advertiser's message. In publishing, art directors work with graphic designers, photographers, copywriters, and editors to develop brochures, catalogs, direct mail, and other printed pieces, all according to the advertising strategy.

Art directors must have a basic knowledge of graphics and design, computer software, printing, photography, and filmmaking. With the help of graphic artists, they decide where to place text and images, choose typefaces, and create storyboard ads and videos. Several layouts are usually submitted to the client, who chooses one or asks for revisions until a layout or conceptualization sketch meets with final approval. The art director then selects an illustrator, graphic artist, photographer, or TV or video producer, and the project moves on to the production department of the agency.

Production departments in large ad agencies may be divided into print production and broadcast production divisions, each with its own managers and staff. *Production managers* and their assistants convert and reproduce written copy and artwork into printed, filmed, or tape-recorded form so that they can be presented to the public. Production employees work closely with imaging, printing, engraving, and other art reproduction firms and must be familiar with various printing processes, papers, inks, typography, still and motion picture photography, digital imaging, and other processes and materials.

In addition to the principal employees in the five major departments, advertising organizations work with a variety of staff or freelance employees who have specialized knowledge, education, and skill, including photographers, photoengravers, typographers, printers, telemarketers, product and package designers, and producers of display materials. Finally, rounding out most advertising establishments are various support employees, such as production coordinators, video editors, word processors, statisticians, accountants, administrators, secretaries, and clerks.

The work of advertising employees is fast-paced, dynamic, and ever changing, depending on each client's strategies and budgets and the creative ideas generated by agency workers. In addition to innovative techniques, methods, media, and materials used by agency workers, new and emerging technologies affect the work of everyone in the advertising arena, from marketing executives to graphic designers. The Internet is undoubtedly the most revolutionary medium to hit the advertising scene. Through this worldwide, computer-based network, researchers are able to precisely target markets and clearly identify consumer needs. In addition, the Web pages provide media specialists with a powerful vehicle for advertising their clients' products and services. New technology has also been playing an important role in the creative area. Most art directors, for example, use a variety of computer software programs, and many create and oversee websites for their clients. Other interactive materials and vehicles, such as CD catalogs, touch-screens, multidimensional visuals, and voice-mail shopping, are changing the way today's advertising workers are doing their jobs.

REQUIREMENTS
High School

You can prepare for a career as an advertising worker by taking a variety of courses at the high school level. General liberal arts courses, such as English, journalism, communications, economics, psychology, speech, business, social science, and mathematics, are important for aspiring advertising employees. In addition, those interested in the creative side of the field should take such classes as art, drawing, graphic design, illustration, and art history. Finally, since computers play a vital role in the advertising field, you should become familiar with word processing and layout programs, as well as the World Wide Web.

Postsecondary Training

The American Association of Advertising Agencies notes that most advertising agencies prefer college graduates for entry-level positions. Copywriters are best prepared with a college degree in English, journalism, or communications; research workers need college training in statistics, market research, and social studies; and most account executives have business or related degrees. Media positions are increasingly requiring a college degree in communications or a technology-related area. Media directors and research directors with a master's degree have a distinct advantage over those with only an undergraduate degree. Some research department heads even have doctorates.

While the requirements from agency to agency may vary somewhat, graduates of liberal arts colleges or those with majors in fields such as communications, journalism, business administration, or marketing research are preferred. Good language skills, as well as a broad liberal arts background, are necessary for advertising workers. College students interested in the field should therefore take such courses as English, writing, art, philosophy, foreign languages, social studies, sociology, psychology, economics, mathematics, statistics, advertising, and marketing. Some 900 degree-granting institutions throughout the United States offer specialized majors in advertising as part of their curriculum.

Other Requirements

In addition to the variety of educational and work experiences necessary for those aspiring to advertising careers, many personal characteristics are also important. Although you will perform many tasks of your job independently as an advertising worker, you will also interact with others as part of a team. In addition to working with other staff members, you may be responsible for initiating and maintaining client contact. You must therefore be able to get along well with people and communicate clearly.

Advertising is not a job that involves routine, and you must be able to meet and adjust to the challenges presented by each new client and product or service. The ability to think clearly and logically is important, because commonsense approaches rather than gimmicks persuade people that something is worth buying. You must also be creative, flexible, and imaginative in order to anticipate consumer demand and trends, to develop effective concepts, and to sell the ideas, products, and services of your clients.

Finally, with technology evolving at breakneck speed, keeping up with technological advances and trends is vital. In addition to being able to work with the most current software and hardware, you should be familiar with the Web, as well as with other technology that is shaping and redefining this industry.

EXPLORING

If you aspire to a career in the advertising industry, you can gain valuable insight by taking writing and art courses offered either in school or by private organizations. In addition to the theoretical ideas and techniques that such classes provide, you can actually apply what you learn by working full or part time at local department stores or newspaper offices. Some advertising agencies or research firms also employ students to interview people or to conduct other market research. Work as an agency clerk or messenger may also be available. Participating in internships at an advertising or marketing organization is yet another way to explore the field, as well as to determine your aptitude for advertising work. You may find it helpful to read publications dedicated to this industry, such as *Advertising Age* (http://www.adage.com).

EMPLOYERS

Most advertising workers are employed by advertising agencies that plan and prepare advertising material for their clients on a commission or service fee basis. However, some large companies and nearly all department stores prefer to handle their own advertising. Advertising workers in such organizations prepare advertising materials for in-house clients, such as the marketing or catalog department. They also may be involved in the planning, preparation, and production of special promotional materials, such as sales brochures, articles describing the activities of the organization, or websites. Some advertising workers are employed by owners of various media, including newspapers, magazines, radio and television networks, and outdoor advertising. Workers employed in these media are mainly sales representatives who sell advertising space or broadcast time to advertising agencies or companies that maintain their own advertising departments.

In addition to agencies, large companies, and department stores, advertising services and supply houses employ such advertising specialists as photographers, photoengravers, typographers, printers, product and package designers, display producers, and others who assist in the production of various advertising materials.

Of the 21,000 advertising agencies in the United States, most of the large firms are located in Chicago, Los Angeles, and New York. Employment opportunities are also available, however, at a variety of "small shops," four out of five of which employ fewer than 10 workers each. In addition, a growing number of self-employment and home-based business opportunities are resulting in a variety of industry jobs located in outlying areas rather than in big cities.

STARTING OUT

Although competition for advertising jobs is fierce and getting your foot in the door can be difficult, there are a variety of ways to launch a career in the field. Some large advertising agencies recruit college graduates and place them in training programs designed to acquaint beginners with all aspects of advertising work, but these opportunities are limited and highly competitive.

Instead, many graduates simply send resumes to businesses that employ entry-level advertising workers. Newspapers, radio and television stations, printers, photographers, and advertising agencies are but a few of the businesses that will hire beginners. The *Standard Directory of Advertising Agencies* (New Providence, N.J.: National Register Publishing Company, 2003) lists the names and addresses of ad agencies all across the nation. You can find the directory in almost any public library.

Those who have had work experience in sales positions often enter the advertising field as account executives. High school graduates and other people without experience who want to work in advertising, however, may find it necessary to begin as clerks or assistants to research and production staff members or to copywriters.

ADVANCEMENT

The career path in an advertising agency generally leads from trainee to skilled worker to division head and then to department head. It may also take employees from department to department, allowing them to gain more responsibility with each move. Opportunities abound for those with talent, leadership capability, and ambition.

Management positions require experience in all aspects of advertising, including agency work, communication with advertisers, and knowledge of various advertising media. Copywriters, account executives, and other advertising agency workers who demonstrate outstanding ability to deal with clients and supervise co-workers usually have a good chance of advancing to management positions. Other workers, however, prefer to acquire specialized skills. For them, advancement may mean more responsibility, the opportunity to perform more specialized tasks, and increased pay.

Advertising workers at various department stores, mail order houses, and other large firms that have their own advertising departments can also earn promotions. Advancement in any phase of advertising work is usually dependent on the employee's experience, training, and demonstrated skills.

Some qualified copywriters, artists, and account executives establish their own agencies or become marketing consultants. For these entrepreneurs, advancement may take the form of an increasing number of accounts and/or more prestigious clients.

EARNINGS

Salaries of advertising workers vary depending on the type of work, the size of the agency, its geographic location, the kind of accounts handled, and the agency's gross earnings. Salaries are also determined by a worker's education, aptitude, and experience. The wide range of jobs in advertising makes it difficult to estimate average salaries for all positions.

According to a survey by the National Association of Colleges and Employers, marketing majors entering the job market in 2001 had average starting salaries of $35,000, while advertising majors averaged $29,700.

According to a 2002 salary survey by *Advertising Age,* creative directors at mid-sized advertising agencies (grossing $7.6 to $15 million) earned an average of $124,000 annually. Copywriters at these agencies earned $54,000, account executives earned $47,000, and media directors made $82,000 per year. CEOs at large agencies made more than $270,000 annually, while CEOs at smaller agencies reported yearly earnings of $123,000.

The U.S. Department of Labor's *Occupational Outlook Handbook* reports that the average annual earnings for advertising and promotions managers in 2000 were $53,360. For marketing managers the average was $71,240, sales managers earned $68,520, and public relations managers made $54,540 per year. The lowest paid 10 percent of advertising and promotions managers averaged less than $27,840, while the highest-paid earned more than $137,780. The *2001 National Occupational Employment and Wage Estimates,* also published by the Department of Labor, reported that advertising sales agents earned an average of $36,560 per year; the lowest paid earned less than $18,960 per year and the highest-paid earned more than $88,170 annually.

In advertising agencies, chief executives can earn from $80,000 annually upward to $750,000. In the research and media departments, research directors average $61,000 annually, experienced analysts up to $51,800 per year, media directors between $46,000 and $92,400 annually, and media planners and buyers $27,500 to $32,500 per year. In the creative department, art directors earn between $44,500 and $60,000 or more annually, and creative directors $92,000 per year. Finally, production managers make about $31,000 per year.

In other businesses and industries, individual earnings vary widely. Salaries of advertising workers are generally higher, however, at consumer product firms than at industrial product organizations because of the competition among consumer product producers. The majority of companies offer insurance benefits, a retirement plan, and other incentives and bonuses.

WORK ENVIRONMENT

Conditions at most agencies are similar to those found in other offices throughout the country, except that employees must frequently work under great pressure to meet deadlines. While a traditional 40-hour workweek is the norm at some companies, one-third of the advertising industry's full-time employees report that they work 50 hours or more per week, including evenings and weekends. Bonuses and time off during slow periods are sometimes provided as a means of compensation for unusual workloads and hours.

Although some advertising employees, such as researchers, work independently on a great many tasks, most must function as part of a team. With frequent meetings with coworkers, clients, and media representatives alike, the work environment is usually energized, with ideas being exchanged, contracts being negotiated, and schedules being modified.

Advertising work is fast-paced and exciting. As a result, many employees often feel stressed out as they are constantly challenged to take initiative and be creative. Nevertheless, advertising workers enjoy both professional and personal satisfaction in seeing the culmination of their work communicated to sometimes millions of people.

OUTLOOK

Employment opportunities in the advertising field are expected to increase faster than the average for all industries. Demand for advertising workers will grow as a result of increased production of goods and services, both in the United States and abroad. Network and cable television, radio, newspapers, the Web, and certain other media (particularly interactive vehicles) will offer advertising workers an increasing number of employment opportunities. Some media, such as magazines, direct mail, and event marketing, are expected to provide fewer job opportunities.

Advertising agencies will enjoy faster than average employment growth, as will industries that service ad agencies and other businesses in the advertising field, such as those that offer commercial photography, imaging, art, and graphics services.

At the two extremes, enormous "mega-agencies" and small shops employing up to only 10 workers each offer employment opportunities for people with experience, talent, flexibility, and drive. In addition, self-employment and home-based businesses are on the rise. Many nonindustrial companies, such as banks, schools, and hospitals, will also be creating advertising positions.

In general, openings will become available to replace workers who change positions, retire, or leave the field for other reasons. Competition for these jobs will be keen, however, because of the large number of qualified professionals in this traditionally desirable field. Opportunities will be best for the well-qualified and well-trained applicant. Employers favor college graduates with experience, a high level of creativity, and strong communications skills. People who are not well qualified or prepared for agency work will find the advertising field increasingly difficult to enter. The same is also true for those who seek work in companies that service ad agencies.

FOR MORE INFORMATION

For information on student chapters, scholarships, and internships, contact:
American Advertising Federation
1101 Vermont Avenue, NW, Suite 500
Washington, DC 20005-6306
Tel: 202-898-0089
Email: aaf@aaf.org
http://www.aaf.org

For industry information, contact:
American Association of Advertising Agencies
405 Lexington, 18th Floor
New York, NY 10174-1801

Tel: 212-682-2500
http://www.aaaa.org

For career and salary information, contact:
American Marketing Association
311 South Wacker Drive, Suite 5800
Chicago, IL 60606
Tel: 800-AMA-1150
Email: info@ama.org
http://www.marketingpower.com

The Art Directors Club is an international, nonprofit organization for creative people in advertising, graphic design, interactive media, broadcast design, typography, packaging, environmental design, photography, illustration, and related disciplines.
Art Directors Club
106 West 29th Street
New York, NY 10001
Tel: 212-643-1440
Email: info@adcny.org
http://www.adcny.org

For information on student membership and careers, contact:
Direct Marketing Educational Foundation
1120 Avenue of the Americas
New York, NY 10036-6700
Tel: 212-768-7277
http://www.the-dma.org

The Graphic Artists Guild promotes and protects the economic interests of the artist/designer and is committed to improving conditions for all creators of graphic art and raising standards for the entire industry.
Graphic Artists Guild
90 John Street, Suite 403
New York, NY 10038-3202
Tel: 800-500-2672
Email: pr@gag.org
http://www.gag.org

ANNOUNCERS

QUICK FACTS

School Subjects English Journalism Speech	**Certification or Licensing** None available
	Outlook Decline
Personal Skills Communication/ideas Leadership/management	**DOT** 131
Work Environment Primarily indoors Primarily one location	**GOE** 11.08.03 **NOC** 5231
Minimum Education Level Some postsecondary training	**O*NET-SOC** 27-3011.00
Salary Range $12,000 to $20,270 to $300,000+	

OVERVIEW

Announcers work at television or radio stations, presenting news and commercial messages from a script. They identify the station, announce station breaks, and introduce and close shows. Interviewing guests, making public service announcements, and conducting panel discussions may also be part of the announcer's work. In small stations, the local announcer may keep the program log, run the transmitter, and cue the changeover to network broadcasting as well as write scripts or rewrite news releases. Approximately 71,000 people are employed as announcers and newscasters at radio and television stations in the United States.

HISTORY

Guglielmo Marconi, a young Italian engineer, first transmitted a radio signal in his home in 1895. Radio developed rapidly as people began to comprehend the tremendous possibilities. The stations KDKA in Pittsburgh and WWWJ in Detroit began broadcasting in

1920. Within 10 years, there were radio stations in all the major cities in the United States, and broadcasting became big business. The National Broadcasting Company became the first network in 1926 when it linked together 25 stations across the country. The Columbia Broadcasting System was organized in the following year. In 1934, the Mutual Broadcasting Company was founded. The years between 1930 and 1950 may be considered the zenith of the radio industry. With the coming of television, radio broadcasting took second place in importance as home entertainment—but radio's commercial and communications value should not be underestimated.

Discoveries that led to the development of television can be traced as far back as 1878, when William Crookes invented a tube that produced the cathode ray. Other inventors who contributed to the development of television were: Vladimir Zworykin, a Russian-born scientist who came to the United States at the age of 20 and invented the iconoscope before he was 30; Charles Jenkins, who invented a scanning disk using certain vacuum tubes and photoelectric cells; and Philo Farnsworth, who invented an image dissector. WNBT and WCBW, the first commercially licensed television stations, went on the air in 1941 in New York. Both suspended operations during World War II but resumed them in 1946 when television sets began to be manufactured on a commercial scale.

As radio broadcasting was growing across the country in its early days, the need for announcers grew. They identified the station and brought continuity to broadcast time by linking one program with the next, as well as participating in many programs. In the early days (and even today in smaller stations) announcers performed a variety of jobs around the station. When television began, many radio announcers and newscasters started to work in the new medium. The need for men and women in radio and television broadcasting has continued to grow. Television news broadcasting requires specialized "on-camera" personnel—anchors, television news reporters, broadcast news analysts, consumer reporters, and sports reporters (sportscasters).

THE JOB

Some announcers merely announce; others do a multitude of other jobs, depending on the size of the station. But the nature of their announcing work remains the same. An announcer is engaged in an exacting career. The necessity for finishing a sentence or a program at a precisely planned moment makes this a demanding and often tense career. It is absolutely essential that announcers project a sense of calm to their audiences, regardless of the activity and tension behind the scenes.

The announcer who specializes in reporting the news to the listening or viewing public is called a *newscaster*. This job may require simply reporting facts, or it may include editorial commentary. Employers may grant newscasters the authority to express their opinions on news items or the philosophies of others. Newscasters must make judgments about which news is important and which is not. In some instances they write their own scripts based on facts that are furnished by international news bureaus. In other instances, they read text exactly as it comes in over a teletype machine. They may make as few as one or two reports each day if they work on a major news program, or they may broadcast news for five minutes every hour or half-hour. Their delivery is usually dignified, measured, and impersonal.

The newscaster may specialize in certain aspects of the news, such as economics, politics, or military activity. Newscasters also introduce films and interviews prepared by *news reporters* that provide in-depth coverage and information on the event being reported. *News analysts* are often called *commentators,* and they interpret specific events and discuss how these may affect individuals or the nation. They may have a specified daily slot for which material must be written, recorded, or presented live. They gather information that is analyzed and interpreted through research and interviews and cover public functions such as political conventions, press conferences, and social events.

Smaller television stations may have an announcer who performs all the functions of reporting, presenting, and commenting on the news, as well as introducing network and news service reports.

The announcer who plays recorded music interspersed with a variety of advertising material and informal commentary is called a *disc jockey*. This title arose when most music was recorded on conventional flat records or discs. Today much of the recorded music used in commercial radio stations is on magnetic tape or compact discs. Disc jockeys serve as a bridge between the music itself and the listener. They may perform such public services as announcing the time, the weather forecast, or important news. It can be a lonely job, since many disc jockeys are alone in the studio. But because their job is to maintain the good spirits of their audience and to attract new listeners, disc jockeys must possess the ability to be relaxed and cheerful.

Unlike the more conventional radio or television announcer, the disc jockey is not bound by a written script. Except for the commercial

Advances in Broadcasting

Imagine listening to the radio and browsing through hundreds of stations without ever hearing static. This scenario is now a reality for people all around the world, thanks to the introduction of *satellite radio*—just one of the many advances in broadcasting that have occurred in recent years.

The concept of satellite radio was introduced in 1992, when the Federal Communications Commission (FCC) allotted a spectrum in one of the radio bands (the "S" band) for satellite broadcasting. Satellites that have been placed in orbit more than 22,000 miles above the Earth now enable this type of radio technology. Ground stations transmit signals to these satellites, which bounce the signal back to radio receivers on the ground. These receivers then unscramble the digital signals, which include audio information, as well as additional data including song title, artist, and genre. Satellite radios stations have crystal clear reception (with no static) and there are few, if any, commercials. If listeners choose satellite radio, they do not have access to local stations, but they can access hundreds of other radio stations.

As of March 2003, there were three space-based radio broadcasters: Sirius Satellite Radio, XM Satellite Radio, and WorldSpace. The effects of satellite radio have been compared to cable TV's effect on television when it was introduced 30 years ago. Satellite radio is now available for as little as $9.99 a month, according to How Stuff Works (http://www.howstuffworks.com).

Digital Television (DTV) is another revolutionary advance in broadcasting. Digital televisions have the ability to produce up to 10 percent more detail than regular analog televisions, and all you need is a digital TV receiver and an antenna. The FCC gave each broadcaster a new frequency to use for digital broadcasting, and if the broadcaster chooses, this one channel can be broken into many subchannels. As of March 2003, there were 801 stations that had the capability to broadcast digitally nationwide, according to the National Association of Broadcasters. The association also reports that DTV is now being broadcast in 97.4 percent of households with televisions in the United States. Viewers with access to DTV can also obtain electronic newspapers, telephone directories, and other information that can be translated into digital code. To find out more about digital television, visit http://www.titantv.com or http://www.digitaltelevision.com.

announcements, which must be read as written, the disc jockey's state-ments are usually spontaneous. Disc jockeys usually are not required to play a musical selection to the end; they may fade out a record when it interferes with a predetermined schedule for commercials, news, time checks, or weather reports.

Announcers who cover sports events for the benefit of the listen-ing or viewing audience are known as *sportscasters.* This is a highly specialized form of announcing, as sportscasters must have exten-sive knowledge of the sports that they are covering, plus the ability to describe events quickly and accurately.

Often the sportscaster will spend several days with team mem-bers, observing practice sessions, interviewing people, and research-ing the history of an event or of the teams to be covered. The more information that a sportscaster can acquire about individual team members, the company they represent, tradition of the contest, rat-ings of the team, and community in which the event takes place, the more interesting the coverage is to the audience.

Many radio and television announcers become well known in their communities. They may participate in community activities as masters of ceremonies at banquets and other public events.

REQUIREMENTS
High School

Although there are no formal educational requirements for entering the field of radio and television announcing, most large stations prefer college-educated applicants. This is generally because announcers with broad educational and cultural backgrounds are better prepared to meet a variety of unexpected or emergency situ-ations. The greater the knowledge of geography, history, literature, the arts, political science, music, science, and of the sound and struc-ture of the English language, the greater the announcer's value.

In high school, therefore, you should focus on a college prepara-tory curriculum, according to Steve Bell, a professor of telecom-munications at Ball State University. A former network anchor who now teaches broadcast journalism, he says, "One trend that con-cerns me is that some high schools are developing elaborate radio and television journalism programs that take up large chunks of academic time, and I think that is getting the cart before the horse. There's nothing wrong with one broadcast journalism course or extracurricular activities, but not at the expense of academic hours."

In that college preparatory curriculum, you should learn how to write and use the English language in literature and communication classes, including speech. Subjects such as history, government, economics, and a foreign language are also important.

Postsecondary Training

When it comes to college, having your focus in the right place is essential, according to Professor Bell. "You want to be sure you're going to a college or university that has a strong program in broadcast journalism, where they also put a strong emphasis on the liberal arts core."

Some advocate a more vocational type of training in preparation for broadcast journalism, but Bell cautions against strictly vocational training. "The ultimate purpose of college is to have more of an education than you have from a trade school. It is important to obtain a broad-based understanding of the world we live in, especially if your career goal is to become an anchor."

A strong liberal arts background with emphasis in journalism, English, political science, or economics, as well as a telecommunications or communications major, is advised.

Certification or Licensing

A Federal Communications Commission license or permit is no longer required for broadcasting positions. Union membership may be required for employment with large stations in major cities and is a necessity with the networks. The largest talent union is the American Federation of Television and Radio Artists. Most small stations, however, are nonunion.

Other Requirements

You must have a pleasing voice and personality to be a successful announcer. You must be levelheaded and able to react calmly in the face of a major crisis. People's lives may depend on your ability to remain calm during a disaster. There are also many unexpected circumstances that demand the skill of quick thinking. For example, if guests who are to appear on a program do not arrive or become too nervous to go on the air, you must compensate immediately and fill the airtime. You must smooth over an awkward phrase, breakdown in equipment, or other technical difficulty.

Good diction and English usage, thorough knowledge of correct pronunciation, and freedom from regional dialects are very important.

A factual error, grammatical error, or mispronounced word can bring letters of criticism to station managers.

If you aspire to a career as a television announcer, you must present a good appearance and have no nervous mannerisms. Neatness, cleanliness, and careful attention to the details of proper dress are important. Successful television announcers have a combination of sincerity and showmanship that attracts and captures an audience.

Broadcast announcing is a highly competitive field. Station officials will pay particular attention to taped auditions of your delivery or, in the case of television, to videotaped demos of sample presentations.

EXPLORING

If you are interested in a career as an announcer, try to get a summer job at a radio or television station. Although you will probably not have the opportunity to broadcast, you may be able to judge whether or not the type of work appeals to you as a career.

Any chance to speak or perform before an audience should be welcomed. Join the speech or debate team to build strong speaking skills. Appearing as a speaker or performer can show whether or not you have the stage presence necessary for a career in front of a microphone or camera.

Many colleges and universities have their own radio and television stations and offer courses in radio and television. You can gain valuable experience working at college-owned stations. Some radio stations, cable systems, and TV stations offer financial assistance, internships, and co-op work programs, as well as scholarships and fellowships.

EMPLOYERS

Of the roughly 71,000 announcers working in the United States, almost all are on staff at one of the 13,012 radio stations or 1,686 television stations around the country. Some, however, work on a freelance basis on individual assignments for networks, stations, advertising agencies, and other producers of commercials. Worldwide, as of January 2000, there were an estimated 21,500 television stations and more than 44,000 radio stations.

Some companies own several television or radio stations; some stations belong to networks such as ABC, CBS, NBC, WB, or Fox, while others are independent. While radio and television stations are located throughout the United States, major markets where better paying jobs are found are generally near large metropolitan areas.

STARTING OUT

One way to enter this field is to apply for an entry-level job rather than an announcer position. It is also advisable to start at a small station. Most announcers start in jobs such as production secretary, production assistant, researcher, or reporter in small stations. As opportunities arise, it is common for announcers to move from one job to another. You may be able to find work as a disc jockey, sportscaster, or news reporter. Network jobs are few, and the competition for them is great. You must have several years of experience as well as a college education to be considered for these positions.

You must audition before you will be employed as an announcer. You should carefully select audition material to show a prospective employer the full range of your abilities. In addition to presenting prepared materials, you may be asked to read material that you have not seen previously, such as a commercial, news release, dramatic selection, or poem.

ADVANCEMENT

Most successful announcers advance from small stations to large ones. Experienced announcers usually have held several jobs. The most successful announcers may be those who work for the networks. Usually, because of network locations, announcers must live in or near the country's largest cities.

Some careers lead from announcing to other aspects of radio or television work. More people are employed in sales, promotion, and planning than in performing; often they are paid more than announcers. Because the networks employ relatively few announcers in proportion to the rest of the broadcasting professionals, a candidate must have several years of experience and specific background in several news areas before being considered for an audition. These top announcers generally are college graduates.

EARNINGS

According to a salary survey by the Radio and Television News Directors Association, there is a wide range of salaries for announcers. For radio announcers, the median salary was $22,000 in 2001 with a low of $12,000 and a high of $45,000 or more. For television reporters and announcers, the median salary was $26,000 with a low of $17,000 and a high of $300,000 or more.

The U.S. Bureau of Labor Statistics reported in its *2001 National Occupational Employment and Wage Estimates* that median annual earnings of all announcers in 2001 were $20,270. Salaries ranged from less than $12,630 to $49,850 or more.

For both radio and television, salaries are higher in the larger markets. Salaries are also generally higher in commercial than in public broadcasting. Nationally known announcers and newscasters who appear regularly on network television programs receive salaries that may be quite impressive. For those who become top television personalities in large metropolitan areas, salaries also are quite high.

Most radio or television stations broadcast 24 hours a day. Although much of the material may be prerecorded, announcing staff must often be available and, as a result, may work considerable overtime or split shifts, especially at smaller stations. Evening, night, weekend, and holiday duty may provide additional compensation.

WORK ENVIRONMENT

Work in radio and television stations is usually very pleasant. Almost all stations are housed in modern facilities. The maintenance of technical electronic equipment requires temperature and dust control, and people who work around such equipment benefit from the precautions taken to preserve it.

Announcers' jobs may provide opportunities to meet well-known or celebrity persons. Being at the center of an important communications medium can make the broadcaster more keenly aware of current issues and divergent points of view than the average person.

Announcers and newscasters usually work a 40-hour week, but they may work irregular hours. They may report for work very early in the morning or work late into the night. Some radio stations operate on a 24-hour basis. All-night announcers may be alone in the station during their working hours.

OUTLOOK

Competition for entry-level employment in announcing during the coming years is expected to be keen, as the broadcasting industry always attracts more applicants than are needed to fill available openings. There is a better chance of working in radio than in television because there are more radio stations. Local television stations usually carry a high percentage of network programs and need only a very small staff to carry out local operations.

The U.S. Department of Labor predicts that opportunities for announcers will decline over the next several years due to the slowing growth of new radio and television stations. Openings will result mainly from those who leave the industry or the labor force. The trend among major networks, and to some extent among many smaller radio and TV stations, is toward specialization. Newscasters who specialize in such areas as business, sports, weather, consumer, and health news should have an advantage over other job applicants.

FOR MORE INFORMATION

For information on its summer internship program, contact:
Association of Local Television Stations
1320 19th Street, NW, Suite 300
Washington, DC 20036
Tel: 202-887-1970

For a list of schools offering degrees in broadcasting as well as scholarship information, contact:
Broadcast Education Association
1771 N Street, NW
Washington, DC 20036-2891
Tel: 888-380-7222
Email: beainfo@beaweb.org
http://www.beaweb.org

For college programs and union information, contact:
National Association of Broadcast Employees and Technicians
501 Third Street, NW, 8th Floor
Washington, DC 20001
Tel: 202-434-1254
Email: nabet@nabetcwa.org
http://nabetcwa.org

For broadcast education and scholarship information, contact:
National Association of Broadcasters
1771 N Street, NW
Washington, DC 20036
Tel: 202-429-5300
Email: nab@nab.org
http://www.nab.org

For general information, contact:
National Association of Farm Broadcasters
PO Box 500
Platte City, MO 64079
Tel: 816-431-4032
Email: info@nafb.com
http://nafb.com

For a booklet on careers in cable television, contact:
National Cable Television Association
1724 Massachusetts Avenue, NW
Washington, DC 20036
Tel: 202-775-3550
http://www.ncta.com

For scholarship and internship information, contact:
Radio-Television News Directors Foundation
1600 K Street, NW, Suite 700
Washington, DC 20006-2838
Tel: 202-659-6510
Email: rtnda@rtnda.org
http://www.rtnda.org

BOOK EDITORS

School Subjects Computer science English Journalism	**Certification or Licensing** None available
Personal Skills Artistic Communication/ideas	**Outlook** Faster than the average
Work Environment Primarily indoors Primarily one location	**DOT** 132
Minimum Education Level Bachelor's degree	**GOE** 01.01.01
Salary Range $23,090 to $37,550 to $73,460+	**NOC** 5122
	O*NET-SOC 27-3041.00

OVERVIEW

Book editors acquire and prepare written material for publication in book form. Such formats include trade books (fiction and nonfiction), textbooks, and technical and professional books (which include reference books). A book editor's duties include evaluating a manuscript, accepting or rejecting it, rewriting, correcting spelling and grammar, researching, and fact checking. Book editors may work directly with printers in arranging for proofs and with artists and designers in arranging for illustration matter and determining the physical specifications of the book.

Approximately 122,000 editors work for newspapers, magazines, and book publishers in the United States. Book editors are employed at small and large publishing houses, book packagers (companies that specialize in book production), associations, and government agencies.

HISTORY

Though the origins of publishing remain unknown, experts have proposed that publishing came into existence soon after people developed written language, perhaps in Sumer in approximately 4000 B.C. After it became possible to record information in writing, somebody had to decide which information was worth recording. Technically speaking, the first record-keepers were the first publishers and editors. Some of the first things deemed suitable for publication were accounting records, genealogies, laws, and religious rituals and beliefs.

In the early years of European publishing, the published works were intended for the small, elite group of educated people who could read and afford to buy books. For the most part, these people were clergymen and members of the upper class who had intellectual interests. Publishing was the business of printers, who also often performed what we would now call editorial tasks. Books of that era generally were written and edited in Latin, which was the language of intellectuals. Over time, however, literacy spread and books began to be written in the languages of the countries in which they were published.

Beginning in the 19th century, the various tasks performed by publishing concerns became more specialized. Whereas in early publishing a single person would often perform various functions, in later publishing employees performed a narrow range of tasks. Instead of having a single editor, a publication would have an editorial staff. One person would be responsible for acquisitions, another would copyedit, another would be responsible for editorial tasks that related to production, and so forth.

Editing has also been powerfully affected by technology. Publishing came into existence only after Gutenberg had invented the necessary technology, and it has changed in various ways as technology has developed. The most important recent developments have been those that have made it possible to transfer and edit information rapidly and efficiently. The development of the computer has revolutionized editing, making it possible to write and rewrite texts electronically and transmit corrected stories almost instantaneously from one part of the world to another.

THE JOB

The editorial department is generally the main core of any publishing house. Procedures and terminology may vary from one type of publishing house to another, but there is some general agreement among the essentials. Publishers of trade books, textbooks, and reference books all have somewhat different needs for which they have developed different editorial practices.

The editor has the principal responsibility in evaluating the manuscript. The editor responsible for seeing a book through to publication may hold any of several titles. The highest level editorial executive in a publishing house is usually the *editor in chief* or *editorial director.* The person holding either of these titles directs the overall operation of the editorial department. Sometimes an *executive editor* occupies the highest position in an editorial department. The next level of editor is often the *managing editor,* who keeps track of schedules and deadlines and must know where all manuscripts are at any given time. Other editors who handle copy include the *senior editors, associate editors, assistant editors, editorial assistants,* and *copy editors.*

In a trade-book house, the editor, usually at the senior or associate position, works with manuscripts that he or she has solicited from authors or that have been submitted by known authors or their agents. Editors who seek out authors to write manuscripts are also known as *acquisitions editors.*

In technical/professional book houses, editors commonly do more researching, revising, and rewriting than trade-book editors do. These editors are often required to be skilled in certain subjects. Editors must be sure that the subject is comprehensively covered and organized according to an agreed-upon outline. Editors contract for virtually all of the material that comes into technical/professional book houses. The authors they solicit are often scholars.

Editors who edit heavily or ask an author to revise extensively must learn to be highly diplomatic; the art of author–editor relations is a critical aspect of the editor's job.

When the editor is satisfied with the manuscript, it goes to the copy editor. The copy editor usually does the final editing of the manuscript before it goes to the typesetter. On almost any type of manuscript, the copy editor is responsible for correcting errors of spelling, punctuation, grammar, and usage.

The copy editor marks up the manuscript to indicate where different kinds of typefaces are used and where charts, illustrations, and photos may be inserted. It is important for the copy editor to discover any inconsistencies in the text and to query the author about them. The copy editor then usually acts as a liaison between the typesetter, the editor, and the author as the manuscript is typeset into galley proofs and then page proofs.

In a small house, one editor might do the work of all of the editors described here. There can also be separate fact checkers, proofreaders, style editors (also called line editors), and indexers. An assistant editor could be assigned to do many of the kinds of jobs handled by the senior or associate editors. Editorial assistants provide support for the other editors and may be required to proofread and handle some administrative duties.

REQUIREMENTS
High School

If you have an interest in a career as an editor, the most obvious classes that English, literature, and composition classes will offer good preparation. You should also become comfortable working with word processing programs, either through taking a computer science class or through your own schoolwork. Taking journalism classes will give you the opportunity to practice different writing styles, including short feature pieces and long investigative stories. Take advantage of any clubs or extracurricular activities that will give you a chance to write or edit. Joining the school newspaper staff is a great way to explore different tasks in publishing, such as writing, editing, layout, and printing.

Postsecondary Training

A college degree is a requirement for entry into the field of book editing. For general editing, a degree in English or journalism is particularly valuable, although most degrees in the liberal arts are acceptable. Degrees in other fields, such as the sciences, psychology, mathematics, or applied arts, can be useful in publishing houses that produce books related to those fields. Textbook and technical/professional book houses in particular seek out editors with strengths in certain subject areas.

Other Requirements

Book editors should have a sharp eye for detail and a compulsion for accuracy (of both grammar and content). Intellectual curiosity, self-motivation, and a respect for deadlines are important characteristics for book editors to have. Knowledge of word processing and desktop publishing programs is necessary as well.

It goes without saying that if you are seeking a career in book editing, you should not only love to read, but love books for their own sake, as well. If you are not an avid reader, you are not likely to go far as a book editor. The craft and history of bookmaking itself is also something in which a young book editor should be interested. A keen interest in any subject, be it a sport, a hobby, or an avocation, can lead you into special areas of book publishing.

EXPLORING

As previously mentioned, joining your school's newspaper staff is a great way to explore editing and writing while in high school. Even if your duties are not strictly editorial, gaining experience by writing, doing layout work, or even securing advertisements will help you to understand how the editing stage relates to the entire field of publishing. Joining your school's yearbook staff or starting your own literary magazine are other ways to gain valuable experience.

You might be able to find a part-time job with a local book publisher or newspaper. You could also try to publish your own magazine or newsletter. Combine one of your other interests with your desire to edit. For example, if you are interested in sports, you could try writing and editing your own sports report to distribute to family and friends.

Since editing and writing are inextricably linked, be sure to keep your writing skills sharp. Outside of any class assignments, try keeping a journal. Try to write something every day and gain practice at reworking your writing until it is as good as you can make it. Explore different kinds of writing, such as short stories, poetry, fiction, essays, comedic prose, and plays.

If you are interested in becoming a book editor, you might consider joining a book club. Check Web Magic's list of book clubs at http://www.literature.com. Other interesting book websites, such as http://www.literarymarketplace.com, may be of interest if you'd like to learn more about publishing companies.

EMPLOYERS

Book editors may find employment with small publishing houses, large publishing houses, the federal government, or book packagers, or they may be self-employed as freelancers. The major book publishers are located in larger cities, such as New York, Chicago, Los Angeles, Boston, Philadelphia, San Francisco, and Washington, D.C. Publishers of professional, religious, business, and technical books are dispersed throughout the country. There are approximately 122,000 editors employed in the United States (including book editors and all other editors).

STARTING OUT

New graduates can find editing positions through their local newspaper or through contacts made in college. College career counselors may be able to assist in finding book publishers to apply for jobs. Another option is to simply look them up in the Yellow Pages or Internet and apply for positions directly. Many publishers will advertise job openings on their corporate websites or on job sites such as monster.com. Starting positions are generally at the assistant level and can include administrative duties in addition to basic editing tasks.

ADVANCEMENT

An editor's career path is dependent on the size and structure of the book publisher. Those who start as editorial assistants or proofreaders generally become copy editors. The next step may be a position as a senior copy editor, which involves overseeing the work of junior copy editors, or as a *project editor.* The project editor performs a wide variety of tasks, including copyediting, coordinating the work of in-house and freelance copy editors, and managing the schedule of a particular project. From this position, an editor may move up to become first assistant editor, then managing editor, then editor in chief. As editors advance, they are usually involved in more management work and decision-making. The editor in chief works with the publisher to ensure that a suitable editorial policy is being followed, while the managing editor is responsible for all aspects of the editorial department. Head editors employed by a publisher may choose to start their own editing business, freelancing full time.

WORK ENVIRONMENT

Book editors do most of their work on a computer, either in an office setting or at home. When working alone, the environment is generally quiet to allow the editor to concentrate on the work at hand. Editors also work in teams, allowing for an exchange of ideas and collaboration. They typically work a normal workweek schedule of 40 hours per week, though if a book is near a deadline, they may work longer hours to get assignments done on schedule.

EARNINGS

Earnings for book editors vary based on the size of the employer and the types of books it publishes, geographic location, and experience of the editor. The U.S. Department of Labor reports the median yearly salary for book editors was $37,550 in 2000. For all editors in 2001, the salaries ranged from a low of less than $23,090 to a high of more than $73,460 annually. The median salary for all editors in 2001 was $39,960. In general, editors are paid higher salaries at large companies, in major cities, and on the east and west coasts.

Publishers usually offer employee benefits that are about average for U.S. industry. There are other benefits, however. Most editors enjoy working with people who like books, and the atmosphere of an editorial department is generally intellectual and stimulating. Some book editors have the opportunity to travel in order to attend meetings, to meet with authors, or to do research.

OUTLOOK

According to the U.S. Department of Labor, job growth for writers and editors should be faster than the average, although competition for positions will be strong. The growth of online publishing will increase the need for editors who are Web experts. Other areas where editors may find work include advertising, public relations, and businesses with their own publications, such as company newsletters. Turnover is relatively high in publishing—editors often advance by moving to another firm or by establishing a freelance business. There are many publishers and organizations that operate with a minimal salaried staff and hire freelance editors for everything from project management to proofreading and production.

FOR MORE INFORMATION

Literary Market Place, *published annually by R. R. Bowker, lists the names of publishing companies in the United States and Canada as well as their specialties and the names of their key personnel. For additional information about careers in publishing, contact the following:*

Association of American Publishers
71 Fifth Avenue
New York, NY 10003-3004
Tel: 212-255-0200
http://www.publishers.org

Publishers Marketing Association
627 Aviation Way
Manhattan Beach, CA 90266
Tel: 310-372-2732
Email: info@pma-online.org
http://www.pma-online.org

Small Publishers Association of North America
PO Box 1306
425 Cedar Street
Buena Vista, CO 81211
Tel: 719-395-4790
Email: span@spannet.org
http://www.spannet.org

COLLEGE ADMINISTRATORS

QUICK FACTS

School Subjects
Business
English
Speech

Personal Skills
Helping/teaching
Leadership/management

Work Environment
Primarily indoors
Primarily one location

Minimum Education Level
Bachelor's degree

Salary Range
$33,640 to $61,700 to
$272,200+

Certification or Licensing
None available

Outlook
About as fast as the
average

DOT
090

GOE
11.05.02

NOC
0312

O*NET-SOC
11-9033.00

OVERVIEW

College administrators coordinate and oversee programs such as admissions and financial aid in public and private colleges and universities. They frequently work with teams of people to develop and manage student services. Administrators also oversee specific academic divisions of colleges and universities.

HISTORY

Before the Civil War, most U.S. colleges and universities managed their administration with a president, a treasurer, and a part-time librarian. Members of the faculty often were responsible for the administrative tasks of the day, and there was no uniformity in college admissions requirements.

By 1860, the average number of administrative officers in U.S. colleges was still only four. However, as the job of running an institution expanded in scope in response to ever-increasing student enrollment, the responsibilities of administration began to splinter. After creating positions for registrar, secretary of faculty, chief business officer, and a number of departmental deans, most schools next hired a director of admissions to oversee the application and acceptance of students. In addition, several eastern schools and a few prominent college presidents, Charles Eliot of Harvard and Nicholas Butler of Columbia among them, saw the need to establish organizations whose purpose would be to put an end to the chaos. The College Entrance Examination Board was formed to create standardized college entrance requirements. By 1910, there were 25 leading eastern colleges using the Board's exams. Today, most colleges require that a student submit standardized test scores, such as the SAT or ACT, when applying.

After World War II, returning veterans entered America's colleges and universities by the thousands. With this great influx of students, college administrators were needed to better organize the university system. During this time, financial aid administration also became a major program. Today, as the costs of a college education continue to rise dramatically, college financial aid administrators are needed to help students and parents find loans, grants, scholarships, and work-study programs.

THE JOB

A college administrator's work is demanding and diverse. An administrator is responsible for a wide range of tasks in areas such as counseling services, admissions, alumni affairs, financial aid, academics, and business. The following are some of the different types of college administrators, but keep in mind that this is only a partial list. It takes many administrators in many different departments to run a college.

Many college and university administrators are known as *deans.* Deans are the administrative heads of specific divisions or groups within the university, and are in charge of overseeing the activities and policies of that division. One type of dean is an *academic dean.* Academic deans are concerned with such issues as the requirements for a major, the courses offered, and the faculty hired within a specific academic department or division. The field of academic dean includes such titles as dean of the college of humanities, dean of social and behavioral sciences, and dean of the graduate school, just to name a few. The *dean of students* is responsible for the student-affairs program, often including such areas as student housing, organizations, clubs, and activities.

Registrars prepare class schedules and final exam schedules. They maintain computer records of student data, such as grades and degree requirements. They prepare school catalogs and student handbooks. *Associate registrars* assist in running the school registrar's office.

Recruiters visit high school campuses and college fairs to provide information about their school and to interest students in applying for admission. They develop relationships with high school administrators and arrange to meet with counselors, students, and parents.

Financial aid administrators direct the scholarship, grant, and loan programs that provide financial assistance to students and help them meet the costs of tuition, fees, books, and other living expenses. The administrator keeps students informed of the financial assistance available to them and helps answer student and parent questions and concerns. At smaller colleges, this work might be done by a single person, the *financial aid officer.* At larger colleges and universities, the staff might be bigger, and the financial aid officer will head a department and direct the activities of *financial aid counselors,* who handle most of the personal contact with students.

Other college administrators include *college admissions counselors,* who review records, interview prospective students, and process applications for admission. *Alumni directors* oversee the alumni associations of colleges and universities. An alumni director maintains relationships with the graduates of the college primarily for fundraising purposes.

Such jobs as university *president, vice president,* and *provost* are among the highest-ranking college and university administrative positions. Generally the president and vice president act as high-level managers, overseeing the rest of a college's administration. They handle business concerns, press relations, public image, and community involvement, and they listen to faculty and administration concerns, often casting the final vote on issues such as compensation, advancement, and tenure. At most schools, the provost is in charge of the many collegiate deans. Working through the authority of the deans, the provost manages the college faculty. The provost also oversees budgets, the academic schedule, event planning, and participates in faculty hiring and promotion decisions.

REQUIREMENTS
High School

A well-rounded education is important for anyone pursuing some of the top administrative positions. To prepare for a job in college administration, take accounting and math courses, as you may be dealing with financial records and student statistics. To be a dean of a college, you must have good communication skills, so you should take courses in English literature and composition. Also, speech courses are important, as you'll be required to give presentations and represent your department at meetings and conferences. Follow your guidance counselor's college preparatory plan, which will likely include courses in science, foreign language, history, and sociology.

Postsecondary Training

Education requirements for jobs in college administration depend on the size of the school and the job position. Some assistant positions may not require anything more than a few years of experience in an office. For most jobs in college administration, however, you'll need at least a bachelor's degree. For the top administrative positions, you'll need a master's or a doctorate. A bachelor's degree in any field is usually acceptable for pursuing this career. After you've received your bachelor's, you may choose to pursue a master's in student personnel, administration, or subjects such as economics, psychology, and sociology. Other important studies include education, counseling, information processing, business, and finance. In order to become a college dean, you'll need a doctoral degree and many years of experience with a college or university. Your degree may be in your area of study or in college administration.

Other Requirements

As a college administrator, you should be very organized and able to manage a busy office of assistants. Some offices require more organization than others; for example, a financial aid office handles the records and aid disbursement for the entire student body and requires a director with an eye for efficiency and the ability to keep track of the various sources of student funding. As a dean, however, you'll work in a smaller office, concentrating more on issues concerning faculty and committees, and you'll rely on your diplomatic skills for maintaining an efficient and successful department. People skills are valuable for college deans, as you'll be representing your department both within the university and at national conferences.

Whatever the administrative position, it is important to have patience and tact to handle a wide range of personalities as well as an emotional steadiness when confronted with unusual and unexpected situations.

EXPLORING

To learn something about what the job of administrator entails, talk to your high school principal and superintendent. Also, interview administrators at colleges and universities. Many of their office phone numbers are listed in college directories. The email addresses of the administrators of many different departments, from deans to registrars, are often published on college websites. You should also discuss the career with the college recruiters who visit your high school. Also, familiarize yourself with all the various aspects of running a college and university by looking at college student handbooks and course catalogs. Most handbooks list all the offices and administrators and how they assist students and faculty.

EMPLOYERS

Administrators are needed all across the country to run colleges and universities. Job opportunities exist at public and private institutions, community colleges, and universities both large and small. In a smaller college, an administrator may run more than one department. There are more job openings for administrators in universities serving large student bodies.

STARTING OUT

There are several different types of entry-level positions available in the typical college administrative office. If you can gain part-time work or an internship in admissions or another office while you are still in school, you will have a great advantage when seeking work in this field after graduation. Any other experience in an administrative or managerial position that involves working with people or with computerized data is also helpful. Entry-level positions often involve filing, data processing, and updating records or charts. You might also move into a position as an administrator after working as a college professor. Deans in colleges and universities have usually worked many years as tenured professors.

The department of human resources in most colleges and universities maintains a listing of job openings at the institution and will often advertise the positions nationally. *The Chronicle of Higher Education* (http://www.chronicle.com) is a newspaper with national job listings. The College and University Professional Association for Human Resources (http://www.cupahr.org) also maintains a job list.

ADVANCEMENT

Entry-level positions, which usually require only a bachelor's degree, include *admissions counselors,* who advise students regarding admissions requirements and decisions, and *evaluators,* who check high school transcripts and college transfer records to determine whether applying students may be admitted. Administrative assistants are hired for the offices of registrars, financial aid departments, and deans.

Advancement from any of these positions will depend on the manner in which an office is organized as well as how large it is. One may move up to assistant director or associate director, or, in a larger office, into any specialized divisions such as minority admissions, financial aid counseling, or disabled student services. Advancement also may come through transferring to other departments, schools, or systems.

Workshops and seminars are available through professional associations for those interested in staying informed and becoming more knowledgeable in the field, but it is highly unlikely that an office employee will gain the top administrative level without a graduate degree.

EARNINGS

Salaries for college administrators vary widely among two-year and four-year colleges and among public and private institutions, but they are generally comparable to those of college faculty. According to the U.S. Department of Labor's *2001 National Occupational Employment and Wage Estimates,* the median salary for education administrators was $61,700. The lowest paid 10 percent of administrators earned $33,640 per year, while the highest-paid made $112,620 annually.

According to findings by the CUPA-HR, the following academic deans had these median annual salaries for 2000–2001: dean of medicine, $272,200; dean of engineering, $146,938; dean of arts and sciences, $94,666; and dean of mathematics, $69,449. The CUPA-HR also reports the median annual salary for registrars as $58,241, for dean of students as $67,000, and for director of student activities as $39,292.

According to a study done by the *Chronicle of Higher Education,* the average pay for college presidents was $207,000 a year in 2000. Though college presidents can earn high salaries, they are often not as high as earnings of other top administrators and even some college coaches. For example, competition can drive up the pay for highly desired medical specialists, economics educators, or football coaches.

Most colleges and universities provide excellent benefits packages including health insurance, paid vacation, sick leave, and tuition remission. Higher level administrators such as presidents, deans, and provosts often receive such bonuses as access to special university clubs, tickets to sporting events, expense accounts for entertaining university guests, and other privileges.

WORK ENVIRONMENT

College and universities are usually pleasant places to be employed. Offices are often spacious and comfortable, and the campus may be a scenic, relaxing work setting.

Employment in most administrative positions is usually on a 12-month basis. Many of the positions, such as admissions director, financial aid counselor, and dean of students, require a great deal of direct contact with students, and so working hours may vary according to student needs. It is not unusual for college administrators to work long hours during peak enrollment periods, such as the beginning of each quarter or semester. During these periods, the office can be fast paced and stressful as administrators work to assist as many students as possible. Directors are sometimes required to work evenings and weekends to provide broader student access to administrative services. In addition, administrators are sometimes required to travel to other colleges, career fairs, high schools, and professional conferences to provide information about the school for which they work.

OUTLOOK

The U.S. Department of Labor predicts that overall employment for education administrators will grow about as fast as the average. Competition for these prestigious positions, however, will be stiff. Many faculty at institutions of higher learning have the educational and experience requirements for these jobs. Candidates may face less competition for positions in nonacademic areas, such as admissions or fund-raising. Those who are already working within a department seeking an administrator and those willing to relocate will have the best chances of getting administrative positions.

FOR MORE INFORMATION

For information about publications, current legislation, and membership, contact the following organizations:

American Association of University Administrators
PO Box 261363
Plano, TX 75026-1363
http://www.aaua.org

College and University Professional Association for Human Resources
1233 20th Street, NW, Suite 301
Washington, DC 20036-1250
Tel: 202-429-0311
http://www.cupahr.org

COLUMNISTS

School Subjects	Certification or Licensing
Computer science	None available
English	
Journalism	**Outlook**
	Little change or more
Personal Skills	slowly than the average
Communication/ideas	
Helping/teaching	**DOT**
	131
Work Environment	
Indoors and outdoors	**GOE**
Primarily multiple locations	01.01.03
Minimum Education Level	**NOC**
Bachelor's degree	5123
Salary Range	**O*NET-SOC**
$17,320 to $30,060 to	27-3022.00
$68,020+	

OVERVIEW

Columnists write opinion pieces for publication in newspapers or magazines. Some columnists work for syndicates, which are organizations that sell articles to many media at once.

Columnists can be generalists who write about whatever strikes them on any topic. They generally focus on a specialty, such as government, politics, local issues, health, humor, sports, gossip, or other themes.

Most newspapers employ local columnists or run columns from syndicates. Some syndicated columnists work out of their homes or private offices.

HISTORY

Because the earliest American newspapers were political vehicles, much of their news stories brimmed with commentary and opinion. This practice continued up until the Civil War. Horace Greeley, a popular editor who had regularly espoused partisanship in his *New York Tribune*, was the first to give editorial opinion its own page separate from the news.

As newspapers grew into instruments of mass communication, their editors sought balance and fairness on the editorial pages and began publishing a number of columns with varying viewpoints.

Famous Washington, D.C.-based columnist Jack Anderson is known for bringing an investigative slant to the editorial page. Art Buchwald and Molly Ivins became well known for their satirical look at government and politicians.

The growth of news and commentary on the Internet has only added to the power of columnists.

THE JOB

Columnists often take news stories and enhance the facts with personal opinions and panache. Columnists may also write from their personal experiences. Either way, a column usually has a punchy start, a pithy middle, and a strong, sometimes poignant, ending.

Columnists are responsible for writing columns on a regular basis according to a schedule, depending on the frequency of publication. They may write a column daily, weekly, quarterly, or monthly. Like other journalists, they face pressure to meet a deadline.

Most columnists are free to select their own story ideas. The need to constantly come up with new and interesting ideas may be one of the hardest parts of the job, but also one of the most rewarding. Columnists search through newspapers, magazines, and the Internet, watch television, and listen to the radio. The various types of media suggest ideas and keep the writer aware of current events and social issues.

Next, they do research, delving into a topic much like an investigative reporter would, so that they can back up their arguments with facts.

Finally, they write, usually on a computer. After a column is written, at least one editor goes over it to check for clarity and correct mistakes. Then the cycle begins again. Often a columnist will write a few relatively timeless pieces to keep for use as backups in a pinch, in case a new idea can't be found or falls through.

Most columnists work in newsrooms or magazine offices, although some, especially those who are syndicated but not affiliated with a particular newspaper, work out of their homes or private offices. Many well-known syndicated columnists work out of Washington, D.C.

Newspapers often run small pictures of columnists, called head shots, next to their columns. This, and a consistent placement of a column in a particular spot in the paper, usually gives a columnist greater recognition than a reporter or editor.

REQUIREMENTS
High School

You'll need a broad-based education to do this job well, so take a college prep curriculum in high school. Concentrate on English and
journalism classes that will help you develop research and writing
skills. Keep your computer skills up to date with computer science
courses. History, psychology, science, and math should round out
your education. If you interested in writing about a particular topic,
such as sports, politics, or medicine, take classes that will help you
develop your knowledge in that area. In the future, you'll be able to
draw on this knowledge when you write your column.

Postsecondary Training

As is the case for other journalists, at least a bachelor's degree in
journalism is usually required, although some journalists graduate
with degrees in political science or English. Experience may be
gained by writing for the college or university newspaper and
through a summer internship at a newspaper or other publication.
It also may be helpful to submit freelance opinion columns to local
or national publications. The more published articles, called "clips,"
you can show to prospective employers, the better.

Other Requirements

Being a columnist requires similar characteristics to those required
for reporters: curiosity, a genuine interest in people, the ability to
write clearly and succinctly, and the strength to thrive under deadline pressure. But as a columnist, you will also require a certain wit
and wisdom, the compunction to express strong opinions, and the
ability to take apart an issue and debate it.

EXPLORING

A good way to explore this career is to work for your school newspaper and perhaps write your own column. Participation in debate
clubs will help you form opinions and express them clearly. Read
your city's newspaper regularly, and take a look at national papers
as well as magazines. Which columnists, on the local and national
level, interest you? Why do you feel their columns are well done?
Try to incorporate these good qualities into your own writing.
Contact your local newspaper and ask for a tour of the facilities. This
will give you a sense of what the office atmosphere is like and what
technologies are used there. Ask to speak with one of the paper's

regular columnists about his or her job. He or she may be able to provide you with valuable insights. Visit the Dow Jones Newspaper
Fund website (http://djnewspaperfund.dowjones.com/fund) for
information on careers, summer programs, internships, and more.
Try getting a part-time or summer job at the newspaper, even if it's
just answering phones and doing data entry. In this way you'll be
able to test out how well you like working in such an atmosphere.

EMPLOYERS

Newspapers of all kinds run columns, as do certain magazines and
even public radio stations, where a tape is played over the airways
of the author reading the column. Some columnists are self-
employed, preferring to market their work to syndicates instead of
working for a single newspaper or magazine.

STARTING OUT

Most columnists start out as reporters. Experienced reporters are the
ones most likely to become columnists. Occasionally, however, a
relatively new reporter may suggest a weekly column if the beat
being covered warrants it, for example, politics.

Another route is to start out by freelancing, sending columns out
to a multitude of newspapers and magazines in the hopes that someone will pick them up. Also, columns can be marketed to syndicates.
A list of these, and magazines that may also be interested in columns,
is provided in the *Writer's Market* (http://www.writersmarket.com).

ADVANCEMENT

Newspaper columnists can advance in national exposure by having
their work syndicated. They also may try to get a collection of their
columns published in book form. Moving from a small newspaper or
magazine to a large national publication is another way to advance.

Columnists also may choose to work in other editorial positions,
such as editor, editorial writer or page editor, or foreign correspondent.

EARNINGS

Like reporters' salaries, the incomes of columnists vary greatly
according to experience, newspaper size and location, and whether
the columnist is under a union contract. But generally, columnists
earn higher salaries than reporters.

The U.S. Department of Labor classifies columnists with news analysts, reporters, and correspondents, and reports that the median
annual income for these professionals was $30,060 in 2001. Ten percent

of those in this group earned less than $17,320, and 10 percent made more than $68,020 annually. According to the *Annual Survey of Journalism & Mass Communication Graduates,* directed by the University of Georgia, the median salary for those who graduated in 2000 with bachelor's degrees in journalism or mass communication was approximately $27,000. Median earnings varied somewhat by employer; for example, those working for weekly papers earned $22,880, while those working for consumer magazines earned $28,236. Although these salary figures are for all journalists (not just columnists), they provide a general range for those working in this field. However, popular columnists at large papers earn considerably higher salaries.

Freelancers may be paid by the column. Syndicates pay columnists 40 percent to 60 percent of the sales income generated by their columns or a flat fee if only one column is being sold.

Freelancers must provide their own benefits. Columnists working on staff at newspapers and magazines receive typical benefits such as health insurance, paid vacation days, sick days, and retirement plans.

WORK ENVIRONMENT

Columnists work mostly indoors in newspaper or magazine offices, although they may occasionally conduct interviews or do research on location out of the office. Some columnists may work as much as 48 to 52 hours a week. Some columnists do the majority of their writing at home or in a private office, and come to the newsroom primarily for meetings and to have their work approved or changed by editors. The atmosphere in a newsroom is generally fast paced and loud, so columnists must be able to concentrate and meet deadlines in this type of environment.

OUTLOOK

The U.S. Department of Labor predicts that employment growth for news analysts, reporters, and correspondents (including columnists) will be slower than the average over the next several years. Growth will be hindered by such factors as mergers and closures of newspapers, decreasing circulation, and lower profits from advertising revenue. Online publications may be a source for new jobs. Competition for newspaper and magazine positions is very competitive, and competition for the position of columnist is even stiffer because these are prestigious jobs that are limited in number. Smaller daily and weekly newspapers may be easier places to find employment than major metropolitan newspapers, and movement up the ladder to columnist will also likely be quicker. Pay, however, is less than at bigger papers. Journalism and mass communication graduates will have the best opportunities, and writers will be needed to replace those who leave the field for other work or retirement.

FOR MORE INFORMATION

For information on careers in newspaper reporting, education, and financial aid opportunities, contact:
American Society of Journalists and Authors
1501 Broadway, Suite 302
New York, NY 10036
Tel: 212-997-0947
Email: info@asja.org
http://www.asja.org

This association provides general educational information on all areas of journalism, including newspapers, magazines, television, and radio.
**Association for Education in Journalism and Mass
  Communication**
234 Outlet Pointe Boulevard
Columbia, SC 29210-5667
Tel: 803-798-0271
Email: aejmc@aejmc.org
http://www.aejmc.org

For information on jobs, scholarships, internships, college programs, and other resources, contact:
National Association of Broadcasters
1771 N Street, NW
Washington, DC 20036
Tel: 202-429-5300
Email: nab@nab.org
http://www.nab.org

The SPJ has student chapters all over the United States and offers information on scholarships and internships.
Society of Professional Journalists (SPJ)
3909 North Meridian Street
Indianapolis, IN 46208
Tel: 317-927-8000
Email: questions@spj.org
http://www.spj.org

DISC JOCKEYS

QUICK FACTS

<table>
<tr><td>School Subjects
English
Journalism
Speech</td><td>Certification or Licensing
None available</td></tr>
<tr><td>Personal Skills
Artistic
Communication/ideas</td><td>Outlook
Decline</td></tr>
<tr><td></td><td>DOT
159</td></tr>
<tr><td>Work Environment
Primarily indoors
Primarily one location</td><td>GOE
01.03.03</td></tr>
<tr><td></td><td>NOC
5231</td></tr>
<tr><td>Minimum Education Level
Some postsecondary training</td><td>O*NET-SOC
27-3011.00</td></tr>
<tr><td>Salary Range
$7,000 to $31,251 to
$100,000</td><td></td></tr>
</table>

OVERVIEW

Disc jockeys (DJs) play recorded music for radio stations or for parties, dances, and special events. On the radio, they intersperse the music with a variety of advertising material and informal commentary. They may also perform such public services as announcing the time, the weather forecast, travel times, or important news. Interviewing guests and making public service announcements may also be part of the DJ's work.

HISTORY

The first major contemporary disc jockey in the United States was Alan Freed (1921–1965), who worked in the 1950s on WINS radio in New York. In 1957, his rock and roll stage shows at the Paramount Theater made front-page news in the *New York Times* because of the huge crowds they attracted. The title "disc jockey" arose originally because most music was recorded on conventional flat records or discs. The term is still in use today, except that much of the recorded music used in commercial radio stations is on magnetic tape or compact disc.

Disc jockeys often play a major role in shaping a radio station's public image. A station's choice of on-air personalities can vary according to timeslots (e.g., high-energy morning DJs versus more sedate late-night personalities), the format of the station (e.g., classical, rock, or R&B), and the demographics of its listeners. DJs that establish a name for themselves and the station they work for are given more creative freedom and often command salaries at the top of the range.

THE JOB

Disc jockeys serve as a bridge between the music itself and the listener. They also perform such public services as announcing the time, the weather forecast, or important news. Working at a radio station can be a lonely job, since often the DJ is the only person in the studio. But because their job is to maintain the good spirits of their audience and attract new listeners, disc jockeys must possess the ability to sound relaxed and cheerful.

Dave Wineland is a disc jockey at WRZQ 107.3 in Columbus, Indiana. He once covered the popular 5:30 to 10 A.M. morning shift that many commuters listen to on their way to work, but now works the afternoon shift. Like many DJs, his duties extend beyond on-the-air announcements. He also works as production director at the station and writes and produces many of the commercials and promotion announcements. "I spend a lot of time in the production room," says Wineland, who also delegates some of the production duties to other DJs on the staff.

Unlike the more conventional radio or television announcer, the disc jockey is not bound by a written script. Except for the commercial announcements, which must be read as it is written, the DJ's statements are usually spontaneous. DJs are not usually required to play a musical selection to the end; they may fade out a record when it interferes with a predetermined schedule for commercials, news, time checks, or weather reports. DJs are not always free to play what they want; at some radio stations, especially the larger ones, the program director or the music director makes the decisions about the music that will be played. And while some stations may encourage their disc jockeys to talk, others emphasize music over commentary and restrict the amount of ad-libbing allowed by DJs.

Top 50 Radio Markets
(in number of listeners)

1. New York, NY
2. Los Angeles, CA
3. Chicago, IL
4. San Francisco, CA
5. Dallas-Ft. Worth, TX
6. Philadelphia, PA
7. Houston–Galveston, TX
8. Washington, DC
9. Boston, MA
10. Detroit, MI
11. Atlanta, GA
12. Miami-Ft. Lauderdale-Hollywood, FL
13. Puerto Rico
14. Seattle-Tacoma, WA
15. Phoenix, AZ
16. Minneapolis-St. Paul, MN
17. San Diego, CA
18. Nassau–Suffolk (Long Island), NY
19. Baltimore, MD
20. St. Louis, MO
21. Tampa-St. Petersburg–Clearwater, FL
22. Denver-Boulder, CO
23. Pittsburgh, PA
24. Portland, OR
25. Cleveland, OH
26. Cincinnati, OH
27. Sacramento, CA
28. Riverside-San Bernadino, CA
29. Kansas City
30. San Jose, CA
31. San Antonio, TX
32. Salt Lake City-Ogden-Provo, UT
33. Milwaukee-Racine, WI
34. Providence-Warwick-Pawtucket, RI
35. Columbus, OH
36. Middlesex-Somerset-Union, NJ
37. Charlotte-Gastonia-Rock Hill, NC
38. Orlando, FL
39. Las Vegas, NV
40. Norfolk-Virginia Beach-Newport News, VA
41. Indianapolis, IN
42. Austin, TX
43. Greensboro–Winston-Salem–High Point, NC
44. New Orleans, LA
45. Nashville, TN
46. Raleigh–Durham, NC
47. West Palm Beach-Boca Raton, FL
48. Memphis, TN
49. Hartford-New Britain-Middletown, CT
50. Jacksonville, FL

Source: Arbitron Inc. (http://www.arbitron.com)

Many DJs have become well-known public personalities in broadcasting; they may participate in community activities and public events.

Disc jockeys who work at parties, weddings, and other special events usually work on a part-time basis. They are often called *party DJs*. A DJ who works for a supplying company receives training, equipment, music, and job assignments from the company. Self-employed DJs must provide everything they need themselves. Party DJs have more contact with people than radio DJs, so they must be personable with clients.

REQUIREMENTS
High School

In high school, you can start to prepare for a career as a disc jockey. A good knowledge of the English language, correct pronunciation, and diction are important. High school English classes as well as speech classes are helpful in getting a good familiarity with the language. Extracurricular activities such as debating and theater will also help with learning good pronunciation and projection.

Many high schools have radio stations on site where students can work as DJs, production managers, or technicians. This experience can be a good starting point to learn more about the field. Dave Wineland's first radio job was at the radio station at Carmel High School in Indianapolis.

Postsecondary Training

Although there are no formal educational requirements for becoming a disc jockey, many large stations prefer applicants with a college education. Some students choose to attend a school specifically for broadcasting, taking courses specific to becoming an announcer. However, students should research the school's reputation by getting references from the school or the local Better Business Bureau. Many other hopeful DJs obtain a more general degree in communications. Like many disc jockeys today, Wineland has a college degree. He earned a degree in telecommunications from Ball State University.

Although there may not be any specific training program required by prospective employers, station officials pay particular attention to an applicant's taped auditions. Companies that hire DJs for parties will often train them; experience is not always necessary if the applicant has a suitable personality.

Other Requirements

Disc jockeys should be levelheaded and able to react calmly even in the face of a crisis. Many unexpected circumstances can arise that demand the skill of quick thinking. For example, if guests who are to appear on a program either do not arrive or become too nervous to go on the air, the DJ must fill the airtime. He or she must also smooth over a breakdown in equipment or some other technical difficulty.

Union membership may be required for employment with large stations in major cities. The largest talent union is the American Federation of Television and Radio Artists. Most small stations, however, hire nonunion workers.

EXPLORING

If a career as a DJ sounds interesting, you might try to get a summer job at a radio station. Although you may not get a chance to work on air, but working behind the scenes will enable you to meet and observe DJs at work. This can help you gauge whether you might like this kind of work, or perhaps another position in the radio field.

Take advantage of any opportunity you get to speak or perform before an audience. Appearing as a speaker or a performer can help you decide whether or not you have the necessary stage presence for a career on the air.

Many colleges and universities have their own radio stations and offer courses in radio. Students can gain valuable experience working at college-owned stations. Some radio stations offer students financial assistance and on-the-job training to students who take on leadership roles and help manage the station. This often takes the form of internships and co-op work programs, as well as scholarships and fellowships.

EMPLOYERS

There has been a steady growth in the number of radio stations in the United States. According to 2002 statistics from the National Association of Broadcasters, the United States alone has 13,296 radio stations.

Radio is a 24-hour-a-day, seven-day-a-week medium, so there are many slots to fill. Most of these stations are small stations where disc jockeys are required to perform many other duties for a lower salary than at larger stations in bigger metropolitan areas.

Due to the Telecommunications Act of 1996, companies can own an unlimited number of radio stations nationwide with an eight-station limit within one market area, depending on the size of the market. When this legislation took effect, mergers and acquisitions changed the face of the radio industry. So, while the pool of employers is smaller, the number of stations continues to rise.

STARTING OUT

One way to enter this field is to apply for an entry-level job, such as an office or production assistant, rather than a job as a disc jockey. It is also advisable to start at a small local station. As opportunities arise, DJs commonly move from one station to another.

While still a high school student, Dave Wineland applied for a position at his local radio station in Monticello, Indiana. "I was willing to work long hours for low pay," he says, acknowledging that starting out in radio can require some sacrifices. However, on-air experience is a must.

DJs must undergo an audition before a station hires them. Audition material should be selected carefully to show the prospective employer the range of the applicant's abilities. A prospective DJ should practice talking aloud, alone, then make a tape of him- or herself with five to seven minutes of material to send to radio stations. The tape should include a news story, two 60-second commercials, and a sample of the applicant introducing and coming out of a record. (Tapes should not include the whole song, just the first and final few seconds, with the aspiring DJ introducing and finishing the music; this is called "telescoping.") In addition to presenting prepared materials, applicants may also be asked to read material that they have not seen previously. This may be a commercial, news release, dramatic selection, or poem.

ADVANCEMENT

Most successful disc jockeys advance from small stations to large ones. The typical experienced DJ will have held several jobs at different types of stations.

Some careers lead from being a DJ to other types of radio or television work. More people are employed in sales, promotion, and planning than in performing, and they are often paid more than DJs.

EARNINGS

The salary range for disc jockeys is extremely broad, with a low of $7,000 and a high of $100,000. The average salary in the late 1990s was $31,251, according to a survey conducted by the National

Association of Broadcasters (NAB) and the Broadcast Cable Financial Management Association.

Smaller market areas and smaller stations fall closer to the bottom of the range, while the top markets and top-rated stations offer DJs higher salaries.

Benefits vary according to the size of the market and station. However, vacation and sick time is somewhat limited because the medium requires that radio personalities be on the air nearly every day.

WORK ENVIRONMENT

Work in radio stations is usually very pleasant. Almost all stations are housed in modern facilities. Temperature and dust control are important factors in the proper maintenance of technical electronic equipment, and people who work around such machinery benefit from the precautions taken to preserve it.

The work can be demanding. It requires that every activity or comment on the air begin and end exactly on time. This can be difficult, especially when the disc jockey has to handle news, commercials, music, weather, and guests within a certain time frame. It takes a lot of skill to work the controls, watch the clock, select music, talk with a caller or guest, read reports, and entertain the audience; often several of these tasks must be performed simultaneously. A DJ must be able to plan ahead and stay alert so that when one song ends he or she is ready with the next song or with a scheduled commercial.

Because radio audiences listen to DJs who play the music they like and talk about the things that interest them, DJs must always be aware of pleasing their audience. If listeners begin switching stations, ratings go down and disc jockeys can lose their jobs.

Disc jockeys do not always have job security; if the owner or manager of a radio station changes, the DJ may lose his or her job. The consolidation of radio stations to form larger, cost-efficient stations has caused some employees to lose their jobs.

DJs may work irregular hours. They may have to report for work at a very early hour in the morning. Sometimes they will be free during the daytime hours, but will have to work late into the night. Some radio stations operate on a 24-hour basis. All-night announcers may be alone in the station during their working hours.

The disc jockey who stays with a station for a period of time becomes a well-known personality in the community. Such celebrities are sought after as participants in community activities and may be recognized on the street.

DJs who work at parties and other events work in a variety of settings. They generally have more freedom to choose music selections but little opportunity to ad-lib. Their work is primarily on evenings and weekends.

OUTLOOK

According to the National Association of Broadcasters, radio reaches 77 percent of people over the age of 12 every day. Despite radio's popularity, the *Occupational Outlook Handbook* projects that employment of announcers will decline slightly over the next several years. Due to this decline, competition for jobs will be great in an already competitive field.

While small stations will still hire beginners, on-air experience will be increasingly important. Another area where job seekers can push ahead of the competition is in specialization. Knowledge of specific areas such as business, consumer, and health news may be advantageous.

While on-air radio personalities are not necessarily affected by economic downturns, mergers and changes in the industry can affect employment. If a radio station has to make cuts due to a weak economy, it will most likely do so in a behind-the-scenes area, which means that the disc jockeys who remain may face a further diversity in their duties.

FOR MORE INFORMATION

For a list of schools offering degrees in broadcasting as well as scholarship information, contact:
Broadcast Education Association
1771 N Street, NW
Washington, D.C. 20036-2891
Tel: 888-380-7222
Email: beainfo@beaweb.org
http://www.beaweb.org

For broadcast education, support, and scholarship information, contact:
National Association of Broadcasters
1771 N Street, NW
Washington, D.C. 20036
Tel: 202-429-5300
Email: nab@nab.org
http://www.nab.org

For scholarship and internship information, contact:
Radio-Television News Directors Association and Foundation
1600 K Street, NW, Suite 700
Washington, D.C. 20006-2838
Tel: 202-659-6510
Email: rtnda@rtnda.org
http://www.rtnda.org

For college programs and union information, contact:
National Association of Broadcast Employees and Technicians
Email: nabet@nabetcwa.org
http://nabetcwa.org

EVENT PLANNERS

QUICK FACTS

School Subjects Business English Foreign language	**Certification or Licensing** Voluntary
	Outlook Faster than the average
Personal Skills Communication/ideas Leadership/management	**DOT** 169
Work Environment Primarily indoors One location with some travel	**GOE** N/A
	NOC 1226
Minimum Education Level Bachelor's degree	**O*NET-SOC** 13-1121.00
Salary Range $30,000 to $54,613 to $60,230+	

OVERVIEW

The duties of *event planners* are varied and may include the following: establishing a site for an event; making travel, hotel, and food arrangements; and planning the program and overseeing guest registration. The planner may be responsible for all of the negotiating, planning, and coordinating for a major worldwide convention, or the planner may be involved with a small, in-house meeting involving only a few people. Some professional associations, government agencies, nonprofit organizations, political groups, and educational institutions hire event planners or have employees on staff who have these responsibilities. Many of these organizations and companies outsource their event planning responsibilities to firms that specialize in these services, such as marketing, public relations, and event planning firms. Many event and meeting planners are independent consultants.

Some event planners' services are also used on a personal level to plan class or family reunions, birthday parties, weddings, or anniversaries. There are approximately 34,000 event planners employed in the United States.

HISTORY

According to the *National Directory of Occupational Titles and Codes,* the meeting management profession was recognized as a career in the early 1990s. As corporations have specialized and expanded their business to include facilities and employees worldwide, company meeting logistics have become more complex. Planning a meeting that brings together employees and directors from around the world requires advanced planning to acquire a site, make travel and hotel arrangements, book speakers and entertainment, and arrange for catering.

Similarly, the growth of the convention and trade show industry has resulted in the need for persons with skills specific to the planning, marketing, and execution of a successful show. Conventions, trade shows, meetings, and corporate travel have become a big business in recent years, accounting for approximately $80 billion in annual spending.

The scope of meetings has changed as well. Technological advances now allow meetings to be conducted via the Internet, through videoconferencing or closed circuit television, or by setting up conference calls.

THE JOB

Event planners have a variety of duties depending on their specific title and the firms they work for or with. Generally, planners organize and plan an event such as a meeting, open house, convention, or a specific celebration.

Meetings might consist of a small inter-department meeting, a board meeting, an all-employee meeting, an in-house training session, a stockholders' meeting, or a meeting with vendors or distributors. When planning for these events, meeting planners usually check the calendars of key executives to establish a meeting time that fits into their schedules. Planners reserve meeting rooms, training rooms, or outside facilities for the event. They visit outside sites to make sure they are appropriate for that specific event. Planners notify people of the time, place, and date of the event and set up registration procedures, if necessary. They arrange for food, room layout, audiovisual equipment, instructors, computers, sound equipment, and telephone equipment as required.

In some cases, a company may employ an in-house meeting planner who is responsible for small- to medium-sized events. When a large meeting, trade show, conference, open house, or convention is planned, the in-house event planner may contract with outside meeting planners to assist with specific responsibilities such as registration, catering, and display setup. Some companies have their own trade show or convention managers on staff.

Convention, trade show, or conference managers negotiate and communicate with other enterprises related to the convention or trade show industry such as hotel and catering sales staff, speakers' bureaus, and trade staff such as *electricians* or *laborers* who set up convention display areas. They may also be responsible for contracting the transportation of the equipment and supplies to and from the event site. The manager usually works with an established budget and negotiates fees with these enterprises and enters contracts with them. Managers may also negotiate contracts with professionals to handle registration, marketing, and public relations for the event.

Managers and planners need to be aware of legal aspects of trade show setups, such as fire code regulations, floor plan, and space limitations, and make sure they are within these guidelines. They often need to obtain written approval for these arrangements. Good record-keeping and communication skills are daily essentials. The convention manager may have staff to handle the sales, registration, marketing, logistics, or other specific aspects of the event, or these duties may be subcontracted to another firm.

Some convention planners are employed specifically by convention and visitors' bureaus, the tourism industry, or by exhibit halls or convention facilities. Their job responsibilities may be specific to one aspect of the show, or they may be required to do any or all of the above-mentioned duties. Some convention and trade show managers may work for the exposition center or association and be responsible for selling booth space at large events.

Special event coordinators are usually employed by large corporations who hold numerous special events, or by firms who contract their special event planning services to companies, associations, or religious, political, or educational groups. A special event coordinator is responsible for planning, organizing, and implementing a special event such as an open house, an anniversary, the dedication of a new facility, a special promotion or sale, an ordination, a political rally, or a victory celebration. This coordinator works with the company or organization and determines the purpose of the special event, the type of celebration desired, the site, the budget, the attendees, the food and entertainment preferences, and the anticipated outcome. The special event planner then coordinates the vendors and equipment necessary tomake the event successful. The coordinator works closely with the client at all times to ensure that the event is being planned as expected. Follow-up assessment of the event is usually part of the services offered by the special event coordinator.

Party planners are often employed by individuals, families, or small companies to help them plan a small party for a special occasion. Many party planners are independent contractors who work out of their homes or are employees of small firms. Party planners may help plan weddings, birthdays, christenings, bar or bat mitzvahs, anniversaries, or other events. They may be responsible for the entire event including the invitations, catering, decorating, entertainment, serving, and cleanup, or planners may simply perform one or two duties, such as contracting with a magician for a children's birthday party, recommending a menu, or greeting and serving guests.

REQUIREMENTS
High School
If you are interested in entering the field of event planning, you should take high school classes in business, English, and speech. Because many conferences and meetings are international in scope, you may also want to take foreign language and geography courses. In addition, computer science classes will be beneficial for the large amount of record-keeping involved in this field.

Postsecondary Training
Almost all coordinators and planners must have a four-year college degree to work for a company, corporation, convention, or travel center. Some institutions offer bachelor's degrees in meeting planning; however, degrees in business, English, communications, marketing, public relations, sales, or travel would also be a good fit for a career as a meetings manager, convention planner, or special event coordinator. Many directors and planners who become company heads have earned graduate degrees.

Some small firms, convention centers, or exhibit facilities may accept persons with associate degrees or travel industry certification for certain planning positions. Party planners may not always need education beyond high school, but advancement opportunities will be more plentiful with additional education.

Certification or Licensing

There are some professional associations for planners that offer certification programs. For example, Meeting Professionals International offers the Certification in Meeting Management designation. The International Association for Exhibition Management offers the Certified in Exhibition Management designation. (See "For More Information" at the end of this article for contact information.)

Other Requirements

To be an event planner, you must have excellent organizational skills, the ability to plan projects and events, and the ability to think creatively. You must be able to work well with people and anticipate their needs in advance. You should be willing to pitch in to get a job done even though it may not be part of your duties. In a situation where there is an unforeseen crisis, you need to react quickly and professionally. Planners should have good negotiating and communication skills and be assertive but tactful.

EXPLORING

High school guidance counselors can supply information on event planners or convention coordinators. Public and school librarians may also be able to provide useful books, magazines, and pamphlets. Searching the Internet for companies that provide event-planning services can give you an idea of the types of services that they offer. Professional associations related to the travel, convention, and meeting industries may have career information for students. Some of these organizations are listed at the end of this article.

Attending local trade shows and conventions will provide insight into the operations of this industry. Also, some exhibit and convention halls may hire students to assist with various aspects of trade show operations. You can learn more about this profession by subscribing to magazines such as *Meetings & Conventions* (http://www.meetings-conventions.com).

Some party planners may hire assistants to help with children's birthday parties or other special events. Organize and plan a large family event, such as a birthday, anniversary, graduation, or retirement celebration. You will have to find a location, hire catering or assign family members to bring specific food items, send invitations, purchase and arrange decorations, and organize entertainment, all according to what your budget allows.

You can also gain business experience through school activities. Join the business club, run for student council, or head up the prom committee to learn how to plan and carry out events.

EMPLOYERS

Many large corporations or institutions worldwide hire meeting managers, convention managers, or event planners to handle their specific activities. Although some companies may not have employees with the specific title of event planner or meeting manager, these skills are very marketable and these duties may be part of another job title. In many companies, these duties may be part of a position within the marketing, public relations, or corporate communications department.

Convention facilities, exhibit halls, training and educational institutions, travel companies, and health care facilities also hire event planners. Hotels often hire planners to handle meetings and events held within their facilities. Large associations usually maintain an event planning staff for one or more annual conventions or business meetings for their members.

Job opportunities are also available with companies that contract out event and meeting planning services. Many of these companies have positions that specialize in certain aspects of the planning service, such as travel coordinator, exhibit planner, or facilities negotiator, or they have people who perform specific functions such as trade show display setup, registration, and follow-up reporting.

Planners interested in jobs with the convention and trade show industries or hotels may find that larger cities have more demand for planners and offer higher salaries.

Experienced meeting planners or convention managers may choose to establish their own businesses or independently contract out their services. Party planning may also be a good independent business venture. Approximately 34,000 event planners are employed in the United States.

STARTING OUT

An internship at a visitors and convention bureau, exhibit center, or with a travel agency or meeting planning company is a good way to meet and network with other people in this field. Attending trade shows might offer a chance to speak with people about the field and to discuss any contacts they might have.

Some colleges and universities may offer job placement for people seeking careers in meeting planning or in the convention and trade show industries. Professional associations related to these industries are also good contacts for someone starting out. Classified ads and trade magazines may also offer some job leads.

ADVANCEMENT

Advancement opportunities for people in the event planning field are good. Experienced planners can expect to move into positions of increased responsibility. They may become senior managers and executive directors of private businesses, hotels, convention facilities, exhibit halls, travel corporations, museums, or other facilities. They can advance within a corporation to a position with more responsibilities or they may go into the planning business for themselves. Planners who have established a good reputation in the industry are often recruited by other firms or facilities and can advance their careers with these opportunities.

EARNINGS

According to a salary survey by *Special Events* magazine online, the average annual base salary for event planners was $36,079 in 2000. Nearly 40 percent of event planners were offered bonuses or commission, and the average bonus was $4,187.

Meeting Professionals International reports that in 2000, the average salary for U.S. meeting planners was $54,613. In the Northeast, meeting planners earned an average $58,146; in the West, $57,136; in the Midwest, $51,650; and in the South, $51,164. Corporate meeting planners earned an average of $56,120; association meeting professionals earned $46,539; and independent planners earned an average of $60,230.

Benefits may vary depending on the position and the employer but generally include vacation, sick leave, insurance, and other work-related benefits.

WORK ENVIRONMENT

Work environments vary with the planner's title and job responsibilities, but generally planners can expect to work in a business setting as part of a team. Usually, the planner's initial planning work is done in a clean environment with modern equipment prior to the opening of a convention or trade show. Working in convention and trade show environments, however, can be noisy, crowded, and distracting. In addition, the days can be long and may require standing for hours. If the planner is involved with supervising the setup or dismantling of a trade show or convention, the work can be dirty and physically demanding.

Although most facilities have crews that assist with setup, meeting planners occasionally get involved with last-minute changes and may need to do some physical lifting of equipment, tables, or chairs.

Event planners can usually expect to work erratic hours, often putting in long days prior to the event and the day the event is actually held. Travel is often part of the job requirements and may include working and/or traveling nights and on the weekends.

OUTLOOK

Job opportunities for event planners will continue to grow at a faster-than-average rate. The introduction of new technology enables more meetings to take place than ever before. Conventions, trade shows, meetings, and incentive travel support more than 1.5 million American jobs, according to the Professional Convention Management Association (PCMA). These events account for more than $80 billion in annual spending.

FOR MORE INFORMATION

For information on careers in the field of event planning, contact the following organizations.

International Association for Exposition Management
8111 LBJ Freeway, Suite 750
Dallas, TX 75251-1313
Tel: 972-458-8002
http://www.iaem.org

International Association of Assembly Managers
4425 West Airport Freeway, Suite 590
Irving, TX 75062-5835
Tel: 972-255-8020
http://www.iaam.org

Meeting Professionals International
4455 LBJ Freeway, Suite 1200
Dallas, TX 75244-5903
Tel: 972-702-3000
http://www.mpiweb.org

Professional Convention Management Association
2301 South Lake Shore Drive, Suite 1001
Chicago, IL 60616-1419
Tel: 312-423-7262
Email: students@pcma.org
http://www.pcma.org

EXECUTIVE RECRUITERS

QUICK FACTS

School Subjects
Business
Psychology
Speech

Personal Skills
Communication/ideas
Leadership/management

Work Environment
Primarily indoors
Primarily multiple locations

Minimum Education Level
Bachelor's degree

Salary Range
$50,000 to $175,000 to
$250,000+

Certification or Licensing
None available

Outlook
Faster than the average

DOT
166

GOE
N/A

NOC
N/A

O*NET-SOC
13-1071.02

OVERVIEW

Executive recruiters are hired by businesses to locate, research, and interview candidates for hard-to-fill employment positions, mainly on the junior to senior management level. Such recruiters work for executive search firms and are paid by clients on a commission basis, or flat fee. There are approximately 10,000 executive recruiters employed by search firms located throughout the United States.

HISTORY

Although most companies have competent in-house human resource departments, a search for a top management position is often lengthy and difficult. Many times, human resource departments are not able to reach, or identify, the most qualified candidates. Also, a measure of privacy is lost if an entire department is aware of the need for a replacement. Companies are increasingly turning to a third party for their employment needs: the executive recruiter.

Executive search firms fall into one of two categories: retained or contingency. *Retainer recruiters* work with upper-level management positions, such as CEOs or CFOs, with salary expectations averaging $150,000 or higher. Companies or other entities contract these firms exclusively to bring new executives on board. Retainer recruiters work on a flat-fee basis or, more commonly, for a percentage of the candidate's first-year salary and bonus. Commission percentages can range anywhere from 10 to 35 percent, although the industry standard is about a third of the candidate's proposed salary package. Executive recruiters, because of the high-level management positions they are assigned to fill and the exclusivity of their contract, usually take longer to complete their task—anywhere from three to six months or more. The more qualities the company is looking for in a candidate, the longer the search.

The *contingency recruiter* deals with junior- to mid-level executive positions paying $50,000 to $150,000. Such recruiters are paid only if the candidate they present is hired for the job; pay is usually a percentage of the first-year salary package. Many times, however, a company will have more than one contingency firm working to fill a single position. Because of this, contingency recruiters are not guaranteed a fee and they may spend less time on their search. Some contingency recruiters also charge on an hourly basis or may work for a flat fee.

THE JOB

Most companies—from *Fortune 500* firms to colleges and universities to small businesses—at one time or another have come across the need to replace an important executive or administrator. Because of restraints such as time, privacy, or resources, many businesses opt to use the services of an executive recruiter. The task begins once the search firm is retained, or notified of the job opening, and is asked to find the best possible candidate.

The recruiter first evaluates the needs and structure of the company and the specifications of the open position. Then a written draft of the job description is made, detailing the title, job definition, responsibilities, and compensation. At this time, a wish list is composed of every possible quality, talent, skill, and educational background the perfect job candidate should possess. It is up to the recruiter to match these specifications as closely as possible.

Once the client approves a written contract the real work begins. The three traditional job functions in the recruitment industry are researcher, associate, and consultant. *Researchers* conduct research to find possible candidates. They look through directories and databases and network with contacts familiar with the field. They read trade papers and magazines as well as national newspapers such as the *Wall Street Journal* and the *New York Times.* Business sections of newspapers often include write-ups of industry leaders. Recruiters also receive resumes from people looking to change employment, which they may use for future reference. Recruiters must stay current with the field they specialize in; they need to be familiar with the key players as well as important technological advances that may change the scope of the industry. They must also have a solid understanding of the workings of their specialty field so they can assess a candidate's ability to meet the demands of a position.

Once a long list is assembled, *associates* contact the prospective candidates, usually by telephone. Candidates who are interested and qualified are screened further and their references are checked fully. *Consultants* conduct personal interviews with promising candidates who make the short list of hopefuls. Consultants also manage client relationships and develop new business for the firm.

The goal of retainer executive recruiters is to present three to five of the best candidates to a client for final interviews. Contingency recruiters, on the other hand, present many qualified candidates to the client to better their chance of filling the position. Executive recruiters will not edit resumes or coach on the interview process, but some will offer information on where candidates stand after the initial interview and give advice on strengths and perceived weaknesses.

A search for the perfect executive is a lengthy process. Most searches take anywhere from one month to a year or more. Once the position is filled, recruiters conduct one or more follow-ups to make sure the employee's transition into the company is smooth. Any conflicts or discrepancies are addressed and often mediated by, or along with, the search firm. Some executive search firms offer some kind of guarantee with their work. If the hired employee leaves a firm within a specified period of time or does not work out as anticipated, then the recruiter will find a replacement for a reduced fee or at no charge.

REQUIREMENTS
High School

To prepare for a career as an executive recruiter, you should take business, speech, English, and mathematics classes in high school.

Psychology and sociology courses will teach you how to recognize personality characteristics that may be key in helping you determine which job candidates would best fit a position.

Postsecondary Training

You will need at least a bachelor's degree and several years of work experience to become an executive recruiter. Postsecondary courses helpful for this career include communications, marketing, and business administration. Some colleges offer undergraduate degrees in human resources management or business degrees with a concentration in human resources management. To have more job opportunities, you may also consider getting a master's degree in one of these fields. Most recruiters move into this industry after successful careers in their particular areas of expertise (for example, health care, finance, publishing, or computers) and they come to the field with a variety of educational backgrounds.

Certification or Licensing

There are no certification or licensing requirements for this industry. Most executive search professionals belong to the Association of Executive Search Consultants or the National Association of Executive Recruiters.

Other Requirements

Executive recruiters need to possess strong people skills. Good communicators are in demand, especially those who can maintain a high level of integrity and confidentiality. Recruiters are privy to sensitive company and employee information that may prove disastrous if leaked to the public.

The most powerful tool in this industry is a network of good contacts. Since executive recruiters come on board after working in the field for which they are now recruiting, they are usually familiar with who's who in the business.

EXPLORING

Familiarize yourself with business practices by joining or starting a business club at your school. Being a part of a speech or debate team is a great way to develop excellent speaking skills, which are necessary in this field. Hold mock interviews with family or friends, and get work and volunteer experience in your specialized field (for example, health care or publishing). Professional associations, such as The International Association of Corporate and Professional Recruiters, are also good sources of information. Visit this association's website at http://www.iacpr.org to learn more.

EMPLOYERS

Executive search firms of all sizes are located throughout the United States. Most specialize in placement in a particular field, for example, chemical engineering or advertising. For a list of search firms, you may want to refer to the *Directory of Executive Recruiters,* also known in the industry as the "Red Book." Search firms in the United States employ approximately 10,000 executive recruiters, according to an estimate by *Executive Recruiter News.*

STARTING OUT

A common starting point in this industry is a position at a contingency search firm, or even an outplacement center. Responsibilities may be limited at first, but a successful, and consistent track record should lead to bigger clients, more placements, and higher commissions. Many executive recruiters were recruited into the field themselves, especially if they were well known in their industry. It is important to market yourself and your accomplishments while you work in entry-level positions. Circulate among the movers and shakers of your company, as well as those of the competition. They may prove to be valuable contacts for the future. Most importantly, cultivate relationships with any recruitment firms that may call; you'll never know when you may need their assistance.

ADVANCEMENT

A typical advancement path in this industry would be a transfer to a retainer-based search firm. Retained search firms deal with the upper-echelon administrative positions that pay top salaries, translating to higher commissions for the recruiter.

Let's say you've already paid your dues and worked successfully at a retainer search firm. What next? You may want to negotiate for partnership or opt to call the shots and start a firm of your own.

EARNINGS

Executive recruiters are paid well for their efforts. Contingency recruiters, who are paid only if their candidate is hired, typically charge a fee from 25 percent to 35 percent of the candidate's first-year cash compensation.

Retained recruiters average fees of one-third of the candidate's first-year cash compensation. Any expenses incurred by the recruiter are usually paid by the employer. According to *U.S. News & World Report*, average entry-level positions pay from $50,000 to $100,000 annually, while mid-level recruiters earn from $100,000 to $250,000. Top earners, those working for larger retainer recruiting firms, can make more than $250,000 a year. Along with their salary, all recruiters are offered a benefit package including health insurance, paid vacations, and sick time or paid disability.

WORK ENVIRONMENT

Many recruiters work 50 to 70 hours a week; it's not uncommon for recruiters to spend several days a week on the road meeting clients, interviewing, or doing candidate research. Also, aspiring recruiters should expect to spend most of their day on the phone.

OUTLOOK

The executive search industry should have a good future. Potential clients include not only large international corporations but also universities, the government, and smaller businesses. Smaller operations are aware that having a solid executive or administrator may make the difference between turning a profit or not being in business at all. Many times, search firm services are used to conduct industry research or to scope out the competition. Executive search firms now specialize in many fields of employment—health care, engineering, or accounting, for example.

The era of company loyalty and employment for life is over in the corporate world. Many savvy workers campaign aggressively, and will transfer given a larger salary, improved benefits, and stock options—in short, a better employment future. Employers, on the other hand, realize the importance in having qualified and experienced employees at the helm of their business. Most companies are willing to pay the price, whether a retainer fee or commission, to find just the right person for the job.

According to the Association of Executive Search Consultants, it is becoming more important for executive recruiters to operate on a global basis. They must be able to conduct searches for clients and candidates in other countries. Peter Felix, president of AESC, says, "Today, the retained executive search business is a $10 billion industry operating in all the major economies of the world. In this era of the knowledge society where executive talent is so important, executive search is seen increasingly as a critical management tool."

FOR MORE INFORMATION

For industry information, contact:

The Association of Executive Search Consultants
500 Fifth Avenue, Suite 930
New York, NY 10110-0900
Tel: 212-398-9556
Email: aesc@aesc.org
http://www.aesc.org

For more industry information, or membership information, contact:

National Association of Executive Recruiters
20 North Wacker Drive, Suite 550
Chicago, IL 60606
Tel: 312-701-0744
http://www.naer.org

For a copy of the industry newsletter, Executive Recruiter News, or the Directory of Executive Recruiters, contact:

Kennedy Information
One Phoenix Mill Lane, 5th Floor
Peterborough, NH 03458
Tel: 800-531-0007
Email: bookstore@kennedyinfo.com
http://www.kennedyinfo.com

FOREIGN CORRESPONDENTS

QUICK FACTS

School Subjects
English
Foreign language
Journalism

Personal Skills
Communication/ideas
Helping/teaching

Work Environment
Indoors and outdoors
Primarily multiple locations

Minimum Education Level
Bachelor's degree

Salary Range
$17,320 to $50,000 to $100,000

Certification or Licensing
None available

Outlook
Little change or more slowly than the average

DOT
N/A

GOE
N/A

NOC
5123

O*NET-SOC
27-3022.00

OVERVIEW

Foreign correspondents report on news from countries outside of where their newspapers, radio or television networks, or wire services are located. They sometimes work for a particular newspaper, but since today's media are more interested in local and national news, they usually rely on reports from news wire services to handle international news coverage rather than dispatching their own reporters to the scene. Only the biggest newspapers and television networks employ foreign correspondents. These reporters are usually stationed in a particular city and cover a wide territory.

HISTORY

James Gordon Bennett, Sr. (1795–1872), a prominent United States journalist and publisher of the *New York Herald*, was responsible for many firsts in the newspaper industry. He was the first publisher to sell papers through newsboys, the first to use illustrations for news stories, the first to publish stock-market prices and daily financial articles, and he was the first to employ European correspondents. Bennett's son, James Gordon Bennett, Jr. (1841–1918), carried on the family business and in 1871 sent Henry M. Stanley to central Africa to find Dr. David Livingstone, a famous British explorer who had disappeared.

In the early days, even magazines employed foreign correspondents. Famous American poet Ezra Pound (1885–1972), for example, reported from London for *Poetry* and *The Little Review*.

The inventions of the telegraph, telephone, typewriter, portable typewriter, the portable laptop computer, and the Internet all have contributed to the field of foreign correspondence.

THE JOB

The foreign correspondent is stationed in a foreign country where his or her job is to report on the news there. Foreign news can range from the violent (wars, coups, and refugee situations) to the calm (cultural events and financial issues). Although a domestic correspondent is responsible for covering specific areas of the news, like politics, health, sports, consumer affairs, business, or religion, foreign correspondents are responsible for all of these areas in the country where they are stationed. A China-based correspondent, for example, could spend a day covering the new trade policy between the United States and China, and the next day report on the religious persecution of Christians by the Chinese government.

A foreign correspondent often is responsible for more than one country. Depending on where he or she is stationed, the foreign correspondent might have to act as a one-person band in gathering and preparing stories.

"There are times when the phone rings at five in the morning and you're told to go to Pakistan," said Michael Lev, Beijing, China, correspondent for the *Chicago Tribune*. "You must keep your wits about you and figure out what to do next."

For the most part, Lev decides on his own story ideas, choosing which ones interest him the most out of a myriad of possibilities. But foreign correspondents alone are responsible for getting the story done, and unlike reporters back home, they have little or no support staff to help them. Broadcast foreign correspondents, for example, may have to do their own audio editing after filming scenes. And just like other news reporters, foreign correspondents work under the pressure of deadlines. In addition, they often are thrown into unfamiliar situations in strange places.

Part of the importance of a foreign correspondent's job is keeping readers or viewers aware of the various cultures and practices held by the rest of the world. Lev says he tries to focus on similarities and differences between the Asian countries he covers and the United States. "If you don't understand another culture, you are more likely to come into conflict with it," he says.

Foreign correspondents are drawn to conflicts of all kinds, especially war. They may choose to go to the front of a battle to get an accurate picture of what's happening. Or they may be able to get the story from a safer position. Sometimes they face weapons targeted directly at them.

Much of a foreign correspondent's time is spent doing research, investigating leads, setting up appointments, making travel arrangements, making on-site observations, and interviewing local people or those involved in the situation. The foreign correspondent often must be experienced in taking photographs or shooting video.

Living conditions can be rough or primitive, sometimes with no running water. The job can sometimes be isolating.

After correspondents have interviewed sources and noted observations about an event or filmed it, they put their stories together, writing on computers and using modern technology like the Internet, email, satellite telephones, and fax machines to finish the job and transmit the story to their newspaper, broadcast station, or wire service. Many times, correspondents work out of hotel rooms.

REQUIREMENTS
High School

In addition to English and creative writing needed for a career in journalism, you should study languages, social studies, political science, history, and geography. Initial experience may be gained by working on your school newspaper or yearbook, or taking advantage of study-abroad programs.

Postsecondary Training

In college, pursuing a journalism major is helpful but may not be crucial to obtaining a job as a foreign correspondent. Classes, or even a major, in political science or literature could be beneficial. Economics and foreign languages also help.

Other Requirements

In addition to a definite love of adventure, to be a foreign correspondent you need to be curios about how other people live, diplo-

Top 25 Media Companies
(by revenue)

1. AOL Time Warner: New York, NY
2. Viacom: New York, NY
3. AT&T Broadband: Denver, CO
4. Walt Disney Co.: New York, NY/Burbank, CA
5. Cox Enterprises: Atlanta, GA
6. NBC-TV (General Electric Co.): New York, NY/ Fairfield, CT
7. News Corp.: Sydney, Australia
8. Clear Channel Communications: San Antonio, TX
9. Gannett Co.: McLean, VA
10. DirecTV (General Motors Corp.): El Segundo, CA
11. Comcast Corp.: Philadelphia, PA
12. Tribune Co.: Chicago, IL
13. Advance Publications: Newark, NJ
14. Hearst Corp.: New York, NY
15. Charter Communications: St. Louis, MO
16. EchoStar Communications Corp.: Littleton, CO
17. Cablevision Systems Corp.: Bethpage, NY
18. Adelphia Communications Corp.: Coudersport, PA
19. New York Times Co.: New York, NY
20. Knight Ridder: San Jose, CA
21. Bloomberg: New York, NY
22. Washington Post Co.: Washington, DC
23. Primedia: New York, NY
24. Dow Jones & Co.: New York, NY
25. Belo: Dallas, TX

Source: *Advertising Age* (http://www.adage.com)

matic when conducting interviews, courageous when confronting people on uncomfortable topics, very communicative, and disciplined enough to act as your own boss. You also need to be strong enough to hold up under pressure yet flexible enough to adapt to other cultures.

EXPLORING

To explore this field, you can begin by honing your skills in different journalism media. Join your high school newspaper staff to become a regular columnist or write special feature articles. Check out your high school's TV station and audition to be an anchor. Is there a radio station at your school? If so, volunteer to be on the staff there. And what about the Web? If your school has an online newspaper, get involved with that project. Gain as much experience as you can with different media; learn about the strengths and weaknesses of each and decide which suits you best. You can also ask your high school journalism teacher or guidance counselor to help you set up an informational interview with a local journalist. Most are happy to speak with you when they know you are interested in their careers. It may be possible to get a part-time or summer job working at a local TV or radio station or at the newspaper office. Competition for one of these jobs, however, is strong because many college students take such positions as interns and do the work for little or no pay.

EMPLOYERS

Foreign correspondents work for news wire services, such as the Associated Press, Reuters, and Agence-France Press; major metropolitan newspapers; news magazines; and television and radio networks. These media are located in the largest cities in the United States and, in the case of Reuters and Agence-France Press, in Europe.

STARTING OUT

College graduates can pursue a couple of paths to become a foreign correspondent. They can decide to experience what being a foreign correspondent is like immediately by going to another country, perhaps one whose language is familiar to them, and freelancing or working as a *stringer*. That means writing stories and offering them to anyone who will buy them. This method can be hard to accomplish financially in the short run but can pay off substantially in the long run.

Another path is to take the traditional route of a journalist and try to get hired upon graduation at any newspaper, radio station, or television station you can. It helps in this regard to have worked at a summer internship during your college years. Recent college graduates generally get hired at small newspapers or media stations,

although a few major metropolitan dailies will employ top graduates for a year with no guarantee of their being kept on afterward.
After building experience at a small paper or station, a reporter can
try to find work at progressively bigger ones. Reporters who find
employment at a major metropolitan daily that uses foreign correspondents can work their way through the ranks to become one.
This is the path Michael Lev took, and he became a foreign correspondent when he was in his early 30s. He suggests that working for
a wire service may allow a reporter to get abroad faster, but he
thinks more freedom can be found working for a newspaper.

ADVANCEMENT

Foreign correspondents can advance to other locations that are more
appealing to them or that offer a bigger challenge. Or they can return
home to become columnists, editorial writers, editors, or network
news directors.

EARNINGS

Salaries vary greatly depending on the publication, network, or station, and the cost of living and tax structure in various places around
the world where foreign correspondents work. Generally, salaries
range from $50,000 to an average of about $75,000 to a peak of
$100,000 or more. Some media will pay for living expenses, such as
the costs of a home, school for the reporter's children, and a car.

According to the Bureau of Labor Statistics, correspondents and
other news reporters earned a median salary of $30,060 in 2001. The
lowest 10 percent earned $17,320 or less, and the highest 10 percent
earned $68,020 or more.

WORK ENVIRONMENT

Correspondents and other reporters may face a hectic work environment if they have tight deadlines and have to produce their reports
with little time for preparation. Correspondents who work in countries
that face great political or social problems risk their health and even
their lives to report breaking news. Covering wars, political uprisings, fires, floods, and similar events can be extremely dangerous.

Working hours vary depending on the correspondent's deadlines.
Their work often demands irregular or long hours. Because foreign
correspondents report from international locations, this job involves
travel. The amount of travel depends on the size of the region the
correspondent covers.

OUTLOOK

Although employment at newspapers, radio stations, and television stations in general is expected to continue to decline, the number of foreign correspondent jobs has leveled off. The employment outlook is expected to remain relatively stable, or even increase should more major conflicts or wars occur.

Factors that keep the number of foreign correspondents low are the high cost of maintaining a foreign news bureau and the relative lack of interest Americans show in world news. Despite these factors, the number of correspondents is not expected to decrease. There are simply too few as it is; decreasing the number could put the job in danger of disappearing, which most journalists believe is not an option. For now and the near future, most job openings will arise from the need to replace those correspondents who leave the job.

FOR MORE INFORMATION

The ASJA promotes the interests of freelance writers. It provides information on court rulings dealing with writing issues, has a writers' referral service, and offers a newsletter.

American Society of Journalists and Authors (ASJA)
1501 Broadway, Suite 302
New York, NY 10036
Tel: 212-997-0947
http://www.asja.org

This association provides the annual publication Journalism and Mass Communication Directory with information on educational programs in all areas of journalism (newspapers, magazines, television, and radio).

Association for Education in Journalism and
  Mass Communication
234 Outlet Pointe Boulevard
Columbia, SC 29210-5667
Tel: 803-798-0271
Email: aejmc@aejmc.org
http://www.aejmc.org

The NAB website's Career Center has information on jobs, scholarships, internships, college programs, and other resources. You can also purchase career publications from the online NAB Store.

National Association of Broadcasters (NAB)
1771 N Street, NW
Washington, DC 20036

Tel: 202-429-5300
Email: nab@nab.org
http://www.nab.org

The SPJ has chapters all over the United States. The SPJ website offers career information and information on internships and fellowships.
Society of Professional Journalists (SPJ)
Eugene S. Pulliam National Journalism Center
3909 North Meridian Street
Indianapolis, IN 46208
Tel: 317-927-8000
Email: questions@spj.org
http://www.spj.org

FUND-RAISERS

QUICK FACTS

School Subjects Business English Mathematics	**Certification or Licensing** Recommended
	Outlook About as fast as the average
Personal Skills Communication/ideas Leadership/management	**DOT** 293
Work Environment Primarily indoors Primarily one location	**GOE** 11.09.02
Minimum Education Level Bachelor's degree	**NOC** N/A
Salary Range $20,000 to $54,000 to $200,000+	**O*NET-SOC** N/A

OVERVIEW

Fund-raisers develop and coordinate the plans by which charity organizations gain financial contributions, generate publicity, and fulfill fiscal objectives. Fund-raisers are employed at a variety of nonprofit organizations, including those in the arts, social service, health care, and educational fields, as well as at private consulting firms around the country.

HISTORY

Organized fund-raising, or philanthropy, is a relatively modern refinement of the old notion of charity. It may be surprising to learn that some people make a living by organizing charity appeals and fund drives, but philanthropy ranks among the 10 largest industries in the United States. The most familiar forms of fund-raising are the much publicized and visible types, such as telethons, direct-mail campaigns, and canned food drives. Successful fund-raising does not depend on a high profile; however, it often requires marketing the appeal for funds to the people most likely to donate. Successful fund-raising requires careful planning, staffing, and execution. An experienced fund-raiser can make all the difference between a successful revenue campaign and a disappointing one.

THE JOB

Fund-raising combines many different skills, such as financial management and accounting, public relations, marketing, human resources, management, and media communications. To be successful, the appeal for funds has to target the people most likely to donate, and donors have to be convinced of the good work being done by the cause they are supporting. To do this, fund-raisers need strong media support and savvy public relations. Fund-raisers also have to bring together people, including volunteers, paid staff, board members, and other community contacts, and direct them toward the common goal of enriching the charity.

To illustrate how a revenue-raising campaign might be conducted, consider the example of Branton Academy, a private high school that is trying to raise money to build a new facility. The principal of Branton approaches a fund-raising consulting firm to study the possible approaches to take. Building a new facility and acquiring the land would cost the academy approximately $800,000. The fund-raising firm's first job is to ask difficult questions about the realism of the academy's goal. What were the results of the academy's last fund-raising effort? Do the local alumni tend to respond to solicitations for revenue? Are the alumni active leaders in the community, and can their support be counted on? Are there enough potential givers besides alumni in the area to reach the goal? Are there enough volunteers on hand to launch a revenue campaign? What kind of publicity, good and bad, has the academy recently generated? What other charities, especially private schools, are trying to raise money in the area at that time?

Once the fund-raising consulting firm has a solid understanding of what the academy is trying to accomplish, it conducts a feasibility study to determine whether there is community support for such a project. If community support exists—that is, if it appears that the fund-raising drive could be a success—the consulting firm works with officials at Branton to draft a fund-raising plan. The plan will describe in detail the goals of the fund-raising appeal, the steps to be taken to meet those goals, the responsibilities of the paid staff and volunteers, budget projections for the campaign, and other important policies. For Branton Academy, the fund-raising consultant might suggest a three-tiered strategy for the campaign: a bicycle marathon by the students to generate interest and initiate the publicity campaign, followed by a month-long phone drive to people in the area, and ending with a formal dinner dance that charges $50 or more per person.

Once the plan is agreed upon, the fund-raising consultants organize training for the volunteers, especially those in phone solicitation, and give them tips on how to present the facts of the campaign to potential contributors and get them to support Branton's efforts. The fund-raisers make arrangements for publicity and press coverage, sometimes employing a professional publicist, so that people will hear about the campaign before they are approached for donations. During the campaign, the consultants and the staff of Branton will research possible large contributors, such as corporations, philanthropic foundations, and wealthy individuals. These potential sources of revenue will receive special attention and personal appeals from fund-raising professionals and Branton's principal and trustees. If the fund-raising effort is a success, Branton Academy will have both the funds it needs to expand and an improved image in the community.

This example is fairly clear and straightforward, but the financial needs of most charities are so complex that a single, month-long campaign would be only part of their fund-raising plans. The American Cancer Society, for instance, holds many charity events in an area every year, in addition to occasional phone drives, marathons, year-round magazine and television advertising, and special appeals to large individual donors. Fund-raisers who work on the staff of charities and nonprofit organizations may need to push several fund drives at the same time, balancing their efforts between long-range endowment funds and special projects. Every nonprofit organization has its own unique goals and financial needs; therefore, fund-raisers have to tailor their efforts to the characteristics of the charity or organization involved. This requires imagination, versatility, and resourcefulness on the fund-raiser's part. The proper allocation of funds is also a weighty responsibility. Fund-raisers also must have strong people skills, especially communications, because their personal contact with volunteers, donors, board members, community groups, local leaders, and members of the press may be an important factor in the success of any revenue appeal.

REQUIREMENTS
High School
To pursue a career in fund-raising, you should follow a college-preparatory curriculum. English, creative writing, speech, mathematics, business, and history classes are recommended, as well as a foreign language, bookkeeping, and computer training. Extracurricular activities such as student council and community outreach programs can help you cultivate important leadership qualities and give you a taste of what fund-raising work requires.

Postsecondary Training
Fund-raising is not a curriculum taught in school, either in high school or at the university level. However, colleges are increasingly offering courses in the broader field of philanthropy. Most fund-raisers have earned a university degree. A broad liberal arts background, with special attention to the social sciences, is a great benefit to fund-raisers because of the nature of most fund-raising work. Specialized degrees that could benefit fund-raisers include communications, psychology, sociology, public relations, business administration, education, and journalism. This type of education will give fund-raisers insight into the concerns and efforts of most nonprofit organizations and how to bring their worthwhile efforts to the public's attention. Courses in economics, accounting, and mathematics are also very useful.

Certification or Licensing
While not required, CFRE International (http://www.cfre.org) offers a Certified Fundraising Executive Program. This certification process is endorsed by leading philanthropic associations, including the Association of Fundraising Professionals. Those who hold certification must become recertified every three years.

Other Requirements
Because fund-raisers need to be able to talk and work with all kinds of people, you will need to be outgoing and friendly. Leadership is also an important quality, because you need to gain the respect of volunteers and inspire them to do their best. Their

enthusiasm for a campaign can be a major factor in other people's commitment to the cause.

EXPLORING

The best way to gauge your interest in a fund-raising career is to volunteer to help at churches, social agencies, health charities, schools, and other organizations for their revenue drives. All of these groups are looking for volunteers and gladly welcome any help they can get. You will be able to observe the various efforts that go into a successful fund-raising drive and the work and dedication of professional fund-raisers. In this way, you can judge whether you enjoy this type of work. Try to interview different fund-raisers and gain helpful advice about acquiring experience and finding employment.

EMPLOYERS

Fund-raisers are usually employed in one of three different ways. They may be members of the staff of the organization or charity in question. For example, many colleges and hospitals maintain fund-raisers on staff, sometimes referred to as *solicitors,* who report to the development director or outreach coordinator. They may also be employed by fund-raising consulting firms, which for a fee will help nonprofit organizations manage their campaigns, budget their money and resources, determine the feasibility of different revenue programs, and counsel them in other ways. Many for-profit companies also have fund-raisers on staff to plan and conduct charity social events, such as fund-raising balls, formal dinners, telethons, walk-a-thons, parties, or carnivals. Corporations perform these philanthropic functions both to help the charity and the community and to generate favorable publicity for themselves.

STARTING OUT

The key to a job in fund-raising is experience. Both private consultants and nonprofit staffs prefer to hire fund-raisers who already have worked on other revenue drives. Because their budgets are always tight, nonprofit organizations are especially reluctant to hire people who need to be trained from scratch. Some small organizations that do not have a budget for hiring full-time fund-raisers may use volunteers.

Colleges offer many opportunities for experience, because nearly every college has at least one staff member (more than likely an entire office) in charge of generating donations from alumni and other sources. These staff members will have useful advice to give on their profession, including private consulting firms that hire fund-raisers. A student may have to serve as a volunteer for such a firm first to get to know the people involved and be considered for a permanent position.

ADVANCEMENT

In a private consulting firm, fund-raisers can advance to higher paying jobs by gaining experience and developing skills. As responsibilities increase, fund-raisers may be put in charge of certain aspects of a campaign, such as the direct-mail or corporate appeal, or may even direct an entire campaign. Those who work for a large social service or nonprofit agency will also find that promotions are determined by skill and creativity in handling difficult assignments. After gaining experience with several nonprofit agencies, some fund-raisers move on and start counseling businesses of their own.

EARNINGS

While beginning fund-raisers do not earn much ($20,000 to $25,000), their salaries will increase as they gain experience or lead successful revenue efforts. Fundraisers with 10–14 years of experience earned a median annual salary of $54,000 in 2000, according to a membership survey conducted by the Association of Fundraising Professionals. The survey also reports that members who held the Certified Fundraising Executive designation earned median salaries that ranged from $60,000 to $75,000. Experienced fund-raisers can be very highly paid, and some of the best earn more than $200,000 a year. To attract and retain experienced fund-raisers, private agencies and nonprofit organizations will also offer competitive salaries and good benefits. While some nonprofit organizations may offer performance bonuses, they are not usually tied directly to the amounts raised.

Benefits for fund-raisers often are equivalent to other professional business positions, including paid vacation, group insurance plans, and paid sick days.

WORK ENVIRONMENT

The working conditions for professional fund-raisers can sometimes be less than ideal. During revenue campaigns, they may have to work in temporary facilities. Their working hours can be irregular, because they have to meet and work with volunteers, potential donors, and other people whenever those people are available.

When campaigns become intense, fund-raisers may have to work long hours, seven days a week. With all the activity that goes on during a campaign, the atmosphere may become stressful, especially as deadlines draw near. So many demands are put on fund-raisers during a campaign—to arrange work schedules, meet with community groups, track finances, and so on—that they must be very organized, flexible, and committed to the overall strategy for the appeal.

OUTLOOK

The job prospects of people who wish to become fund-raisers are good. As federal funding of nonprofit organizations continues to decrease, these groups have to raise operating revenue themselves. They are discovering that hiring full-time fund-raisers is a smart investment. Private fund-raising counseling firms have also reported a need for skilled employees. These firms usually require some experience, but since there are so many fund-raising causes that will eagerly welcome volunteers, interested people should have no problem gaining experience. Both public agencies and private consulting firms keep a full-time staff of fund-raisers, and they may hire part-time workers during special periods and campaigns.

FOR MORE INFORMATION

This organization is a coalition of consulting firms working in the nonprofit sector.

American Association of Fundraising Counsel
10293 North Meridian Street, Suite 175
Indianapolis, IN 46290
Tel: 800-462-2372
Email: info@aafrc.org
http://www.aafrc.org

The following is a professional association for individuals responsible for generating philanthropic support for nonprofits. It provides educational programs, a resource center, conference, and a quarterly journal.

Association of Fundraising Professionals
1101 King Street, Suite 700
Alexandria, VA 22314
Tel: 703-684-0410
http://www.afpnet.org

For information on certification as a Certified Fundraising Executive, contact:
CFRE International
2815 Duke Street
Alexandria, VA 22314
Tel: 703-370-5555
Email: info@cfre.org
http://www.cfre.org

This newspaper for the nonprofit world is published every other week.
The Chronicle of Philanthropy
http://philanthropy.com

HEALTH ADVOCATES

QUICK FACTS

School Subjects
Biology
Health
Speech

Personal Skills
Communication/ideas
Helping/teaching

Work Environment
Primarily indoors
One location with some
travel

Minimum Education Level
Bachelor's degree

Salary Range
$40,000 to $60,000 to
$75,000

Certification or Licensing
None available

Outlook
About as fast as the
average

DOT
N/A

GOE
N/A

NOC
N/A

O*NET-SOC
N/A

OVERVIEW

Health advocates, also known as *patient representatives* and *patient advocates,* work with and on behalf of patients to resolve issues ranging from getting insurance coverage to dealing with complaints about the medical staff to explaining a doctor's treatment plan. In addition to patients, health advocates often deal with physicians, hospitals, health maintenance organizations, insurance companies, and government agencies, to name a few. Advocates are employed by hospitals, nonprofit groups, and other health facilities, such as nursing homes. They also may work as independent contractors.

HISTORY

The world of health care has grown increasingly complex. New scientific discoveries allow doctors to better understand diseases and technology advancements that lead to new and better ways to treat patients. At the same time, government regulations, insurance company policies, hospital rules, and the legal field have all combined to make getting the appropriate health care a complicated process. It can sometimes seem as if the interests of patients get lost in the shuffle. Even the most informed patients may find it difficult to ensure they are getting the most beneficial treatment. This situation has led to the need for someone to work on behalf of patients, promoting their interests everywhere from the doctor's office to the Senate floor.

Although advocates for patients have existed for many years (some cite Florence Nightingale as the first advocate), the recognized profession of health advocate did not really begin do develop until the late 20th century. One step in this development was the acknowledgement by professionals that patients had rights and deserved quality treatment. An example of this occurred in 1973 when the American Hospital Association, a national organization representing hospitals, health care networks, and patients, adopted its first version of a Patient's Bill of Rights. Among other things, the bill recognizes that patients have the right to respectful care, the right to receive understandable information about their treatment, and the right to make their own decisions. Although the profession of health advocates was fairly small in the 1970s, its popularity has increased steadily since then, and health advocates have become important members of the health care community.

THE JOB

As insurance companies, doctors, and even the U.S. government do battle over the health care system, it can sometimes seem as if the interests of patients are being overlooked.

Because the world of health care has become so complex in recent years, it's difficult for patients to know for sure if changes in the system will benefit them. Health advocates enter this struggle on the patients' behalf, using their own health care expertise to promote the interests of patients in the private and public sectors.

For Janet Sell, a registered oncology nurse who works at a nonprofit cancer foundation, health advocacy means working directly with individual patients to help them obtain the treatments they need. Most of Sell's clients come to her when they have been denied insurance coverage for a specific treatment, and she must find a way to reverse the decision. While most rulings arise from simple errors, sometimes insurance companies have decided that crucial treatments are unnecessary or nonstandard, and she must be extremely persistent. As Sell puts it, "You're dealing with bureaucracies. When a clerk tells you a ruling can't be altered, you can't give up until you get the results the patient needs."

For health advocates, though, getting results requires not just persistence but also strong problem-solving skills. Advocates must combine their medical and health administration expertise in creative ways, devising new negotiation strategies all the time. Often, obtaining the best possible outcome for patients means developing a specific plan for each new situation.

As Sell points out, "You have to think ahead, and you have to be strategic. If you say the wrong thing at the wrong time, you can seriously damage your chances of success, and ultimately the patient will be the one to suffer."

For Sell, the best part of advocacy is the knowledge that she is "acting on behalf of patients who desperately need assistance." Because Sell deals primarily with cancer patients, her clients often come to her once they have been significantly weakened by disease. Even patients who have educated themselves about their condition sometimes find themselves too emotionally involved to think clearly about financial or legal details. When Sell acts on behalf of these clients, she supplies both the physical stamina and the emotional distance that her patients lack. As she puts it, "I have the opportunity to do what they would do for themselves if they could."

Although Sell's position at a nonprofit organization may grant her more direct contact with her clients than advocates working to improve legislation or medical standards, to some extent all health advocates share the satisfaction of working for patients' physical and financial well-being. Unfortunately, most health advocates also share the experience that Sell identifies as the worst part of advocacy: working with government agencies involved in health care, such as Medicaid and Medicare. Even for those used to dealing with large corporations and health insurance companies, navigating the bureaucracy of governmental agencies can be a baffling task.

REQUIREMENTS
High School

If you are interested in working as a health advocate, take a broad range of classes in high school. Advocates, after all, need an extensive base of knowledge that covers medical, financial, emotional, and legal areas. Courses that are especially useful include business, mathematics, biology, health, and chemistry. Be sure to take four years of English as well as speech classes, because health advocates need strong oral and written communication skills. Learning a foreign language, such as Spanish, will also be useful. You may also want to take government, psychology, and computer science classes to prepare for this career.

Postsecondary Training

There is no single educational route to take to become a health advocate; the backgrounds that health advocates bring to the field tend to be as varied as their places of employment. Nevertheless, a knowledge of health care systems and medical terminology are vital in this field. Most employers prefer that you have at least a bachelor's degree. Some students choose to get degrees in health administration, premed, biology, or nursing. Helpful courses to take include communications, management, conflict resolution, and medical terminology. Some schools also offer classes in patient representation. As this profession has become more popular, schools have begun to offer specialized programs of study. Sarah Lawrence College, for example, offers a master's degree in health advocacy. Course work for this degree includes nature of illness, position of the health advocate, health law, and ethics, as well as fieldwork.

Other Requirements

Advocates seem to agree that the most important training advocates can bring to this field is a sincere desire to work for the health and well-being of others. You can develop this commitment through community service, volunteer positions at hospitals, or caring for a loved one who has a serious illness. According to Marcia Hurst, head of the health advocacy program at Sarah Lawrence College, the most important skills to add to this sense of commitment are "writing, presentation skills, and analytical thinking." Though knowledge of the health care system is important, you can't do your job as an advocate unless you have the skills to convey that information in a convincing way to your audience, whether that audience is a medical ethics board or an insurance company clerk.

EXPLORING

One way to explore this field is by talking to people in it. Ask your school guidance counselor to help you set up an informational interview with a health advocate in your area. You may also be able to arrange to spend part of a day shadowing the advocate. Another way to learn more about this field is to learn about the issues that relate to patient advocacy. Visit your local library or surf the Internet to learn more. A good way to find out whether this field is for you is by volunteering at an organization that helps people. You might consider joining a religious group that helps the elderly or volunteering at a local hospital. Hospitals and nursing homes may also have paid part-time or summer positions available. Taking such a job will give you experience working in a health care environment and the opportunity to learn about patients' day-to-day needs. Stay up to date in this field by visiting related websites, such as Health Web (http://www.healthweb.org) and Healthfinder (http://www. healthfinder.gov).

EMPLOYERS

In addition to nonprofit organizations, private firms that specialize in patient advocacy have begun to spring up around the country. Some hospitals, specialty practices, and managed-care organizations now hire patient representatives to deal with patients' complaints, and corporations supporting large health care plans for their employees have begun to do the same. Advocates working on more widespread issues in the health care industry often find employment at governmental agencies, community organizations, and schools developing health advocacy courses or programs.

Job descriptions for advocates may also vary significantly, depending on your place of employment. Patient representatives employed by hospitals, doctors' groups, or large corporations still work for improved health care for patients, but also they must balance their employers' interests with those of patients. For that reason, advocates at work on the insurance or treatment side of the industry may find that their jobs resemble more typical customer service positions designed to receive and resolve consumer complaints. Advocates employed by nonprofits don't have the same responsibility to consider the financial needs of the doctors and insurance companies, and they may consequently have more freedom.

STARTING OUT

For Janet Sell, the shift from oncology nurse to patient advocate came naturally. "I wasn't a typical nurse," she remarks. "I was always more of an advocate, always complaining that things weren't right, that we could do better for the patients." Gradually, her interest in patients' rights led her to fight for legislation regarding certain treatments, and soon she made advocacy her full-time job. Sell found that her background in medicine allowed her to speak with authority when confronting insurance companies and doctors.

Contact your college placement office for help in finding your first job. Some hospitals advertise job openings for health advocates in the classified section of the newspaper. You may have to start out in another position in a hospital, and move into health advocacy once you've gained some experience.

ADVANCEMENT

Health advocates who work as members of a staff in a hospital can advance to department manager or other administrative positions. Some health advocates may find jobs in hospices, in AIDS programs, or with the U.S. Department of Health and Human Services.

EARNINGS

Although independent patient advocates may have more opportunities to put the patient first, they sometimes gain that freedom at the expense of job stability and a predictable salary. Patient representatives employed by hospitals, doctors' groups, and corporations can expect to earn a regular salary of $40,000 to $60,000 a year. A self-employed patient advocate or an advocate at a private firm will likely work for consultant fees that tend to vary from job to job. Some independent patient advocates charge flat fees from $75 to $150 to analyze insurance statements; if the advocate identifies any savings for the client, the advocate and client split the savings 50/50. While these rates may work out to significant earnings per year, independent advocates have no guaranteed business, and a slow year will mean a lower income. At nonprofit organizations, advocates can rely on predictable salaries; however, because nonprofits often lack the financial wherewithal of hospitals and corporations, advocates working at nonprofits tend to earn salaries at the lower end of the pay scale.

WORK ENVIRONMENT

The type of employment that an advocate pursues largely determines their work environment. High-profile advocates striving to improve patient conditions on a national level may travel frequently, deliver speeches and seminars, and even lunch with members of Congress. Patient representatives at hospitals or managed care organizations experience a different work environment: a more standard business atmosphere, with little travel outside of the office. While it's not typical, some advocates at nonprofit or small community groups work from home. Any health advocate, though, can expect busy and varied workdays; interaction with many people is part of this job.

OUTLOOK

According to the U.S. Bureau of Labor Statistics, employment in the health services industry will increase as the population ages and new medical technologies evolve. In fact, the U.S. Department of Labor expects the number of jobs will increase by 16.5 percent between 2000 and 2010. While this figure includes all areas of health services, growth in health services is likely to contribute to health advocacy employment in the long run: As the number of patients increases and the field of health services becomes larger and more complex, patients' need for advocates can be expected to increase as well.

As the field of health advocacy grows, it most likely will become more established. New graduate programs can be expected to develop, and eventually undergraduate programs may exist, as well. While the wide range of jobs available means that the field should stay diverse and deregulated, certain areas of health advocacy may develop certification procedures for their subgroups over the next five years.

FOR MORE INFORMATION

For information on education programs and to read selected articles from the Journal of the Health Advocacy Program, contact:
Health Advocacy Program
Sarah Lawrence College
1 Mead Way
Bronxville, New York 10708-5999
Tel: 914-337-0700
Email: occ@mail.slc.edu
http://www.slc.edu

For general information on health advocacy careers, contact:
Society for Healthcare Consumer Advocacy
PO Box 92683
Chicago, IL 60675-2683
http://www.shca-aha.org

LITERARY AGENTS

QUICK FACTS

School Subjects	Certification or Licensing
Business	None available
English	**Outlook**
Personal Skills	Little change or more
Communication/ideas	slowly than the average
Leadership/management	**DOT**
Work Environment	191
Primarily indoors	**GOE**
One location with some	11.12.03
travel	**NOC**
Minimum Education Level	6411
High school diploma	**O*NET-SOC**
Salary Range	13-1011.00
$20,000 to $55,550 to	
$100,000+	

OVERVIEW

Literary agents serve as intermediaries between writers and potential employers such as publishers and television producers. They also represent actors, artists, athletes, musicians, politicians, and other public figures who may seek to undertake writing endeavors. In essence, agents sell a product: their clients' creative talent. In addition to finding work for their clients, agents also may negotiate contracts, pursue publicity, and advise clients in their careers. The majority of literary agents work in New York and Los Angeles, and many others work in San Francisco, Chicago, and Miami.

HISTORY

The business of promoting writers is a product of the 20th century. Modern mass publishing and distribution systems, as well as the advent of the radio, television, and motion picture industries, have created a market for the writer's art that did not exist before. In the past, movie studios used staff writers. Today, independent writers create novels, magazine articles, screenplays, and scripts. It was perhaps only appropriate that brokers should emerge to bring together people who need each other: creators and producers. These brokers are literary agents.

THE JOB

Most agents can be divided into two broad groups: those who represent clients on a case-by-case basis and those who have intensive, ongoing partnerships with clients. Literary agents typically do not have long-term relationships with clients except for established authors. They may work with writers just one time, electing to represent them only after reading manuscripts and determining their viability. Literary agents market their clients' manuscripts to editors, publishers, and television and movie producers, among other buyers. Many of the most prestigious magazines and newspapers will not consider material unless an agent submits it. Busy editors rely on agents to screen manuscripts so that only the best, most professional product reaches them. Sometimes editors go directly to agents with editorial assignments, knowing that the agents will be able to find the best writer for the job.

After taking on a project, such as a book proposal, play, magazine article, or screenplay, agents approach publishers and producers in writing, by phone, or in person and try to convince these decision-makers to use their clients' work. When a publisher or other producer accepts a proposal, agents may negotiate contracts and rights, such as translation and excerpt rights, on behalf of their clients. Rather than pay authors directly, publishers pay their agents, who deduct their commission (anywhere from 4 to 20 percent of the total amount) and return the rest to the author.

Agents who represent established writers perform additional duties for their clients, such as directing them to useful resources, evaluating drafts and offering guidance, speaking for them in matters that must be decided in their absence, and in some instances serving as arbiters between coauthors. Also, to ensure that writers devote as much time as possible to their creative work, agents take care of such business as bookkeeping, processing income checks, and preparing tax forms.

REQUIREMENTS
High School

In order to identify and represent the best writers, you need to be well versed in classic and modern literature and have strong writing skills yourself. While in high school, take classes in literature and composition. Theater and music classes are also beneficial if you are interested in screenplays and scripts.

Postsecondary Training

Desirable areas of study in college include liberal arts, performing arts, and business administration. It is also helpful to study law, although agents need not be lawyers. A college degree is not necessary, but would-be agents with a degree are more likely to be hired than those without a college education.

Other Requirements

Agents need not have any specific education or technical skills, but you must have a knack for recognizing and promoting marketable talent. You must be familiar with the needs of publishers so as to approach them with the most appropriate and timely manuscript. You must be persistent without crossing over the line to harassment, for you must not alienate any of the publishers you will want to contact in the future.

Because continued success depends on the ability to maintain good relationships with clients and potential employers for their clients, you must have good people skills; you must be able to interact tactfully and amicably with a wide variety of people, from demanding clients to busy editors. Moreover, because artists' careers have their ups and downs and production and publishing are fields with high turnover rates, you should not become complacent. You must be flexible, adaptive, and able to establish new relationships quickly and with finesse.

EXPLORING

If you are interested in literary management you can acquaint yourself with current trends in book publishing and with the kinds of books that particular publishing houses issue by working part-time at bookstores and libraries. If you live in a big city, you may be able to get a job with a book or magazine publisher. Some literary agents also sponsor internships.

EMPLOYERS

Literary agents work for established large or small agencies, although many are self-employed. Los Angeles and New York are the country's leading entertainment centers, and most agents work in those two cities. Some agencies have branch offices in other large U.S. cities and affiliate offices overseas, especially in London.

STARTING OUT

Employment within a production facility, publishing house, or entertainment center is a good beginning for agents because it provides an insider's knowledge of agents' target markets. The other optimum approach is to send resumes to any and all agencies and to be willing to start at the bottom, probably as an office worker, then working up to the position of subagent, in order to learn the field.

ADVANCEMENT

How far agents advance depends almost entirely on their entrepreneurial skills. Ability alone isn't enough; successful agents must be persistent and ambitious. In addition to proving themselves to their agency superiors and clients, they must earn the trust and respect of decision-makers in the marketplace, such as publishers and producers. Once agents earn the confidence of a number of successful writers, they can strike out on their own and perhaps even establish their own agencies.

EARNINGS

Literary agents generally earned between $20,000 and $60,000 annually, with a rare few making hundreds of thousands of dollars a year. Because independent agents take a percentage of their clients' earnings (4 to 20 percent), their livelihoods are contingent upon the success of their clients, which is in turn contingent on the agents' ability to promote talent. Some beginning agents can go as long as a year without making any money at all, but, if at the end of that time, their clients begin to gain notice, the agents' investment of time may well pay off.

The Bureau of Labor Statistics reports that agents and business managers of artists, performers, and athletes earned a median salary of $55,550 a year in 2001. The highest 10 percent earned $122,490 or more, while the lowest 10 percent earned $26,790 or less.

According to the Association of Authors' Representatives, New York agency assistants typically earn beginning salaries of about $20,000. Sometimes agency staffers working on commission actually can earn more money than their bosses.

WORK ENVIRONMENT

Agents' hours are often uncertain, for in addition to fairly regular office hours, they often must meet on weekends and evenings with clients and editors with whom they are trying to build relationships.

The majority of their time, however, is spent in the office on the phone. Novices can expect no more than a cubicle, while established agents may enjoy luxurious office suites.

Established agents may frequently travel internationally to meet with clients, to scout out new talent, and find new opportunities for their talent.

OUTLOOK

Agents work in an extremely competitive field. Most agents who attempt to go into business for themselves fail within one year. Most job openings within agencies are the result of turnover, rather than the development of new positions. There are many candidates for few positions.

FOR MORE INFORMATION

For information on the duties, responsibilities, and ethical expectations of agents, and for AAR's newsletter, contact or visit the following website:

Association of Authors' Representatives, Inc. (AAR)
PO Box 237201
Ansonia Station
New York, NY 10003
http://www.aar-online.org

To access the latest news on book publishing, marketing, and selling, visit the Publishers Weekly *website:*
http://publishersweekly.reviewsnews.com

LOBBYISTS

QUICK FACTS

School Subjects
 Government
 Journalism
 Speech

Personal Skills
 Communication/ideas
 Leadership/management

Work Environment
 Primarily indoors
 One location with some
 travel

Minimum Education Level
 Bachelor's degree

Salary Range
 $20,000 to $100,000 to
 $500,000+

Certification or Licensing
 None available

Outlook
 About as fast as the
 average

DOT
 165

GOE
 11.09.03

NOC
 N/A

O*NET-SOC
 N/A

OVERVIEW

A *lobbyist* works to influence legislation on the federal, state, or local level on behalf of clients. Nonprofit organizations, labor unions, trade associations, corporations, and other groups and individuals use lobbyists to voice concerns and opinions to government representatives. Lobbyists use their knowledge of the legislative process and their government contacts to represent their clients' interests. Though most lobbyists are based in Washington, D.C., many work throughout the country representing client issues in city and state government.

HISTORY

Lobbying has been a practice within government since colonial times. In the late 1700s, the term "lobbyist" was used to describe the special-interest representatives who gathered in the anteroom outside the legislative chamber in the New York state capitol. The term often had a negative connotation, with political cartoonists frequently portraying lobbyists as slick, cigar-chomping individuals attempting to buy favors. But in the 20th century, lobbyists came to be seen as experts in the fields that they represented, and members of Congress relied upon them to provide information needed to evaluate legislation. During the New Deal in the 1930s, government spending in Washington greatly increased, and the number of lobbyists proliferated proportionately. A major lobbying law was enacted in 1938, but it wasn't until 1946 that comprehensive legislation in the form of the Federal Regulation of Lobbying Act was passed into law. The act requires that anyone who spends or receives money or anything of value in the interests of passing, modifying, or defeating legislation being considered by the U.S. Congress be registered and provide spending reports. Its effectiveness, however, was reduced by vague language that frequently required legal interpretations. Further regulatory acts have been passed in the years since; most recently, the Lobbying Disclosure Act of 1995 has required registration of all lobbyists working at the federal level.

THE JOB

An example of effective lobbying concerns Medic Alert, an organization that provides bracelets to millions of people in the United States and Canada with health problems. Engraved on the bracelet is a description of the person's medical problem, along with Medic Alert's 24-hour emergency response phone number. The emergency response center is located in a region of California that considered changing the telephone area code. Medic Alert anticipated a lot of confusion—and many possible medical disasters—if the area code was changed from that which is engraved on the millions of bracelets. Medic Alert called upon doctors, nurses, and the media to get word out about the danger to lives. Through this lobbying, the public and the state's policy-makers became aware of an important aspect of the area code change they may not have otherwise known.

The Medic Alert organization, like the thousands of associations, unions, and corporations in the United States, benefited from using lobbyists with an understanding of state politics and influence. The American Society of Association Executives estimates that the number of national trade and charitable associations is over 23,000. With 2,500 of these associations based in Washington, D.C., associations are the third-largest industry in the city, behind government and tourism. Lobbyists may work for one of these associations as a director of government relations, or they may work for an industry, company, or other organization to act on its behalf in government concerns. Lobbyists also work for lobbying firms that work with many different clients on a contractual basis.

Lobbyists have years of experience working with the government, learning about federal and state politics, and meeting career politicians and their staffs. Their job is to make members of Congress aware of the issues of concern to their clients and the effect that legislation and regulations will have on them. They provide the members of Congress with research and analysis to help them make the most informed decisions possible. Lobbyists also keep their clients informed with updates and reports.

Tom McNamara is the president of a government relations firm based in Washington, D.C. He first became involved in politics by working on campaigns before he was even old enough to vote. Throughout his years in government work, he has served as the Chief of Staff for two different members of Congress and was active in both the Reagan and Bush presidential campaigns. "Clients hire me for my advice," McNamara says. "They ask me to do strategic planning, relying on my knowledge of how Congress operates." After learning about a client's problem, McNamara researches the issue, then develops a plan and a proposal to solve the problem. Some of the questions he must ask when seeking a solution are: What are our assets? Who can we talk to who has the necessary influence? Do we need the media? Do we need to talk to Congressional staff members? "With 22 years in the House of Representatives," McNamara says, "I have a tremendous base of people I know. Part of my work is maintaining these relationships, as well as developing relationships with new members and their staff."

Lobbying techniques are generally broken down into two broad categories: direct lobbying and indirect, or "grassroots," lobbying. Direct lobbying techniques include making personal contacts with members of Congress and appointed officials. It is important for lobbyists to know who the key people are in drafting legislation that is significant to their clientele. They hire technical experts to develop reports, charts, graphs, or schematic drawings that may help in the legislative decision-making process that determines the passage, amendment, or defeat of a measure. Sometimes a lobbyist with expertise on a particular issue works directly with a member of Congress in the drafting of a bill. Lobbyists also keep members of Congress tuned in to the voices of their constituents.

Indirect, or grassroots, lobbying involves persuading voters to support a client's view. If the Congress member knows that a majority of voters favor a particular point of view, he or she will support or fight legislation according to the voters' wishes. Probably the most widely used method of indirect lobbying is the letter-writing campaign. Lobbyists use direct mail, newsletters, media advertising, and other methods of communication to reach the constituents and convince them to write to their member of Congress with their supporting views. Lobbyists also use phone campaigns, encouraging the constituents to call their Congress member's office. Aides usually tally the calls that come in and communicate the volume to the legislator.

Indirect lobbying is also done through the media. Lobbyists try to persuade newspaper and magazine editors and radio and television news managers to write or air editorials that reflect the point of view of their clientele. They write op-ed pieces that are submitted to the media for publication. They arrange for experts to speak in favor of a particular position on talk shows or to make statements that are picked up by the media. As a persuasive measure, lobbyists may send a legislator a collection of news clippings indicating public opinion on a forthcoming measure, or provide tapes of aired editorials and news features covering a relevant subject.

REQUIREMENTS
High School
Becoming a lobbyist requires years of experience in other government and related positions. To prepare for a government job, take courses in history, social studies, and civics to learn about the structure of local, state, and federal government. English and composition classes will help you develop your communication skills. Work on the student council or become an officer for a school club. Taking journalism courses and working on the school newspaper will prepare you for the public relations aspect of lobbying. As a reporter, you'll research current issues, meet with policy makers, and write articles.

Postsecondary Training
As a rule, men and women take up lobbying after having left an earlier career. As mentioned earlier, Tom McNamara worked for over 20 years as a congressional staff member before moving on to this other aspect of government work. Schools do not generally offer a specific

curriculum that leads to a career as a lobbyist; your experience with legislation and policy-making is what will prove valuable to employers and clients. Almost all lobbyists have college degrees, and many have graduate degrees. Degrees in law and political science are among the most beneficial for prospective lobbyists, just as they are for other careers in politics and government. Journalism, public relations, and economics are other areas of study that would be helpful in the pursuit of a lobbying career.

Certification or Licensing

Lobbyists do not need a license or certification, but the Lobbying Disclosure Act of 1995 requires all lobbyists working on the federal level to register with the Secretary of the Senate and the Clerk of the House. You may also be required to register with the states in which you lobby and possibly pay a small fee.

There is no union available to lobbyists. Some lobbyists join the American League of Lobbyists, which provides a variety of support services for its members. Membership in a number of other associations, including the American Society of Association Executives and the American Association of Political Consultants, can also be useful to lobbyists.

Other Requirements

"I've had practical, everyday involvement in government and politics," McNamara says about the skills and knowledge most valuable to him as a lobbyist. "I know what motivates Congress members and staff to act."

In addition to this understanding, McNamara emphasizes that lobbyists must be honest in all their professional dealings with others. "The only way to be successful is to be completely honest and straightforward." Your career will be based on your reputation as a reliable person, so you must be very scrupulous in building that reputation.

You also need people skills to develop good relationships with legislators and serve your clients' interests. Your knowledge of the workings of government, along with good communication skills, will help you to explain government legislation to your clients in ways that they can clearly understand.

EXPLORING

To explore this career, become an intern or volunteer in the office of a lobbyist, legislator, government official, special interest group, or nonprofit institution (especially one that relies on government grants). Working in these fields will introduce you to the lobbyist's world and provide early exposure to the workings of government.

Another good way to learn more about this line of work is by becoming involved in your school government; writing for your school newspaper; doing public relations, publicity, and advertising work for school and community organizations; and taking part in fundraising drives. When major legislative issues are being hotly debated, you can write to your congressional representatives to express your views or even organize a letter writing or telephone campaign; these actions are forms of lobbying.

EMPLOYERS

Organizations either hire government liaisons to handle lobbying or they contract with law and lobby firms. Liaisons who work for one organization work on only those issues that affect that organization. Independent lobbyists work on a variety of different issues, taking on clients on a contractual basis. They may contract with large corporations, such as a pharmaceutical or communications company, as well as volunteer services to nonprofit organizations. Lobbying firms are located all across the country. Those executives in charge of government relations for trade associations and other organizations are generally based in Washington, D.C.

STARTING OUT

Lobbyist positions won't be listed in the classifieds. It takes years of experience and an impressive list of connections to find a government relations job in an organization. Tom McNamara retired at age 50 from his work with the House of Representatives. "Lobbying was a natural progression into the private sector," he says. His love for public policy, campaigns, and politics led him to start his own lobbying firm. "I had an institutional understanding that made me valuable," he says.

Professional lobbyists usually have backgrounds as lawyers, public relations executives, congressional aides, legislators, government officials, or professionals in business and industry. Once established in a government or law career, lobbyists begin to hear about corporations and associations that need knowledgeable people for their government relations departments. The American Society of Association Executives (ASAE) hosts a website, http://www.asaenet.org, which lists available positions for executives with trade associations.

ADVANCEMENT

Lobbyists focus on developing long-standing relationships with legislators and clients and become experts on policy-making and legislation. Association or company executives may advance from a position as director of government relations into a position as president or vice-president. Lobbyists who contract their services to various clients advance by taking on more clients and working for larger corporations.

EARNINGS

Because of the wide range of salaries earned by lobbyists, it is difficult to compile an accurate survey. The ASAE, however, regularly conducts surveys of association executives. According to ASAE's 2001 Association Executive Compensation Study, directors of government relations within trade associations earned an average of $93,666 annually. The report notes, however, that compensation varies greatly depending on location. Highest earnings of directors were reported in New York City ($185,300), Washington, D.C. ($174,000), and Chicago ($168,000). The size of an association's staff and budget also affects compensation levels.

Like lawyers, lobbyists are considered very well paid; also like lawyers, a lobbyist's income depends on the size of the organization he or she represents. Experienced contract lobbyists with a solid client base can earn well over $100,000 a year and some make more than $500,000 a year. Beginning lobbyists may make less than $20,000 a year as they build a client base. In many cases, a lobbyist may take on large corporations as clients for the bulk of the annual income, then volunteer services to nonprofit organizations.

WORK ENVIRONMENT

Lobbyists spend much of their time communicating with the people who affect legislation—principally the legislators and officials of federal and state governments. This communication takes place in person, by telephone, and by memoranda. Most of a lobbyist's time is spent gathering information, writing reports, creating publicity, and staying in touch with clients. They respond to the public and the news media when required. Sometimes their expertise is required at hearings or they may testify before a legislature.

Tom McNamara has enjoyed the change from congressional Chief of Staff to lobbyist. "I'm an integral part of the system of government," he says, "albeit in a different role." He feels that every day is distinctly different, and he has the opportunity to meet new and interesting people. "It's intellectually challenging," he says. "You have to stay on top of the issues, and keep track of the personalities as well as the campaigns."

OUTLOOK

The number of special interest groups in the United States continues to grow, and as long as they continue to plead their causes before state and federal governments, lobbyists will be needed. However, lobbying cutbacks often occur in corporations. Because lobbying doesn't directly earn a profit for a business, the government relations department is often the first in a company to receive budget cuts. The American League of Lobbyists anticipates that the career will remain stable, though it's difficult to predict. In recent years, there has been a significant increase in registrations, but that is most likely a result of the Lobbying Disclosure Act of 1995 requiring registration.

The methods of grassroots advocacy will continue to be affected by the Internet and other new communication technology. Lobbyists and organizations use Web pages to inform the public of policy issues. These Web pages often include ways to immediately send email messages to state and federal legislators. Constituents may have the choice of composing their own messages or sending messages already composed. With this method, a member of Congress can easily determine the feelings of the constituents based on the amount of email received.

FOR MORE INFORMATION

For information about a lobbyist career, visit the following website or contact:

American League of Lobbyists
PO Box 30005
Alexandria, VA 22310
Tel: 703-960-3011
Email: alldc.org@erols.com
Web: http://www.alldc.org

For information about government relations and public policy concerns within trade associations, contact:

American Society of Association Executives
1575 I Street, NW
Washington, DC 20005-1103
Tel: 202-626-2723
Web: http://www.asaenet.org

MAGAZINE EDITORS

QUICK FACTS

School Subjects English Journalism **Personal Interests** Communication/ideas Helping/teaching **Work Environment** Primarily indoors Primarily one location **Minimum Education Level** Bachelor's degree **Salary Range** $14,000 to $39,960 to $75,000+	**Certification or Licensing** None available **Outlook** Faster than the average **DOT** 132 **GOE** 01.01.01 **NOC** 5122 **O*NET-SOC** 27-3041.00

OVERVIEW

Magazine editors plan the contents of a magazine, assign articles and select photographs and artwork to enhance articles, and they edit, organize, and sometimes rewrite the articles. They are responsible for making sure that each issue is attractive and readable and maintains the stylistic integrity of the publication. There are approximately 122,000 editors (all types) employed in the United States.

HISTORY

For the most part, the magazines that existed before the 19th century were designed for relatively small, highly educated audiences. In the early 19th century, however, inexpensive magazines that catered to a larger audience began to appear. At the same time, magazines began to specialize, targeting specific audiences. That trend continues today, with close to 20,000 magazines currently in production.

Beginning in the 19th century, magazine staffs became more specialized. Whereas in early publishing a single person would perform various functions, in 19th century and later publishing, employees performed individual tasks. Instead of having a single editor, for example, a magazine would have an editorial staff. One person would be responsible for acquisitions, another would copyedit, another would be responsible for editorial tasks related to production, and so forth.

Starting with Gutenberg's invention of movable type, changes in technology have altered the publishing industry. The development of the computer has revolutionized the running of magazines and other publications. Editing, design, and layout programs have considerably shortened the time in which a publication goes to press. The worldwide scope of magazine reporting is, of course, dependent upon technology that makes it possible to transmit stories and photographs almost instantaneously from one part of the world to another.

Finally, the Internet has provided an entirely new medium for magazine publishing, with many magazines maintaining both print and online versions. Online publishers avoid paper and printing costs, but still collect revenue from online subscriptions and advertising.

THE JOB

The duties of a magazine editor are numerous, varied, and unpredictable. The editor determines each article's placement in the magazine, working closely with the sales, art, and production departments to ensure that the publication's components complement one another and are appealing and readable.

Most magazines focus on a particular topic, such as fashion, news, or sports. Current topics of interest in the magazine's specialty area dictate a magazine's content. In some cases, magazines themselves set trends, generating interest in topics that become popular. Therefore, the editor should know the latest trends in the field that the magazine represents.

Depending on the magazine's size, editors may specialize in a particular area. For example, a fashion magazine may have a beauty editor, features editor, short story editor, and fashion editor. Each editor is responsible for acquiring, proofing, rewriting, and sometimes writing articles.

After determining the magazine's contents, the editor assigns articles to writers and photographers. The editor may have a clear vision of the topic or merely a rough outline. In any case, the editor supervises the article from writing through production, assisted by copy editors, assistant editors, fact checkers, researchers, and editorial assistants. The editor also sets a department budget and negotiates contracts with freelance writers, photographers, and artists.

The magazine editor reviews each article, checking it for clarity, conciseness, and reader appeal. Frequently, the editor edits the manuscript to highlight particular items. Sometimes the magazine editor writes an editorial to stimulate discussion or mold public opinion. The editor also may write articles on topics of personal interest.

Other editorial positions at magazines include the *editor in chief*, who is responsible for the overall editorial course of the magazine, the *executive editor*, who controls day-to-day scheduling and operations, and the *managing editor*, who coordinates copy flow and supervises production of master pages for each issue.

Some entry-level jobs in magazine editorial departments are stepping stones to more responsible positions. *Editorial assistants* perform various tasks such as answering phones and correspondence, setting up meetings and photography shoots, checking facts, and typing manuscripts. *Editorial production assistants* assist in coordinating the layout of feature articles edited by editors and art designed by *art directors* to prepare the magazine for printing.

Many magazines hire *freelance writers* to write articles on an assignment or contract basis. Most freelance writers write for several different publications; some become *contributing editors* to one or more publications to which they contribute the bulk of their work. Magazines also employ *researchers*, sometimes called *fact checkers*, to ensure the factual accuracy of an article's content. Researchers may be on staff or hired on a freelance basis.

REQUIREMENTS
High School

While in high school, develop your writing, reading, and analyzing skills through English and composition classes. It will also benefit you to be current with the latest news and events of the world, so consider taking history or politics classes. Reading the daily newspaper and news magazines can also keep you fresh on current events and will help you to become familiar with different styles of journalistic writing.

If your school offers journalism classes or, better yet, has a school newspaper, get involved. Any participation in the publishing process will be great experience, whether you are writing articles, proofreading copy, or laying out pages.

Top 10 Magazine Companies
(by revenue)

Company	Top Media Property
1. AOL Time Warner	*People Weekly*
2. Hearst Corporation	*Good Housekeeping*
3. Advance Publications	*Parade*
4. Primedia	*Seventeen*
5. International Data Group	*PC World*
6. Reed Elsevier	*Travel Weekly*
7. Reader's Digest Association	*Reader's Digest*
8. McGraw Hill Cos.	*Business Week*
9. Gruner & Jahr USA	*Family Circle*
10. Meredith Corp.	*Better Homes & Gardens*

Source: Publishers Information Bureau

Postsecondary Training

A college degree is required for entry into this field. A degree in jour-nalism, English, or communications is the most popular and stan-dard degree for a magazine editor. Specialized publications prefer a degree in the magazine's specialty, such as chemistry for a chemistry magazine, and experience in writing and editing. A broad liberal arts background is important for work at any magazine.

Most colleges and universities offer specific courses in magazine design, writing, editing, and photography. Related courses might include newspaper and book editing.

Other Requirements

All entry-level positions in magazine publishing require a work-ing knowledge of typing and word processing, plus a superior command of grammar, punctuation, and spelling. Deadlines are important, so commitment, organization, and resourcefulness are crucial.

Editing is intellectually stimulating work that may involve inves-tigative techniques in politics, history, and business. Magazine editors must be talented wordsmiths with impeccable judgment. Their decisions about which opinions, editorials, or essays to feature may influence a large number of people.

EXPLORING

The best way to get a sense of magazine editing is to work on a high school or college newspaper or newsletter. You will probably start out as a staff writer, but with time and experience, you may be able to move into an editorial position with more responsibility and freedom to choose the topics to cover.

EMPLOYERS

Major magazines are concentrated in New York, Chicago, Los Angeles, Boston, Philadelphia, San Francisco, and Washington, D.C., while professional, technical, and union publications are spread throughout the country.

STARTING OUT

Competition for editorial jobs can be fierce, especially in the popular magazine industry. Recent graduates hoping to break into the business should be willing to work other staff positions before moving into an editorial position.

Many editors enter the field as editorial assistants or proofreaders. Some editorial assistants perform only clerical tasks, whereas others may also proofread or perform basic editorial tasks. Typically, an editorial assistant who performs well will be given the opportunity to take on more and more editorial duties as time passes. Proofreaders have the advantage of being able to look at the work of editors, so they can learn while they do their own work.

Good sources of information about job openings are school placement offices, classified ads in newspapers and specialized publications such as *Publishers Weekly* (http://www.publishersweekly.com).

ADVANCEMENT

Employees who start as editorial assistants or proofreaders and show promise generally become copy editors. Copy editors work their way up to become senior editors, managing editors, and editors-in-chief. In many cases, magazine editors advance by moving from a position on one magazine to the same position with a larger or more prestigious magazine. Such moves often bring significant increases in both pay and status.

EARNINGS

According to the Magazine Publishers of America, the average salary for an editor who has four to 10 years of experience can range from $44,000 to $52,000. Entry-level editors earn from $14,000 to $30,000. Senior editors at large-circulation magazines average more than $75,000 a year. In addition, many editors supplement their salaried income by doing freelance work.

According to the Bureau of Labor statistics, the median annual earnings for salaried editors were $39,960 in 2001. The middle 50 percent earned between $29,740 and $54,930. Salaries ranged from less than $23,090 to more than $73,460.

Full-time editors receive vacation time, medical insurance, and sick time, but freelancers must provide their own benefits.

WORK ENVIRONMENT

Most magazine editors work in quiet offices or cubicles. However, even in relatively quiet surroundings, editors can face many distractions. A project editor who is trying to copyedit or review the editing of others may, for example, have to deal with phone calls from authors, questions from junior editors, meetings with members of the editorial and production staff, and questions from freelancers, among many other distractions.

An often stressful part of the magazine editor's job is meeting deadlines. Magazine editors work in a much more pressurized atmosphere than book editors because they face daily or weekly deadlines, whereas book production usually takes place over several months. Many magazine editors must work long hours during certain phases of the publishing cycle.

OUTLOOK

Magazine publishing is a dynamic industry. Magazines are launched every day of the year, although the majority fail. According to Magazine Publishers of America, 293 new magazines were introduced in 2001. The organization names the Internet, government affairs, and consumer marketing as some of the important issues currently facing the magazine publishing industry. The future of magazines is secure since they are a critical medium for advertisers.

A recent trend in magazine publishing is focus on a special interest. There is increasing opportunity for employment at special-interest, trade, and association magazines for those whose backgrounds complement a magazine's specialty. Internet publishing will provide increasing job opportunities as more businesses develop online publications. Magazine editing is keenly competitive, however, and as with any career, the applicant with the most education and experience has a better chance of getting the job. The *Occupational Outlook Handbook* projects faster-than-average growth in employment for editors and writers.

FOR MORE INFORMATION
For general and summer internship program information, contact:
Magazine Publishers of America
919 Third Avenue
New York, NY 10022
Tel: 212-872-3700
http://www.magazine.org

MEDIA PLANNERS AND BUYERS

QUICK FACTS

School Subjects
Business
English
Speech

Personal Skills
Artistic
Communication/ideas

Work Environment
Primarily indoors
One location with
some travel

Minimum Education Level
Bachelor's degree

Salary Range
$18,000 to $35,850 to
$120,000+

Certification or Licensing
None available

Outlook
Much faster than the
average

DOT
162

GOE
11.09.01

NOC
1225

O*NET-SOC
N/A

OVERVIEW

Media specialists are responsible for placing advertisements that will reach targeted customers and get the best response from the market for the least amount of money. Within the media department, *media planners* gather information about the sizes and types of audiences that can be reached through each of the various media and about the cost of advertising in each medium. *Media buyers* purchase space in printed publications, as well as time on radio or television stations. A *media director*, who is accountable for the overall media plan, supervises advertising media workers. In addition to advertising agencies, media planners and buyers work for large companies that purchase space or broadcast time. There are approximately 155,000 advertising sales agents employed in the United States.

HISTORY

The first formal media that allowed advertisers to deliver messages about their products or services to the public were newspapers and magazines, which began selling space to advertisers in the late 19th century. This system of placing ads gave rise to the first media planners and buyers, who were in charge of deciding what kind of advertising to put in which publications and then actually purchasing the space.

In the broadcast realm, radio stations started offering program time to advertisers in the early 1900s. Although television advertising began just before the end of World War II, producers were quick to realize that they could reach huge audiences by placing ads on TV. Television advertising proved to be beneficial to the TV stations as well, since they relied on sponsors for financial assistance in order to bring programs into people's homes. In the past, programs were sometimes named not for the host or star of the program, but for the sponsoring company that was paying for the broadcast of that particular show.

During the early years of radio and television, one sponsor could pay for an entire 30-minute program. However, the cost of producing shows on radio and television increased dramatically, thereby requiring many sponsors to support a single radio or television program. Media planners and buyers learned to get more for their money by buying smaller amounts of time—60, 30, and even 10 second spots—on a greater number of programs.

Today's media planners and buyers have a wide array of media from which to choose. The newest of these, the World Wide Web, allows advertisers not only to target customers precisely, but to interact with them as well. In addition to Web banner ads, producers can also advertise via sponsorships, their own websites, CD catalogs, voicemail telephone shopping, and more. With so many choices, media planners and buyers must carefully determine target markets and select the ideal media mix in order to reach these markets at the least cost.

THE JOB

While many employees may work in the media department, the primary specialists are the media planner and the media buyer. They work with professionals from a wide range of media—from billboards, direct mail, and magazines to television, radio, and the Internet. Both types of media specialists must be familiar with the markets that each medium reaches, as well as the advantages and disadvantages of advertising in each.

Media planners determine target markets based on their clients' advertising approaches. Considering their clients' products and services, budget, and image, media planners gather information about the public's viewing, reading, and buying habits by administering questionnaires and conducting other forms of market research. Through this research, planners are able to identify target markets by sorting data according to people's ages, incomes, marital status, interests, and leisure activities.

By knowing which groups of people watch certain shows, listen to specific radio stations, or read particular magazines or newspapers, media planners can help clients select air time or print space to reach the consumers most likely to buy their products. For example, Saturday morning television shows attract children, while prime-time programs often draw family audiences. For shows broadcast at these times, media planners will recommend air time to their clients who manufacture products of interest to these viewers, such as toys and automobiles, respectively.

Media planners who work directly for companies selling air time or print space must be sensitive to their clients' budgets and resources. When tailoring their sales pitch to a particular client's needs, planners often go to great lengths to persuade the client to buy air time or advertising space. They produce brochures and reports that detail the characteristics of their viewing or reading market, including the average income of those individuals, the number of people who see the ads, and any other information that may be likely to encourage potential advertisers to promote their products.

Media planners try to land contracts by inviting clients to meetings and presentations and educating them about various marketing strategies. They must not only pursue new clients but also attend to current ones, making sure that they are happy with their existing advertising packages. For both new and existing clients, the media planner's main objective is to sell as much air time or ad space as possible.

Media buyers do the actual purchasing of the time on radio or television or the space in a newspaper or magazine in which an advertisement will run. In addition to tracking the time and space available for purchase, media buyers ensure that ads appear when and where they should, negotiate costs for ad placement, and calculate rates, usage, and budgets. They are also responsible for maintaining contact with clients, keeping them informed of all advertising-related developments and resolving any conflicts that arise. Large companies that generate a lot of advertising or those that place only print ads or only broadcast ads sometimes differentiate between the two main media groups by employing *space buyers* and/or *time buyers.*

Workers who actually sell the print space or air time to advertisers are called *print sales workers* or *broadcast time salespeople.* Like media planners, these professionals are well versed about the target markets served by their organizations and can often provide useful information about editorial content or broadcast programs.

In contrast to print and broadcast planners and buyers, *interactive media specialists* are responsible for managing all critical aspects of their clients' online advertising campaigns. While interactive media planners may have responsibilities similar to those of print or broadcast planners, they also act as new technology specialists, placing and tracking all online ads and maintaining relationships with clients and Webmasters alike.

The typical online media planning process begins with an agency spreadsheet that details the criteria about the media buy. These criteria often include target demographics, start and end dates for the ad campaign, and online objectives. After sending all relevant information to a variety of websites, the media specialist receives cost, market, and other data from the sites. Finally, the media specialist places the order and sends all creative information needed to the selected websites. Once the order has been placed, the media specialist receives tracking and performance data and then compiles and analyzes the information in preparation for future ad campaigns.

Media planners and buyers may have a wide variety of clients. Restaurants, hotel chains, beverage companies, food product manufacturers, and automobile dealers all need to advertise to attract potential customers. While huge companies, such as soft drink manufacturers, major airlines, and vacation resorts, pay a lot of money to have their products or services advertised nationally, many smaller firms need to advertise only in their immediate area. Local advertising may come from a health club that wants to announce a special membership rate or from a retail store promoting a sale. Media planners and buyers must be aware of their various clients' advertising needs and create campaigns that will accomplish their promotional objectives.

Diversity in the Media

In recent years, diversity and multiculturalism have become prominent societal issues, especially in regard to media coverage and employment. Since the U.S. population comprises people of many different origins, the U.S. media should, ideally, reflect this diversity, both in terms of content and the people creating and delivering that content. From television and radio broadcasts to magazine newsrooms and public relations firms, employment numbers for minorities have fluctuated and come under close scrutiny in recent years.

Several surveys have followed the trends of diversity in the media workplace. A study co-sponsored by the Radio-Television News Directors Association and Ball State University found that minority representation in radio and television newsrooms declined in 2002, most notably for Hispanics. However, the survey found that female representation in newsrooms had increased.

In 2002, television news departments were 79.4 percent Caucasian, 9.3 percent African-American, 7.7 percent Hispanic, and 3.1 percent Asian American. The survey also found that on average, radio newsrooms were 92 percent Caucasian, 4.1 percent African-American, 2.4 percent Hispanic, and 0.8 percent Asian-American. Women made up just less than 40 percent of all television newsroom staffs and 32.5 percent of all radio staffs.

According to a study by the Center for Media and Public Affairs (CMPA), 29 percent of the stories airing on the ABC, CBS, and NBC evening newscasts in 2002 were reported by women, while 14 percent of the stories were reported by minorities. Both of these figures are record highs for this study, which began in 1990. In addition, for the first time, two Asian-American reporters made the top of CMPA's list of the 50 busiest reporters.

According to a 2002 study by Children Now, the 8:00–9:00 P.M. television timeslot, which many consider a prime family television-viewing hour, is among the least ethnically diverse, with only 16 percent of programs having an ethnically diverse cast. Many consider this sort of misrepresentation in television to be dangerous, as it could lead to skewed perceptions of society, especially among younger viewers.

Some other areas of the media are more diverse. The American Society of Newspaper Editors reported in 2002 that of the 54,400 total newspaper employees in the workforce, 6,600 were minorities. This is an increase of nearly half of one percentage point from 2001.

(continues)

Diversity in the Media *(continued)*

The Screen Actors Guild is also active in watching workforce trends, collecting ethnicity data on all casting roles in TV and film. The Guild has addressed the issue of underrepresentation of Hispanics and other minority groups in Hollywood.

Diversity in the media will continue to be an important issue, as media professionals are often very public figures whose viewpoints are shared with a large audience. The following are a few organizations that research and report on diversity in the media:

- Asian American Journalists Association
  (http://www.aaja.org)
- Bay Area Black Media Coalition
  (http://www.babmc.org)
- Black Broadcasters Alliance
  (http://www.thebba.org)
- California Chicano News Media Association
  (http://www.ccnma.org)
- Freedom Forum
  (http://www.freedomforum.org)
- International Women's Media Foundation
  (http://www.iwmf.org)
- National Association of Black Journalists
  (http://www.nabj.org)
- National Association of Hispanic Journalists
  (http://www.nahj.org)
- National Association of Minority Media Executives
  (http://www.namme.org)
- Native American Journalists Association
  (http://www.naja.com)

REQUIREMENTS
High School

Although most media positions, including those at the entry level, require a bachelor's degree, you can prepare for a future job as media planner and/or buyer by taking specific courses offered at the high school level. These include business, marketing, advertising, cinematography, radio and television, and film and video. General liberal arts classes, such as economics, English, communication, and journalism, are also important, since media planners and buyers must be able to communicate clearly with both clients and co-workers. Mathematics classes will give you the skills to work accurately with budget figures and placement costs.

Postsecondary Training

Increasingly media planners and buyers have college degrees, often with majors in marketing or advertising. Even if you have prior work experience or training in media, you should select college classes that provide a good balance of business coursework, broadcast and print experience, and liberal arts studies.

Business classes may include economics, marketing, sales, and advertising. In addition, courses that focus on specific media, such as cinematography, film and video, radio and television, and new technologies (like the Internet), are important. Additional classes in journalism, English, and speech will also prove helpful. Media directors often need to have a master's degree, as well as extensive experience working with the various media.

Other Requirements

Media planners and buyers in broadcasting should have a keen understanding of programming and consumer buying trends, as well as a knowledge of each potential client's business. Print media specialists must be familiar with the process involved in creating print ads and the markets reached by various publications. In addition, all media workers need to be capable of maintaining good relationships with current clients, as well as pursuing new clients on a continual basis.

Communication and problem solving skills are important, as are creativity, common sense, patience, and persistence. Media planners and buyers must also have excellent oral, written, and analytical skills, knowledge of interactive media planning trends and tools, and the ability to handle multiple assignments in a fast-paced work environment. Strategic thinking skills, industry interest, and computer experience with both database and word processing programs are also vital.

EXPLORING

Many high schools and two-year colleges and most four-year colleges have media departments that may include radio stations and public access or cable television channels. In order to gain worthwhile experience in media, you can work for these departments as aides, production assistants, programmers, or writers. In addition, high school and college newspapers and yearbooks often need students to sell advertising to local merchants. Theater departments also frequently look for people to sell ads for performance programs.

In the local community, newspapers and other publications often hire high school students to work part-time and/or in the summer in sales and clerical positions for the classified advertising department. Some towns have cable television stations that regularly look for volunteers to operate cameras, sell advertising, and coordinate various programs. In addition, a variety of church- and synagogue-sponsored activities, such as craft fairs, holiday boutiques, and rummage sales, can provide you with opportunities to create and place ads and work with the local media to get exposure for the events.

EMPLOYERS

Media planners and buyers often work for advertising agencies in large cities, such as Chicago, New York, and Los Angeles. These agencies represent various clients who are trying to sell everything from financial services to dishwasher soap. Other media specialists work directly for radio and television networks, newspapers, magazines, and websites selling air time and print space. While many of these media organizations are located in large urban areas, particularly radio and television stations, most small towns put out newspapers and therefore need specialists to sell ad space and coordinate accounts. Approximately 155,000 advertising sales agents work in the United States.

STARTING OUT

More than half of the jobs in print and broadcast media do not remain open long enough for companies to advertise available positions in the classified sections of newspapers. As a result, many media organizations, such as radio and television stations, do not usually advertise job openings in the want ads. Media planners and buyers often hear about available positions through friends, acquaintances, or family members and frequently enter the field as entry-level broadcasting or sales associates. Both broadcasting and sales can provide employees just starting out with experience in approaching and working for clients, as well as knowledge about the specifics of programming and its relationship with air-time sales.

Advertising agencies sometimes do advertise job openings, both in local and national papers and on the Web. Competition is quite fierce for entry-level jobs, however, particularly at large agencies in big cities.

Print media employees often start working on smaller publications as in-house sales staff members, answering telephones and taking orders from customers. Other duties may include handling classified ads or coordinating the production and placement of small print ads created by in-house artists and typesetters. While publications often advertise for entry-level positions, the best way to find work in advertising is to send resumes to as many agencies, publications, and broadcasting offices as possible.

While you are enrolled in a college program, you should investigate opportunities for internships or on-campus employment in related areas. Your school's career planning center or placement office should have information on such positions. Previous experience often provides a competitive edge for all job seekers, but it is crucial to aspiring media planners and buyers.

ADVANCEMENT

Large agencies and networks often hire only experienced people, so it is common for media planners and buyers to learn the business at smaller companies. These opportunities allow media specialists to gain the experience and confidence they need to move up to more advanced positions. Jobs at smaller agencies and television and radio stations also provide possibilities for more rapid promotion than those at larger organizations.

Media planners and buyers climbing the company ladder can advance to the position of media director or may earn promotions to executive-level positions. For those already at the management level, advancement can come in the form of larger clients and more responsibility. In addition, many media planners and buyers who have experience with traditional media are investigating the opportunities and challenges that come with the job of interactive media planner/buyer or Web media specialist.

EARNINGS

Because media planners and buyers work for a variety of organizations all across the country and abroad, earnings can vary greatly. In general, however, those just entering the field as marketing assistants make an average of $25,750 to $30,500 per year, according to

OfficeTeam's *2002 Salary Guide*. A *media desk coordinator* makes $27,500 to $32,500 annually, according to *Advertising Age*.

Media directors can earn between $46,000 and $118,400, depending on the type of employer and the director's experience level. For example, directors at small agencies make an average of $42,100, while those at large agencies can earn more than $120,000, according to a 2002 *Advertising Age* salary survey.

Media planners and buyers in television typically earn higher salaries than those in radio. In general, however, beginning broadcasting salespeople usually earn between $18,000 and $35,000 per year and can advance to as much as $46,000 after a few years of experience.

Starting salaries for print advertising salespeople range from $24,500 to $30,500 a year. Experienced workers may earn salaries up to $44,200 a year, on average. Some salespeople draw straight salaries, some receive bonuses that reflect their level of sales, and still others earn their entire wage based on commissions. These commissions are usually calculated as a percentage of sales that the employee brings into the company.

According to the U.S. Bureau of Labor Statistics, advertising sales agents had median annual earnings of $35,850 in 2000. Salaries ranged from $18,570 to more than $87,240.

Most employers of media planners and buyers offer a variety of benefits, including health and life insurance, a retirement plan, and paid vacation and sick days.

WORK ENVIRONMENT

Although media planners and buyers often work a 40-hour week, their hours are not strictly nine to five. Service calls, presentations, and meetings with ad space reps and clients are important parts of the job that usually have a profound effect on work schedules. In addition, media planners and buyers must invest considerable time investigating and reading about trends in programming, buying, and advertising.

The variety of opportunities for media planners and buyers results in a wide diversity of working conditions. Larger advertising agencies, publications, and networks may have modern and comfortable working facilities. Smaller markets may have more modest working environments.

Whatever the size of the organization, many planners seldom go into the office and must call in to keep in touch with the home organization. Travel is a big part of media planners' responsibilities to their clients, and they may have clients in many different types of businesses and services, as well as in different areas of the country.

While much of the media planner and buyer's job requires interaction with a variety of people, including co-workers, sales reps, supervisors, and clients, most media specialists also perform many tasks that require independent work, such as researching and writing reports. In any case, the media planner and buyer must be able to handle many tasks at the same time in a fast-paced, continually changing environment.

OUTLOOK

The employment outlook for media planners and buyers, like the outlook for the advertising industry itself, depends on the general health of the economy. When the economy thrives, companies produce an increasing number of goods and seek to promote them via newspapers, magazines, television, radio, the Internet, and various other media. The U.S. Department of Labor anticipates that employment in the advertising industry is projected to grow 32 percent over the 2000–10 period, much faster than the average for all occupations.

More and more people are relying on radio and television for their entertainment and information. With cable and local television channels offering a wide variety of programs, advertisers are increasingly turning to TV in order to get exposure for their products and services. Although newspaper sales are in decline, there is growth in special-interest periodicals and other print publications. Interactive media, such as the Internet, CD catalogs, and voicemail shopping, are providing a flurry of advertising activity all around the world. The Web alone promises advertising exposure in 65 million American households. All of this activity will increase market opportunities for media planners and buyers.

Employment possibilities for media specialists are far greater in large cities, such as New York, Los Angeles, and Chicago, where most magazines and many broadcast networks have their headquarters. However, smaller publications are often located in outlying areas, and large national organizations usually have sales offices in several cities across the country.

Competition for all advertising positions, including entry-level jobs, is expected to be intense. Media planners and buyers who have considerable experience will have the best chances of finding employment.

FOR MORE INFORMATION

The AAF is the professional advertising association that binds the mutual interests of corporate advertisers, agencies, media companies, suppliers, and academia. Student membership is available at the college level.

American Advertising Federation (AAF)
1101 Vermont Avenue, NW, Suite 500
Washington, DC 20005-6306
Tel: 202-898-0089
Email: aaf@aaf.org
http://www.aaf.org

The AAAA is the management-oriented national trade organization representing the advertising agency business.

American Association of Advertising Agencies (AAAA)
405 Lexington Avenue, 18th Floor
New York, NY 10174-1801
Tel: 212-682-2500
http://www.aaaa.org

MEDIA RELATIONS SPECIALISTS

QUICK FACTS

School Subjects
Business
English
Speech

Personal Skills
Communication/ideas
Leadership/management

Work Environment
Primarily indoors
Primarily one location

Minimum Education Level
Bachelor's degree

Salary Range
$22,780 to $39,580 to
$70,480+

Certification or Licensing
Voluntary

Outlook
Much faster than the
average

DOT
165

GOE
11.09.03

NOC
0611

O*NET-SOC
27-3031.00

OVERVIEW

Media relations specialists are experienced *public relations specialists* who have a broad working knowledge of television, radio, and print journalism and skills in establishing a controlled, positive image in the media for a company, person, or organization. They are also referred to as *communications consultants*. Media relations specialists serve as the liaison between the company, person, or organization they represent and newspaper, magazine, and broadcast news editors and reporters. The number of people working in media relations and their locations falls within the same parameters as public relations specialists. There are approximately 137,000 public relations specialists employed in the United States.

HISTORY

Similar to public relations, media relations is rooted in the 19th century, when newspapers began running positive articles about businesses that advertised in the paper to encourage future advertising. By the early 20th century, literary bureaus were established to contrive these articles, and publicity agents began surfacing in large cities. However, the articles began to undermine the newspapers' objectivity, and the practice was soon halted in the United States.

But the link between media relations and newspapers endured through reporters who were willing to use language's effects on public image to present a company or organization in a positive light. By the end of World War II, government agencies and politicians followed business's example by hiring public relations specialists to help deliver information to the press and to advise them on their appearances at press conferences and interviews.

Media relations is now an essential function of public relations. Virtually every public relations agency either employs media relations specialists or assigns media relations duties for each client to account executives. Likewise, most large companies and organizations have someone in charge of media relations.

THE JOB

As Wendy Leinhart, media specialist with Marcy Monyak & Associates in Chicago, emphasizes, "Media relations is not a stand-alone job; it is a function of public relations." In other words, media relations is just one, but perhaps the most significant, part of public relations.

Media relations specialists develop corporate or product positioning strategies for specific media outlets; plan photo and editorial opportunities for use in the media and develop editorial ideas to fit a publication's or broadcast medium's special promotions; develop news and feature releases and pitch them to the media; place articles with the media; gain favorable product reviews and publicize them to the media; position the organization they represent as an expert source; execute media events, such as press conferences, interviews, tours, and promotions; handle information requests from the press; and collect and analyze media coverage of the organization they represent.

To understand the media relations specialist's work, suppose a large pharmaceutical company has to recall one of its products because of possible tampering. The company's CEO decides she wants to address the issue with the public. The media relations specialist decides between arranging a press conference or an interview with a newspaper journalist from a major newspaper, contacts the appropriate media (in the case of a press conference) or reporter (in the case of an interview), and then briefs the CEO as to the angles on which the reporter or reporters will be basing questions.

Successful media relations depends on building an authentic rapport with reporters and editors while giving them something they can use. Media relations specialists are aware that most reliable journalists despise news that originates with a public relations slant, but that journalists often must rely on it because of time constraints. This is the reason rapport-building skills are essential in media relations.

Because the press release is at the heart of media relations, and major newspapers and wire services receive thousands of releases per day, the experienced media relations specialist knows when something is actually newsworthy and presents it in the most concise, attractive, and easy-to-read manner possible.

REQUIREMENTS
High School

Although your overall schedule should comprise college preparatory courses, there are a number of classes you should emphasize during your high school career. Naturally, English and communication classes, such as speech or debate, should be a top priority, as they will help you hone your communication skills. Also, take computer classes and other classes that emphasize working with different media, such as radio or television broadcasting classes and journalism classes. Courses in mathematics, economics, and business will help you develop the skills you will need to work with budgets and project planning. Be sure to take advertising or marketing classes if your high school offers them. Finally, since a media relations specialist is involved with current events, take any history or social studies class that emphasizes this subject. Such a class will give you the opportunity to observe how current events are related to the public through different media and the influences these media can have.

Postsecondary Training

To become a media relations specialist, you should have at least a bachelor's degree in communications, public relations, or journalism. Many college programs require or encourage their students to complete internships in public relations, either during the school year or the summer. These internships often provide valuable hands-on experience. Typical classes for those majoring in public relations include public relations management; writing courses that cover news releases, speeches, and proposals; and visual communications such as computer graphics. Other courses you should take include psychology, sociology, and business administration. A master's degree may be helpful as you advance in your career.

Certification or Licensing

Although certification or licensing are not required, you may find it beneficial to get accreditation in the communications field. The Public Relations Society of America accredits public relations professionals who have at least five years of experience with the Accredited in Public Relations designation, which can be obtained by passing a written and oral examination. The International Association of Business Communicators also offers the Accredited Business Communicator designation.

Other Requirements

In addition to excellent verbal and written communication skills, you need to be creative and aggressive, with the ability to come up with new and appealing ideas to attract media interest in your clients. You also need to be able to work under the pressure of deadlines, be able to make decisions quickly and effectively, and do thorough research. In addition, as a media relations specialist, you should have an interest in continuously learning about new technologies and using these new technologies to promote the interests of your clients.

EXPLORING

During your high school years, become involved with the school newspaper, yearbook, or literary magazine. Try working with these publications' advertising departments or sections by either selling ad space or promoting the publication to the student body. You can also join school committees that plan and publicize events such as school dances, fundraisers, or other functions. Try your hand at other media by working at the school television or radio station. You may even be able to come up with your own ad campaign for a school event.

The best way to explore this career during your college years is to complete an internship at a public relations firm. If you are unable to get such an internship, try getting a part-time or summer job at a local newspaper, radio, or television station where you can work in some type of public relations department. Read publications by the Public Relations Society of America, such as *The Strategist,* to become more familiar with how the public relations field works.

EMPLOYERS

Media relations specialists are employed either by the organization, company, or individual they represent or by a public relations agency. The majority of opportunities exist in major metropolitan areas, but there also may be opportunities even in smaller communities, such as at colleges and universities. Approximately 137,000 public relations managers are employed in the United States.

STARTING OUT

It is not likely that you'll begin your career in media relations right after graduating from college. Even someone with a professional journalism background should not jump into media relations without first working as a public relations generalist. "Most media relations specialists work entry-level PR jobs after working as a journalist, and fall into media relations as a specialty," Wendy Leinhart says. Also important is computer literacy, as the proliferation of online services continues.

College placement counselors can help you find a position that will prepare you for media relations. Other effective routes include completing an internship at a public relations agency or in a corporate public relations or communications department.

ADVANCEMENT

Entry-level public relations specialists might assemble media clippings or create media lists for different clients. As they gain experience, they may be assigned to write news releases, conduct a poll or survey, or write speeches for company officials.

As prospective media relations specialists become more experienced and knowledgeable about the organization they represent, they may be called on to help seasoned media relations specialists pitch news releases, place articles with the media, and plan media events.

Seasoned media relations specialists can move into managerial positions where they take an active role in shaping media strategies and positioning the organization they represent.

EARNINGS

The U.S. Department of Labor reports that the lowest paid 10 percent of public relations specialists made approximately $22,780 or less in 2000, while the highest paid 10 percent earned $70,480 or more. Salaried public relations specialists earned an average of $39,580 in 2000.

Media relations specialists working for consulting firms, agencies, and large corporations earn the most, while those in the nonprofit sector earn less.

Media relations specialists receive standard benefits, including health insurance, paid vacations, and sick days. They also receive regular salary increases and are often given expense accounts.

WORK ENVIRONMENT
Media relations specialists usually work in a traditional office environment and work between 40 and 50 hours per week. From time to time, tight project deadlines may call for more overtime than usual. Media relations specialists are expected to be tastefully dressed and socially poised and to maintain a professional demeanor. Often, they must entertain editors and reporters at lunches or dinners. Frequently, their conduct in their personal life is important if they are employed by a public relations agency or as a consultant to a client. Media relations specialists also are required to travel from time to time for business.

OUTLOOK
Competition among corporations continues to grow, as does the competition for funding between nonprofit organizations. In addition, individuals in the public eye, such as politicians and sports figures, continue to want expert advice on shaping their images. Thus, public relations will remain among the fastest growing fields, and media relations as a component of public relations will continue to grow. The U.S. Department of Labor predicts that employment for public relations specialists will grow much faster than the average over the next several years.

Competition for media relations positions will be stiff because, as with public relations, so many job seekers are enticed by the perceived glamour and appeal of the field. However, those with journalism backgrounds will have an advantage.

FOR MORE INFORMATION
For information on certification and Communications World *magazine, contact:*

International Association of Business Communicators
One Halladie Plaza, Suite 600
San Francisco, CA 94102
Tel: 415-544-4700

Email: service centre@iabc.com
http://www.iabc.com

For career and certification information, contact:
Public Relations Society of America
Career Information
33 Irving Place
New York, NY 10003-2376
Tel: 212-995-2230
Email: hq@prsa.org
http://www.prsa.org

For information on program accreditation and professional development, contact:
Canadian Public Relations Society, Inc.
4195 Dundas Street West, Suite 340
Toronto, ON M8X 1Y4 Canada
Tel: 416-239-7034
Email: cprs@netcom.ca
http://www.cprs.ca

NEWSPAPER EDITORS

QUICK FACTS

School Subjects English Journalism	**Certification or Licensing** None available
Personal Interests Communication/ideas Helping/teaching	**Outlook** Faster than the average
Work Environment Primarily indoors Primarily one location	**DOT** 132
Minimum Education Level Bachelor's degree	**GOE** 11.08.01
Salary Range $23,090 to $39,960 to $73,460+	**NOC** 5122
	O*NET-SOC 27-3041.00

OVERVIEW

Newspaper editors assign, review, edit, rewrite, and lay out all copy in a newspaper except advertisements. Editors sometimes write stories or editorials that offer opinions on issues. Editors review the editorial page and copy written by staff or syndicated columnists. A large metropolitan daily newspaper staff may include various editors who process thousands of words into print daily. A small town staff of a weekly newspaper, however, may include only one editor, who might be both owner and star reporter. Large metropolitan areas, such as New York, Los Angeles, Chicago, and Washington, D.C. employ many editors. Approximately 122,000 editors work for publications of all types in the United States.

HISTORY

The primary function of the newspaper publishing industry is to inform the public. Newspapers provide details, eyewitness interviews, and interpretations of current events in all areas of our society, such as politics, entertainment, and international affairs, to name a few.

The first American newspaper, *Publick Occurrences Both Foreign and Domestick,* appeared in Boston in 1690 and lasted only one issue due to censorship by the British government. The first continuously published paper in America was the *Boston News-Letter,* first published in 1704. It appeared regularly until 1776. The first daily newspaper, the *Pennsylvania Evening Post and Daily Advertiser,* began publication in 1783.

Early newspaper publishers were jacks-of-all-trades. They interviewed newsmakers; researched, wrote, and edited stories; solicited advertising; and typeset and printed their publications. As newspapers became larger and circulation increased, one person alone could no longer handle all of these tasks. By the late 19th century, every newspaper employed full-time reporters and editors who were skilled at research, writing, and editing. Today, most large newspapers employ a wide range of editors.

Computer technology and the Internet have had a dramatic impact on the newspaper industry. Internet and email technology allow newspaper editors to research information, confirm stories, and communicate with reporters much faster than they have in the past. Most major newspapers publish online versions, which provide some or all of the information that appears simultaneously in print versions. The growth of the Internet as a publishing venue has created many new opportunities for newspaper editors and other professionals in the industry.

THE JOB

Newspaper editors are responsible for the paper's entire news content. The news section includes features, "hard" news, and editorial commentary. Editors of a daily paper plan the contents of each day's issue, assigning articles, reviewing submissions, prioritizing stories, checking wire services, selecting illustrations, and laying out each page with the advertising space allotted.

At a large daily newspaper, an *editor-in-chief* oversees the entire editorial operation, determines its editorial policy, and reports to the publisher. The *managing editor* is responsible for day-to-day operations in an administrative capacity. *Story editors,* or *wire editors,* determine which national news agency (or wire service) stories will be used and edit them. Wire services give smaller papers, without foreign correspondents, access to international stories.

A *city editor* gathers local and sometimes state and national news. The city editor hires copy editors and reporters, hands out assignments to reporters and photographers, reviews and edits stories, confers with executive editors on story content and space availability, and gives stories to copy editors for final editing.

A newspaper may have separate desks for state, national, and foreign news, each with its own head editor. Some papers have separate *editorial page editors.* The *department editors* oversee individual features; they include *business editors, fashion editors, sports editors, book section editors, entertainment editors,* and more. Department heads make decisions on coverage, recommend story ideas, and make assignments. They often have backgrounds in their department's subject matter and are highly skilled at writing and editing.

The copy desk, the story's last stop, is staffed by *copy editors,* who correct spelling, grammar, and punctuation mistakes; check for readability and sense; edit for clarification; examine stories for factual accuracy; and ensure the story conforms to editorial policy. Copy editors sometimes write headlines or picture captions and may crop photos. Occasionally they find serious problems that cause them to kick stories back to the editors or the writer.

Editors, particularly copy editors, base many of their decisions on a style book that provides preferences in spelling, grammar, and word usage; it indicates when to use foreign spellings or English translations and the preferred system of transliteration. Some houses develop their own style books, but often they use or adapt the *Associated Press Stylebook.*

After editors approve the story's organization, coverage, writing quality, and accuracy, they turn it over to the *news editors,* who supervise article placement and determine page layout with the advertising department. News and executive editors discuss the relative priorities of major news stories. If a paper is divided into several sections, each has its own priorities.

Modern newspaper editors depend heavily on computers. Generally, a reporter types the story directly onto the computer network, providing editors with immediate access. Some editorial departments are situated remotely from printing facilities, but computers allow the printer to receive copy immediately upon approval. Today, designers computerize page layout. Many columnists send their finished columns from home computers to the editorial department via modem.

REQUIREMENTS
High School

English is the most important school subject for any future editor. You must have a strong grasp of the English language, including vocabulary, grammar, and punctuation, and you must be able to write well in various styles. Study journalism and take communications-related courses. Work as a writer or editor for your school paper or yearbook. Computer classes that teach word processing software and how to navigate the Internet will be invaluable in your future research. You absolutely must learn to type. If you cannot type accurately and rapidly, you will be at an extreme disadvantage.

Other subjects are important, too. Editors have knowledge in a wide range of topics, and the more you know about history, geography, math, the sciences, the arts, and culture, the better a writer and editor you will be.

Postsecondary Training

Look for a school with strong journalism and communications programs. Many programs require you to complete two years of liberal arts studies before concentrating on journalism studies. Journalism courses include reporting, writing, and editing; press law and ethics; journalism history; and photojournalism. Advanced classes include feature writing, investigative reporting, and graphics. Some schools offer internships for credit.

When hiring, newspapers look closely at a candidate's extracurricular activities, putting special emphasis on internships, school newspaper and freelance writing and editing, and part-time newspaper work (called *stringing*). Typing, computer skills, and knowledge of printing are helpful.

Other Requirements

To be a successful newspaper editor, you must have a love of learning, reading, and writing. You should enjoy the process of discovering information and presenting it to a wide audience in a complete, precise, and understandable way. You must be detail-oriented and care about the finer points of accuracy, not only in writing, but in reporting and presentation. You must be able to work well with coworkers, both giving and taking direction, and you must be able to work alone. Editors can spend long hours sitting at a desk in front of a computer screen.

EXPLORING

One of the best ways to explore this job is by working on your school's newspaper or other publication. You will most probably start as a staff writer or proofreader, which will help you understand editing and how it relates to the entire field of publishing.

Keeping a journal is another good way to polish your writing skills and explore your interest in writing and editing your own work. In fact, any writing project will be helpful, since editing and writing are inextricably linked. Make an effort to write every day, even if it is only a few paragraphs. Try different kinds of writing, such as letters to the editor, short stories, poetry, essays, comedic prose, and plays.

EMPLOYERS

Generally, newspaper editors are employed in every city or town, as most towns have at least one newspaper. As the population multiplies, so do the opportunities. In large metropolitan areas, there may be one or two daily papers, several general-interest weekly papers, ethnic and other special-interest newspapers, trade newspapers, and daily and weekly community and suburban newspapers. All of these publications need managing and department editors. Online papers also provide opportunities for editors.

STARTING OUT

A typical route of entry into this field is by working as an editorial assistant or proofreader. Editorial assistants perform clerical tasks as well as some proofreading and other basic editorial tasks. Proofreaders can learn about editorial jobs while they work on a piece by looking at editors' comments on their work.

Job openings can be found using school placement offices, classified ads in newspapers and trade journals, and specialized publications such as *Publishers Weekly* (http://www.publishersweekly.com). In addition, many publishers have websites that list job openings, and large publishers often have telephone job lines that serve the same purpose.

ADVANCEMENT

Newspaper editors generally begin working on the copy desk, where they progress from less significant stories and projects to major news and feature stories. A common route to advancement is for copy editors to be promoted to a particular department, where they may move up the ranks to management positions. An editor who has achieved success in a department may become a city editor, who is responsible for news, or a managing editor, who runs the entire editorial operation of a newspaper.

EARNINGS

Salaries for newspaper editors vary from small to large communities, but editors generally are well compensated. Other factors affecting compensation include quality of education and previous experience, job level, and the newspaper's circulation. Large metropolitan dailies offer higher paying jobs, while outlying weekly papers pay less.

According to the Bureau of Labor Statistics, the median annual income for editors (including newspaper editors) was $39,960 in 2001. The lowest paid 10 percent of editors earned less than $23,090 annually. The highest paid 10 percent of all editors earned more than $73,460 per year.

On many newspapers, salary ranges and benefits, such as vacation time and health insurance, for most nonmanagerial editorial workers are negotiated by the Newspaper Guild.

WORK ENVIRONMENT

Editors work in a wide variety of environments. For the most part, publishers of all kinds realize that a quiet atmosphere is conducive to work that requires tremendous concentration. It takes an unusual ability to edit in a noisy place. Most editors work in private offices or cubicles. Even in relatively quiet surroundings, however, editors often have many distractions. In many cases, editors have computers that are exclusively for their own use, but in others, editors must share computers that are located in a common area.

Deadlines are an important issue for virtually all editors. Newspaper editors work in a much more pressured atmosphere than other editors because they face daily or weekly deadlines. To meet these deadlines, newspaper editors often work long hours. Some newspaper editors start work at 5 A.M., others work until 11 P.M. or even through the night. Those who work on weekly newspapers, including feature editors, columnists, and editorial page editors, usually work more regular hours.

OUTLOOK

According to the U.S. Department of Labor, employment for editors and writers, while highly competitive, should grow faster than the average. Opportunities will be better on small daily and weekly newspapers, where the pay is lower. Some publications hire free-lance editors to support reduced full-time staffs. And as experienced editors leave the workforce or move to other fields, job openings will be available.

FOR MORE INFORMATION

The ASNE helps editors maintain the highest standards of quality, improve their craft, and better serve their communities. It preserves and promotes core journalistic values.

American Society of Newspaper Editors (ASNE)
11690B Sunrise Valley Drive
Reston, VA 20191-1409
Tel: 703-453-1122
http://www.asne.org

Founded in 1958 by the Wall Street Journal *to improve the quality of journalism education, this organization offers internships, scholarships, and literature for college students. For information on how to receive a copy of* The Journalist's Road to Success, *which lists schools offering degrees in news-editing, and financial aid to those interested in print journalism, contact:*

Dow Jones Newspaper Fund
PO Box 300
Princeton, NJ 08543-0300
Tel: 609-452-2820
Email: newsfund@wsj.dowjones.com
http://djnewspaperfund.dowjones.com

This trade association for African-American owned newspapers has a foundation that offers a scholarship and internship program for inner-city high school juniors.

National Newspaper Publishers Association
3200 13th Street, NW
Washington, DC 20010
Tel: 202-588-8764
http://www.nnpa.org

This organization for journalists has campus and online chapters.
Society of Professional Journalists
Eugene S. Pulliam National Journalism Center
3909 North Meridian Street
Indianapolis, IN 46208
Tel: 317-927-8000
Email: questions@spj.org
http://spj.org

PRESS SECRETARIES

QUICK FACTS

School Subjects English Government Journalism	**Certification or Licensing** None available
	Outlook About as fast as the average
Personal Skills Communication/ideas Leadership/management	**DOT** N/A
Work Environment Primarily indoors One location with some travel	**GOE** N/A
	NOC N/A
Minimum Education Level Bachelor's degree	**O*NET-SOC** N/A
Salary Range $23,930 to $41,010 to $116,573+	

OVERVIEW

Press secretaries help politicians promote themselves and their issues among voters. They advise politicians on how to address the media. Sometimes called "spin doctors," these professionals use the media to either change or strengthen public opinion. Press secretaries work for candidates and elected officials in Washington, D.C.; others work all across the country, involved with local and state government officials and candidates.

HISTORY

The practice of using the media for political purposes is nearly as old as the U.S. government itself. The news media developed right alongside the political parties, and early newspapers served as a battleground for the Federalists and the Republicans. The first media moguls of the late 1800s often saw their newspapers as podiums from which to promote themselves. George Hearst bought the *San Francisco Examiner* in 1885 for the sole purpose of helping him campaign for Congress.

The latter half of the 20th century introduced whole other forms of media, which were quickly exploited by politicians seeking offices. Many historians mark the Kennedy–Nixon debate of 1960 as the moment when television coverage first became a key factor in the election process. Those who read of the debate in the next day's newspapers were under the impression that Nixon had easily won, but it was Kennedy's composure and appeal on camera that made the most powerful impression. Negative campaigning first showed its powerful influence in 1964, when Democratic presidential candidate Lyndon Johnson ran ads featuring a girl picking a flower while a nuclear bomb exploded in the background, which commented on Republican candidate Barry Goldwater's advocacy of strong military action in Vietnam.

Bill Clinton was probably the first president to benefit from the art of "spin," as his press secretaries and political managers were actively involved in dealing with his scandals and keeping his approval ratings high among the public. James Carville and George Stephanopolis, working for Clinton's 1992 campaign, had the task of playing up Clinton's strengths as an intelligent, gifted politician, while down-playing his questionable moral background. Their efforts were portrayed in the documentary *The War Room*, and their success earned them national renown as "spin doctors."

THE JOB

If you were to manage a political campaign, how would you go about publicizing the candidate to the largest number of voters? You'd use TV, of course. The need for TV and radio spots during a campaign is the reason it costs so much today to run for office. And it's also the reason many politicians hire professionals with an understanding of media relations to help them get elected. Once elected, a politician continues to rely on media relations experts, such as press secretaries, to use the media to portray the politician in the best light. In recent years, such words as "spin," "leak," and "sound bite" have entered the daily vocabulary of news and politics to describe elements of political coverage in the media.

Press secretaries serve on the congressional staffs of senators and representatives and on the staffs of governors and mayors. The president also has a press secretary. Press secretaries and their assistants write press releases and opinion pieces to publicize the efforts of the government officials for whom they work. They also help prepare speeches and prepare their employers for press conferences and interviews. They maintain websites, posting press releases and the results of press conferences.

One related job is that of the *political consultant*. These experts usually work independently, or as members of consulting firms, and contract with individuals. Political consultants are involved in producing radio and TV ads, writing campaign plans, and developing themes for these campaigns. A theme may focus on a specific issue or on the differences between their client and the opponent. Their client may be new to the political arena or an established individual looking to maintain an office. They conduct polls and surveys to gauge public opinion and to identify their client's biggest competition. Political consultants advise their clients in the best ways to use the media.

Another related job is that of the *media relations expert*. These professionals are often called *spin doctors* because of their ability to put a good spin on a news story to best suit the purposes of their clients. Media relations experts are often called upon during a political scandal, or after corporate blunders, for damage control. Using the newspapers and radio and TV broadcasts, spin doctors attempt to downplay public relations disasters, helping politicians and corporations save face.

Because of media manipulations, press secretaries and other media representatives may be viewed as people who conceal facts and present lies, prey on the emotions of voters, or even represent clients responsible for illegal practices. However, press secretaries and other media experts are often responsible for bringing public attention to important issues and good political candidates.

REQUIREMENTS
High School

English composition, drama, and speech classes will help you develop good communication skills, while government, history, and civics classes will teach you about the structure of local, state, and federal government. Take math, economics, and accounting courses to prepare for poll-taking and for analyzing statistics and demographics.

While in high school, work with your school newspaper, radio station, or TV station. This will help you recognize how important reporters, editors, and producers are in putting together newspapers and shaping news segments. You should also consider joining your school's speech and debate team to gain experience in research and in persuasive argument.

Postsecondary Training

Most people in media relations have bachelor's degrees, and some also hold master's degrees, doctorates, and law degrees. As an undergraduate, you should enroll in a four-year college and pursue a well-rounded education. Press secretaries need a good understanding of the history and culture of the United States and foreign countries. Some of the majors you should consider as an undergraduate are journalism, political science, communications, English, marketing, and economics. You should take courses in government, psychology, statistics, history of western civilization, and a foreign language. You might then choose to pursue a graduate degree in journalism, political science, public administration, or international relations.

Seek a college with a good internship program. You might also pursue internships with local and state officials and your congressional members in the Senate and House of Representatives. Journalism internships will involve you with local and national publications, or the news departments of radio and TV stations.

Other Requirements

In this career, you need to be very organized and capable of juggling many different tasks, from quickly writing ads and press releases to developing budgets and expense accounts. You need good problem-solving skills and some imagination when putting a positive spin on negative issues. Good people skills are important so that you can develop contacts within government and the media. You should feel comfortable with public speaking, leading press conferences, and speaking on behalf of your employers and clients. You should also enjoy competition. You can't be intimidated by people in power or by journalists questioning the issues addressed in your campaigns.

EXPLORING

Get involved with your school government as well as with committees and clubs that have officers and elections. You can also become involved in local, state, and federal elections by volunteering for campaigns; though you may just be making phone calls and putting up signs, you may also have the opportunity to write press releases and schedule press conferences and interviews, and you will see first-hand how a campaign operates.

Working for your school newspaper will help you learn about conducting research, interviews, and opinion polls, which all play a part in managing media relations. You may be able to get a part-time job or an internship with your city's newspaper or broadcast news station, where you will gain experience with election coverage and political advertising. Visit the websites of U.S. Congress members. Many sites feature lists of recent press releases, which will give you a sense of how a press office publicizes the efforts and actions of Congress members. Read some of the many books examining recent political campaigns and scandals, and read magazines like *Harper's* (http://www.harpers.org), *The Atlantic* (http://www.theatlantic.com), and the online magazine *Salon.com* (http://www.salonmag.com) for political commentary.

EMPLOYERS

Though a majority of press secretaries work in Washington, D.C., others work in state capitals and major cities all across the country, working for local, state, and federal government officials. Media experts outside the government arena work in public relations agencies and the press offices of large corporations.

STARTING OUT

Media relations jobs aren't advertised, and there's no predetermined path to success. It is recommended that you make connections with people in both politics and the media. Volunteer for political campaigns, and also advocate for public policy issues of interest to you. You can make good connections, and gain valuable experience, working or interning in the offices of your state capital. You might also try for an internship with one of your state's members of Congress; contact their offices in Washington, D.C. for internship applications. If you're more interested in the writing and producing aspects of the career, work for local newspapers or the broadcast news media; or work as a producer for a television production crew or for an ad agency that specializes in political campaigns. A political consulting firm may hire assistants for writing and for commercial production. Whereas some people pursue the career directly by working in the press offices of political candidates, others find their way into political consulting after having worked as lawyers, lobbyists, or journalists.

ADVANCEMENT
A press secretary who has worked closely with a successful government official may advance into a higher staff position, like chief of staff or legislative director. Network TV, cable, and radio news departments also hire successful media relations experts to serve as political analysts on the air.

EARNINGS
According to the U.S. Bureau of Labor Statistics, public relations specialists (which includes press secretaries) had median annual earnings of $41,010 in 2001, with salaries ranging from less than $23,930 to more than $72,910. In 2000, median earnings for those who worked in local government were $40,760, and for those in state government, $39,560.

According to the Congressional Management Foundation (CMF), a consulting firm in Washington, D.C., press secretaries working in the U.S. House of Representatives earned less than their counterparts in the Senate. The CMF found that the average pay of a House press secretary was $45,301, while those employed by the Senate earned an average of $116,573. This pay differential is probably even greater, because the CMF info for the Senate is from 1999, while the House data is from 2000.

WORK ENVIRONMENT
Representing politicians can be thankless work. Press secretaries may have to speak to the press about sensitive, volatile issues and deal directly with the frustrations of journalists unable to get the answers they want. When working for prominent politicians, they may become the subject of personal attacks. Their hours are often long and stressful. In some cases, press secretaries have to write, produce, and deliver press releases in a matter of hours. They may also have to be available to the politician around the clock.

Despite these potential conflicts, their work can be exciting and fast-paced. Press secretaries see the results of their efforts in the newspapers and on television, and they have the satisfaction of influencing voters and public opinion.

OUTLOOK
Employment in this field is expected to grow about as fast as the average. Media representatives will become increasingly important to candidates and elected officials. Television ads and Internet campaigns have become necessities for reaching the public. The work of

press secretaries will expand as more news networks and news magazines more closely follow the decisions and actions of government officials.

The Pew Research Center, which surveys public opinion on political issues, has found that most Americans are concerned about negative campaigning, while most political consultants see nothing wrong with using negative tactics in advertising. Despite how the general public may feel about negative campaigning, it remains a very effective tool. In some local elections, candidates may mutually agree to avoid the mud-slinging, but the use of negative ads in general is likely to increase.

FOR MORE INFORMATION

This organization provides professional guidance, assistance, and education to members and maintains a code of ethics.

American Association of Political Consultants
600 Pennsylvania Avenue, SE, Suite 330
Washington, DC 20003
Tel: 202-544-9815
http://www.theaapc.org

For general information about careers in broadcast media, contact:
National Association of Broadcasters
1771 N Street, NW
Washington, DC 20036
Tel: 202-429-5300
Email: nab@nab.org
http://www.nab.org

Visit the websites of the House and the Senate for press releases and links to sites for individual members of Congress. To write to your state representatives, contact:
Office of Senator (Name)
United States Senate
Washington, DC 20510
http://www.senate.gov

Office of Congressperson (Name)
U.S. House of Representatives
Washington, DC 20510
http://www.house.gov

The Pew Research Center is an opinion research group that studies atti-tudes toward press, politics, and public policy issues. To read some of their survey results, visit their website or write:

The Pew Research Center for the People and the Press
1150 18th Street, NW, Suite 975
Washington, DC 20036
Tel: 202-293-3126
Email: mailprc@people-press.org
http://www.people-press.org

PUBLIC RELATIONS SPECIALISTS

QUICK FACTS

School Subjects
Business
English
Journalism

Personal Skills
Communication/ideas
Leadership/management

Work Environment
Primarily indoors
One location with some travel

Minimum Education Level
Bachelor's degree

Salary Range
$23,930 to $41,010 to
$72,910+

Certification or Licensing
Voluntary

Outlook
Much faster than the
average

DOT
165

GOE
11.09.03

NOC
5124

O*NET-SOC
11-2031.00,
27-3031.00

OVERVIEW

Public relations (PR) specialists develop and maintain programs that present a favorable public image for an individual or organization. They provide information to the target audience (generally, the public at large) about the client, its goals and accomplishments, and any further plans or projects that may be of public interest.

PR specialists may be employed by corporations, government agencies, nonprofit organizations—almost any type of organization. Many PR specialists hold positions in public relations consulting firms or work for advertising agencies. There are approximately 137,000 public relations specialists in the United States.

HISTORY

The first public relations counsel was a reporter named Ivy Ledbetter Lee, who in 1906 was named press representative for coalmine operators. Labor disputes were becoming a large concern of the operators, and they had run into problems because of their continual refusal to talk to the press and the hired miners. Lee convinced the mine operators to start responding to press questions and supply the press with information on the mine activities.

During and after World War II, the rapid advancement of communications techniques prompted firms to realize they needed professional help to ensure their messages were given proper public attention. Manufacturing firms that had turned their production facilities over to the war effort returned to the manufacture of peacetime products and enlisted the aid of public relations professionals to forcefully bring products and the company name before the buying public.

Large business firms, labor unions, and service organizations, such as the American Red Cross, Boy Scouts of America, and the YMCA, began to recognize the value of establishing positive, healthy relationships with the public that they served and depended on for support. The need for effective public relations was often emphasized when circumstances beyond a company's or institution's control created unfavorable reaction from the public.

Public relations specialists must be experts at representing their clients before the media. The rapid growth of the public relations field since 1945 is a testament to an increased awareness by all industries of the power of professional media usage and PR campaigns to maintain good relationships with many different publics: customers, employees, stockholders, contributors, and competitors.

THE JOB

Public relations specialists do a wide variety of tasks. Some work primarily as writers, creating reports, news releases, and booklet texts. Others write speeches or create copy for radio, TV, or film sequences. These workers spend much of their time contacting the press, radio, TV, and magazines on behalf of their employers. Some PR specialists work more as editors than writers, fact-checking and rewriting employee publications, newsletters, shareholder reports, and other management communications.

Specialists may choose to concentrate in graphic design, using their background knowledge of art and layout for developing brochures, booklets, and photographic communications. Other PR workers handle special events, such as press parties, convention exhibits, open houses, or anniversary celebrations.

PR specialists must be alert to any and all company or institutional events that are newsworthy. They prepare news releases and direct them toward the proper media. Specialists working for manufacturers and retailers are concerned with efforts that will promote sales and create goodwill for the firm's products. They work closely with the marketing and sales departments to announce new products, prepare displays, and attend occasional dealers' conventions.

A large firm may have a *director of public relations,* who is a vice president of the company and in charge of a staff that includes writers, artists, researchers, and other specialists. Publicity for an individual or a small organization may involve many of the same areas of expertise but may be carried out by a few people or possibly even one person.

Many PR workers act as consultants (rather than staff) of a corporation, institution, or organization. These workers have the advantage of being able to operate independently, state opinions objectively, and work with more than one type of business or association.

PR specialists are called upon to work with the public-opinion aspects of almost every corporate or institutional problem. These can range from the opening of a new manufacturing plant to a college's dormitory dedication to a merger or sale of a company.

Public relations professionals can also specialize. *Lobbyists* try to persuade legislators and other office holders to pass laws favoring the interests of the firms or people they represent. *Fund-raising directors* develop and direct programs designed to raise funds for social welfare agencies and other nonprofit organizations.

Early in their careers, public relations specialists become accustomed to having others receive credit for their behind-the-scenes work. The speeches they draft will be delivered by company officers, the magazine articles they prepare may be credited to the president of the company, and they may be consulted to prepare the message to stockholders from the chairman of the board that appears in the annual report.

REQUIREMENTS
High School

While in high school, take courses in English, journalism, public speaking, humanities, and languages, because public relations is based on effective communication with others. Courses such as these will develop your skills in written and oral communication as

Top 10 Global Public Relations Firms
(by revenue)

1. Weber Shandwick Worldwide
2. Fleishman-Hillard Inc.
3. Hill and Knowlton, Inc.
4. INCEPTA (CITIGATE)
5. Burson Marsteller
6. Edelman Public Relations Worldwide
7. Ketchum, Inc.
8. Porter Novelli
9. GCI GROUP/APCO Worldwide
10. Ogilvy Public Relations Worldwide

Source: The Council of Public Relations Firms (http://www.prfirms.org)

well as provide a better understanding of different fields and industries to be publicized.

Postsecondary Training

Most people employed in public relations service have a college degree. Major fields of study most beneficial to developing the proper skills are public relations, English, and journalism. Some employers feel that majoring in the area in which the public relations person will eventually work is the best training. A knowledge of business administration is most helpful, as is a native talent for selling. A graduate degree may be required for managerial positions. People with a bachelor's degree in public relations can find staff positions with either an organization or a public relations firm.

More than 200 colleges and about 100 graduate schools offer degree programs or special courses in public relations. In addition, many other colleges offer at least courses in the field. The journalism or communication departments of schools sometimes offer PR programs. In addition to courses in theory and techniques of public relations, PR students may study organization, management and administration, and practical applications; they often specialize in areas such as business, government, and nonprofit organizations.

Other preparation includes courses in creative writing, psychology, communications, advertising, and journalism.

Certification or Licensing

The Public Relations Society of America, the International Association of Business Communicators, and the Canadian Public Relations Society, Inc., accredit public relations workers who have passed a comprehensive examination. Such accreditation is a sign of competence in this field, although it is not a requirement for employment.

Other Requirements

Today's public relations specialist must be a businessperson first, both to understand how to perform successfully in business and to comprehend the needs and goals of the organization or client. Additionally, the public relations specialist needs to be a strong writer and speaker with good interpersonal, leadership, and organizational skills.

EXPLORING

Almost any experience in working with other people will help you to develop strong interpersonal skills, which are crucial in public relations. The possibilities are almost endless. Summer work on a newspaper or trade paper or with a radio or television station may give insight into communications media. Working as a volunteer on a political campaign can help you to understand the ways in which people can be persuaded. Being selected as a page for the U.S. Congress or a state legislature will help you grasp the fundamentals of government processes. A job in retail will help you to understand some of the principles of product presentation. A teaching job will develop your organization and presentation skills.

EMPLOYERS

Public relations specialists hold about 137,000 jobs. Workers may be paid employees of the organization they represent or they may be part of a public relations firm that works for organizations on a contract basis. Others are involved in fund-raising or political campaigning. Public relations may be done for a corporation, retail business, service company, utility, association, nonprofit organization, or educational institution.

Most PR firms are located in large cities that are centers of communications. New York, Chicago, Los Angeles, and Washington, D.C.

are good places to search for a public relations job. Nevertheless, there are many good opportunities in cities across the United States.

STARTING OUT

There is no clear-cut formula for getting a job in public relations. Individuals often enter the field after gaining preliminary experience in another occupation closely allied to the field, usually some segment of communications, frequently journalism. Coming into public relations from newspaper work is still a recommended route. Another good method is to gain initial employment as a public relations trainee or intern, or as a clerk, secretary, or research assistant in a public relations department or a counseling firm.

ADVANCEMENT

In some large companies, an entry-level public relations specialist may start as a trainee in a formal training program for new employees. In others, new employees may expect to receive work that has a minimum of responsibility. They may assemble clippings or do rewrites on material that has already been accepted. They may make posters or assist in conducting polls or surveys, or compile reports from data submitted by others.

As workers acquire experience, they are given more responsibility. They write news releases, direct polls or surveys, or advance to writing speeches for company officials. Progress may seem to be slow, because some skills take a long time to master.

Some lower level PR workers advance in responsibility and salary in the same firm in which they started. Others find that the path to advancement is to accept a more attractive position in another firm.

The goal of many public relations specialists is to open an independent office or to join an established consulting firm. To start an independent office requires a large outlay of capital and an established reputation in the field. However, those who are successful in operating their own consulting firms probably attain the greatest financial success in the public relations field.

EARNINGS

The Bureau of Labor Statistics reports that public relations specialists had median annual earnings of $41,010 in 2001. Salaries ranged from less than $23,930 to more than $72,910.

The U.S. Department of Labor reports the following 2000 median salaries for public relations specialists by type of employer: management and public relations, $43,690; state government, $39,560; local government, $40,760; and colleges and universities, $35,080.

Many PR workers receive a range of fringe benefits from corporations and agencies employing them, including bonus/incentive compensation, stock options, profit sharing/pension plans/401-K programs, medical benefits, life insurance, financial planning, maternity/paternity leave, paid vacations, and family college tuition. Bonuses can range from 5 to 100 percent of base compensation and often are based on individual and/or company performance.

WORK ENVIRONMENT

Public relations specialists generally work in offices with adequate secretarial help, regular salary increases, and expense accounts. They are expected to make a good appearance in tasteful, conservative clothing. They must have social poise, and their conduct in their personal life is important to their firms or their clients. The public relations specialist may have to entertain business associates.

The PR specialist seldom works the conventional office hours for many weeks at a time; although the workweek may consist of 35 to 40 hours, these hours may be supplemented by evenings and even weekends when meetings must be attended and other special events covered. Time behind the desk may represent only a small part of the total working schedule. Travel is often an important and necessary part of the job.

The life of the PR worker is so greatly determined by the job that many consider this a disadvantage. Because the work is concerned with public opinion, it is often difficult to measure the results of performance and to sell the worth of a public relations program to an employer or client. Competition in the consulting field is keen, and if a firm loses an account, some of its personnel may be affected. The demands it makes for anonymity will be considered by some as one of the profession's less inviting aspects. Public relations involves much more hard work and a great deal less glamour than is popularly supposed.

OUTLOOK

Employment of public relations professionals is expected to grow much faster than average for all other occupations, according to the U.S. Department of Labor. Competition will be keen for beginning jobs in public relations because so many job seekers are enticed by the perceived glamour and appeal of the field; those with both education and experience will have an advantage.

Most large companies have some sort of public relations resource, either through their own staff or through the use of a firm of consultants. They are expected to expand their public relations activities and create many new jobs. More of the smaller companies are hiring public relations specialists, adding to the demand for these workers.

FOR MORE INFORMATION

To read Communication World Online *and other information for professionals in public relations, employee communications, marketing communications, and public affairs, contact:*

International Association of Business Communicators
One Hallidie Plaza, Suite 600
San Francisco, CA 94102-2818
Tel: 415-544-4700
http://www.iabc.com

For statistics, salary surveys, and other information about the profession, contact:

Public Relations Society of America
33 Irving Place
New York, NY 10003-2376
Tel: 212-995-2230
Email: hq@prsa.org
http://www.prsa.org

This professional association for public relations professionals offers an accreditation program and opportunities for professional development.

Canadian Public Relations Society, Inc.
4195 Dundas Street West, Suite 346
Toronto, ON M8X 1Y4 Canada
Tel: 416-239-7034
http://www.cprs.ca

RADIO PRODUCERS

QUICK FACTS

School Subjects English Journalism Speech	**Certification or Licensing** None available
	Outlook Little change or more slowly than the average
Personal Skills Communication/ideas Leadership/management	**DOT** 159
Work Environment Primarily indoors Primarily one location	**GOE** 01.03.01
Minimum Education Level Bachelor's degree	**NOC** 5131
Salary Range $21,000 to $27,500 to $42,000	**O*NET-SOC** 27-2012.00

OVERVIEW

Radio producers plan, rehearse, and produce live or recorded programs. They work with the music, on-air personalities, sound effects, and technology to put together an entire radio show. They schedule interviews and arrange for promotional events.

According to the Federal Communications Commission (FCC), the United States alone has 13,296 radio stations. Larger stations employ radio producers, while smaller stations may combine those duties with those of the program director or disc jockey. While most radio producers work at radio stations, some work to produce a particular show and then sell that show to various stations.

HISTORY

As long as radio has existed, people have been behind the scenes to make sure that what the audience hears is what the station wants them to hear. A wide variety of administrative, programming, and technical people work behind the scenes of radio shows to create a professional broadcast.

Scheduled broadcasting began with a program broadcast by radio station KDKA in Pittsburgh, and by 1923, 2.5 million radios had been purchased. In the 1930s, radio personalities were household names, and even then, numerous people worked behind the scenes, arranging interviews and coordinating production.

Before television, radio producers would direct the on-air soap operas as well as the news, weather, and music. With the added technology of today's radio broadcast, radio producers are even more important in mixing the special effects, locations, personalities, and formats in ways that create a good radio show.

The Internet has made the radio producer's job easier in some ways and more challenging in others. Websites specifically for producers provide a community where ideas can be exchanged for shows, news, jokes, and more. However, with the new frontier of broadcasting on the Internet, radio producers have one more duty to add to their long list of responsibilities.

THE JOB

The identity and style of a radio program is a result of the collaborations of on-air and off-air professionals. Radio disc jockeys talk the talk during a broadcast, and producers walk the walk behind the scenes. But in many situations, particularly with smaller radio stations, the disc jockey and the show's producer are the same person.

Also, many show producers have disc jockey experience. This experience, combined with technical expertise, helps producers effectively plan their shows.

Brent Lee, a radio producer for WFMS, a country radio station in Indianapolis, began his career while still in high school at the small radio station in his home town. This early on-air experience, combined with his degree in telecommunications and political science from Ball State University, helped to give Lee the necessary background for his current position.

Radio producers rely on the public's very particular tastes—differences in taste allow for many different kinds of radio to exist, to serve many different segments of a community. In developing radio programs, producers take into consideration the marketplace—they listen to other area radio stations and determine what's needed and appreciated in the community, and what there may already be too much of. They conduct surveys and interviews to find out what the public wants to hear. They decide which age groups they want to pursue and develop a format based on what appeals to these listeners. This all results in a station's identity, which is very important. Listeners associate a station with the kind of music it plays, how much music it plays, the type of news and conversation presented, and the station's on-air personalities.

Based on this feedback, and on market research, radio disc jockeys/producers devise music playlists and music libraries. They each develop an individual on-air identity, or personality, and they invite guests who will interest their listeners. Keeping a show running on time is also the responsibility of a producer. This involves carefully weaving many different elements into a show, including music, news reports, traffic reports, and interviews.

As the producer of the "Jim, Kevin, and Bill Show," Lee arrives at the station at about 4:15 A.M. each morning to prep for the morning show. The show broadcasts from 5 A.M. to 9 A.M. each morning, with its main audience to be the "morning drivers" on their way to work or school.

The time of the broadcast is one key to planning a radio show. Because of the typical listeners of the morning show, traffic reports are given every 10 minutes. These reports are mixed with weather, news, and music. While the rest of the day, WFMS listeners will hear 13 songs each hour, the morning show typically plays between six and eight songs per hour. Those songs are interspersed with six traffic reports, four weather forecasts, a variety of national, local, and entertainment news, and morning disc jockey banter.

The audience of the country music radio station is mostly female, and the morning show is billed as "good, clean fun" by the station, promoting the family nature of the program.

In addition to keeping in touch with the listening public, producers keep track of current events. They consult newspapers and other radio programs to determine what subjects to discuss on their morning shows. One of the newest tools that Lee uses is a website designed specifically for morning shows. The site provides a forum to share ideas and ask questions.

"There are a couple of things each day that can be used," says Lee. "Since we're a family show, we have to throw some of it out, but it's a really good resource."

Radio producers write copy for and coordinate on-air commercials, which are usually recorded in advance. They also devise contests, from large public events to small, on-air trivia competitions.

Though a majority of radio stations have music formats, radio producers also work for 24-hour news stations, public broadcasting, and talk radio. Producing news programs and radio documentaries involves a great deal of research, booking guests, writing scripts, and interviewing.

"One of the most attractive qualities about this job is it's fun," says Lee. "Each day, I spend half of my first five hours laughing."

REQUIREMENTS
High School

Writing skills are valuable in any profession, but especially in radio. Take composition and literature courses, and other courses that require essays and term papers. Journalism courses will not only help you develop your writing skills, but they will teach you about the nature and history of media. You'll learn about deadlines and how to put a complete project (such as a newspaper or yearbook) together. Speech courses are also necessary if you plan on getting on-air experience or managing other workers.

Business courses and clubs frequently require students to put together projects; starting any business is similar to producing your own radio show. Use such a project as an opportunity to become familiar with the market research, interviewing, and writing that are all part of a radio producer's job. For both the future radio producer and the future disc jockey, a theater department offers great learning opportunities. Drama or theater classes, which are frequently involved in productions, may provide opportunities for learning about funding, advertising, casting, and other fundamentals similar to a radio production.

If your school has a radio station, get involved with it in any way you can. Check with your local radio stations; some may offer part-time jobs to high school students interested in becoming producers and disc jockeys.

Postsecondary Training

Most journalism and communications schools at universities offer programs in broadcasting. Radio producers and announcers often start their training in journalism schools, and they receive hands-on instruction at campus radio stations. These broadcasting programs are generally news-centered, providing great opportunities for students interested in producing news programs, daily newscasts, and documentaries. News directors and program managers of radio stations generally want to hire people who have a good, well-rounded education with a grounding of history, geography, political science, and literature.

Other Requirements

In order to be a successful radio producer, you should be well versed in the English language (or the language you broadcast in) and be a creative thinker who can combine several elements into one project. The ability to understand technical equipment and coordinate it with on-air events is also necessary.

A healthy curiosity about people and the world will help radio producers find new topics for news shows, new guests for call-ins, and new ideas for music formats. There are no physical requirements to be a radio producer, although those starting as disc jockeys need a strong, clear voice to be heard over the airwaves.

EXPLORING

Getting your feet wet early is a good idea for all radio careers. Small radio stations are often willing to let young, inexperienced people work either behind-the-scenes or on-air. Getting a job or an internship at one of the small stations in your area may be as simple as asking for one.

Many high schools and universities have on-site radio stations where students can get hands-on experience at all different levels. As you explore the career further, you might want to interview a radio producer to make sure that the job requirements and description are still of interest to you.

Since most people don't start out as a producer, experience in any area of radio is helpful, so talk to local disc jockeys or program directors as well.

EMPLOYERS

There has been a steady growth in the number of radio stations in the United States. According to the FCC, there were 13,012 radio stations as of 2001 and over 3,800 station owners.

However, many stations combine the position of radio producer with that of the disc jockey or program director, so depending on the size of the station and market, producers may or may not be able to find a suitable employer.

Due to the Telecommunications Act of 1996, companies can own an unlimited number of radio stations nationwide with an eight-station limit within one market area, depending on the size of the market. When this legislation took effect, mergers and acquisitions changed the face of the radio industry. So, while the pool of employers is smaller, the number of stations continues to rise.

STARTING OUT

Radio producers usually start work at radio stations in any capacity possible. After working for a while in a part-time position gaining experience and making connections, a young, dedicated producer will find opportunities to work in production or on-air.

Both experience and a college education are generally needed to become a radio producer. It is best if both the experience and the education are well rounded with exposure to on-air and off-air positions as well as a good working knowledge of the world in which we live.

Although some future producers begin their first radio jobs in paid positions, many serve unpaid internships or volunteer to help run their college or high school station. Even if this entry-level work is unpaid, the experience gained is one of the key necessities to furthering a career in any type of radio work.

With experience as a disc jockey or behind-the-scenes person, an aspiring radio producer might try to land a position at another station, most likely within a station and format they are used to.

ADVANCEMENT

Radio producers are a key link in putting together a radio show. Once they have experience coordinating all the elements that go into a radio production, it is possible to move into a program director position or, possibly in the future, to general manager.

Another way to advance is to move from being the producer of a small show to a larger one, or move from a small station to a larger one. Some producers move into the freelance arena, producing their own shows that they sell to several radio stations.

EARNINGS

According to a salary survey by the Radio and Television News Directors Association (RTNDA), radio news producers reported salaries ranging from $21,000 to $42,000 per year, with a median of $27,500 in 2001. Like many radio jobs, there is a wide salary range resulting from differences in market size and station size of each radio station. Salaries for radio producers have been relatively flat, according to RTNDA, with little growth over the previous few years.

Most large stations offer full-time employees typical benefits, including health and life insurance.

WORK ENVIRONMENT

Radio producers generally work indoors in a busy environment, although some location and outdoor work might be required. The atmosphere at a radio station is generally very pleasant; however, smaller stations may not be modern, with much of the investment going into high-tech equipment for the broadcasts.

Full-time radio producers usually work more than 40 hours per week planning, scheduling, and producing radio shows. Also, according to the schedule of their shows, early morning, late night, or weekend work might be required. Radio is a 24-hour-a-day, seven-day-a-week production, requiring constant staffing.

Producers work with disc jockeys and program directors in planning radio shows, and they also work with advertising personnel to produce radio commercials. In addition to this collaboration, they may work alone doing research for the show. Working with the public is another aspect of the radio producer's job. Promotions and events may require contact with businesspeople and listeners.

OUTLOOK

The U.S. Department of Labor predicts slower-than-average employment growth in the radio industry over the next several years. In the past, radio station ownership was highly regulated by the government, limiting the number of stations a person or company could own. Recent deregulation has made multiple station ownership possible. Radio stations now are bought and sold at a more rapid pace. This may result in a radio station changing formats as well as entire staffs. Though some radio producers are able to stay at a station over a period of several years, people going into radio should be prepared to change employers at some point in their careers.

Another trend that is affecting radio production jobs is the increasing use of programming created by services outside the broadcasting industry. Satellite radio, in which subscribers pay a monthly fee for access to 100 radio stations, will be a big threat to smaller, marginal stations.

Competition is stiff for all radio jobs. Graduates of college broadcasting programs are finding a scarcity of work in media. Paid internships will also be difficult to find—many students of radio will have to work for free for a while to gain experience. Radio producers may find more opportunities as freelancers, developing their own programs independently and selling them to stations.

FOR MORE INFORMATION

For a list of schools offering degrees in broadcasting as well as scholarship information, contact:

Broadcast Education Association
1771 N Street, NW
Washington, DC 20036-2891
Tel: 202-429-5355
Email: beainfo@beaweb.org
http://www.beaweb.org

The FCC offers information on media guidelines, including all radio laws. For more information, contact:

Federal Communications Commission (FCC)
445 12th Street, SW
Washington, DC 20554
Tel: 888-225-5322
Email: fccinfo@fcc.gov
http://www.fcc.gov

For college programs and union information, contact:

National Association of Broadcast Employees and Technicians
501 3rd Street, NW, 8th Floor
Washington, DC 20001
Tel: 800-882-9174
Email: nabet@nabetcwa.org
http://nabetcwa.org

For broadcast education, support, and scholarship information, contact:

National Association of Broadcasters
1771 N Street, NW
Washington, DC 20036
Tel: 202-429-5300
Email: nab@nab.org
http://www.nab.org

For scholarship and internship information, contact:

Radio-Television News Directors Foundation
1600 K Street, NW, Suite 700
Washington, DC 20006-2838
Tel: 202-659-6510
Email: rtnda@rtnda.org
http://www.rtnda.org

RADIO PROGRAM DIRECTORS

QUICK FACTS

School Subjects
Business
Journalism

Personal Skills
Communication/ideas
Leadership/management

Work Environment
Primarily indoors
Primarily one location

Minimum Education Level
Bachelor's degree

Salary Range
$10,000 to $66,165 to
$72,000

Certification or Licensing
None available

Outlook
Little change or more
slowly than the average

DOT
184

GOE
11.05.02

NOC
2263

O*NET-SOC
27-2012.02, 27-2012.03

OVERVIEW

Radio program directors plan and schedule program material for radio stations. They determine the entertainment programs, news broadcasts, and other program material their organizations offer to the public. At a large station, the program director may supervise a large programming staff. At a small station, one person may manage and handle all programming duties.

HISTORY

Radio broadcasting in the United States began after World War I. The first commercial radio station, KDKA in Pittsburgh, came on the air in 1920 with a broadcast of presidential election returns. About a dozen radio stations were broadcasting by 1921. In 1926 the first national network linked stations across the country. The Federal Communications Commission (FCC) reports that in early 2003, there were 13,331 AM and FM stations broadcasting in the United States.

THE JOB

Program directors plan and schedule program material for radio stations of all sizes. They work in both commercial and public broadcasting and may be employed by individual radio stations or regional/national networks.

The material program directors work with includes entertainment programs, public service programs, newscasts, sportscasts, and commercial announcements. Program directors decide what material is broadcast and when it is scheduled; they work with other staff members to develop programs and buy programs from independent producers. They are guided by such factors as the budget available for program material, the audience their station seeks to attract, their organization's policies on content and other matters, and the kinds of products advertised in the various commercial announcements.

In addition, program directors may set up schedules for the program staff, audition and hire disc jockeys and other on-the-air personnel, and assist the sales department in negotiating contracts with sponsors of commercial announcements. The duties of individual program directors are determined by the size of their organization, and whether they work for a commercial or public operation.

At small radio stations the owner or manager may be responsible for programming, but at larger radio stations, the staff usually includes a program director. At medium to large radio stations, the program director usually has a staff that includes such personnel as music librarians, music directors, editors for prerecorded segments, and writers. Some stations and networks employ *public service directors*. It is the responsibility of these individuals to plan and schedule radio public service programs and announcements in such fields as education, religion, and civic and government affairs.

Program directors must carefully coordinate the various elements for a station while keeping in tune with the listeners, advertisers, and sponsors.

Other managers in radio broadcasting include production managers, operations directors, news directors, and sports directors. The work of program directors usually does not include the duties of *radio directors,* who direct rehearsals and integrate all the elements of a performance.

REQUIREMENTS
High School

If you are interested in this career, take courses that develop your communication skills in high school. Such classes include English, debate, and speech. You also should take business courses to develop your management skills; current events and history courses to develop your understanding of the news and the trends that affect the public's interests; and such courses as dance, drama, music, and painting to expand your understanding of the creative arts. Finally, don't neglect your computer skills. You will probably be using computers throughout your career to file reports, maintain schedules, and plan future programming projects.

Postsecondary Training

Those with the most thorough educational backgrounds will find it easiest to advance in this field. Therefore a college degree is recommended. Possible majors for those interested in this work include radio and television production and broadcasting, communications, liberal arts, or business administration. You will probably take English, economics, business administration, computer, and media classes. You may also wish to acquire some technical training that will help you understand the engineering aspects of broadcasting.

Other Requirements

Program directors must be creative, alert, and adaptable people who stay up to date on the public's interests and attitudes and are able to recognize the potential in new ideas. They must be able to work under pressure for long hours, and they must be able to work with all kinds of people. Program directors also must be good managers who can make decisions, oversee costs and deadlines, and attend to details.

EXPLORING

If your high school or college has a radio station, you should volunteer to work on the staff. You also should look for part-time or summer jobs at local radio stations. You may not be able to plan the programming at a local station, but you will see how a station works and be able to make contacts with those in the field. If you can't find a job at a local station, at least arrange for a visit and ask to talk to the personnel. You may be able to "shadow" a program director for a day—that is, follow that director for the workday and see what his or her job entails.

EMPLOYERS

According to the FCC, there were 13,331 radio stations in the United States in early 2003. Large conglomerates own some radio stations, while others are owned individually. While radio stations are located all over the country, the largest stations with the highest paid positions are located in large metropolitan areas.

STARTING OUT

Program director jobs are not entry-level positions. A degree and extensive experience in the field is required. Most program directors have technical and on-air experience in radio. While you are in college, investigate the availability of internships, since internships are almost essential for prospective job candidates. Your college placement office should also have information on job openings. Private and state employment agencies may also provide useful resources. You can also send resumes to radio stations or apply in person.

Beginners should be willing to relocate, as they are unlikely to find employment in large cities. They usually start at small stations with fewer employees, allowing them a chance to learn a variety of skills.

ADVANCEMENT

Most beginners start in entry-level jobs and work several years before they have enough experience to become program directors. Experienced program directors usually advance by moving from small stations to larger stations and networks or by becoming station managers.

EARNINGS

Salaries for radio program directors vary widely based on such factors as size and location of the station, whether the station is commercial or public, and experience of the director. According to the U.S. Bureau of Labor Statistics, median annual earnings of general and operations managers in both radio and television broadcasting were $66,165 in 2001.

According to the *2002 Radio and Television Salary Survey* by the Radio-Television News Directors Association, radio news directors earned a median of $30,500, and salaries ranged from a low of $10,000 to a high of $72,000.

Program directors usually receive health and life coverage benefits and, sometimes, yearly bonuses.

WORK ENVIRONMENT

Program directors at small radio stations often work 44 to 48 hours a week and frequently work evenings, late at night, and weekends.

At larger stations, which have more personnel, program directors usually work 40-hour weeks.

Program directors frequently work under pressure because of the need to maintain precise timing and meet the needs of sponsors, performers, and other staff members.

Although the work is sometimes stressful and demanding, radio program directors usually work in pleasant environments with creative staffs. They also interact with the community to arrange programming and deal with a variety of people.

OUTLOOK

All radio stations employ program directors or have other employees whose duties include programming. According to the U.S. Department of Labor, employment in radio and television broadcasting is expected to increase 10 percent over the 2000–10 period, which is slower than the average for all industries. The slow growth rate is attributed to industry consolidation, introduction of new technologies, greater use of prepared programming, and competition from other media.

Competition for radio jobs is strong; however, there are more opportunities for beginners in radio than there are in television. In larger cities, most stations hire only experienced workers.

Newer radio stations are expected to create additional openings for program directors, but some radio stations are eliminating program director positions by installing automatic programming equipment or combining those responsibilities with other positions.

FOR MORE INFORMATION

For a list of schools offering degrees in broadcasting, contact:
Broadcast Education Association
1771 N Street, NW
Washington, DC 20036-2891
Tel: 888-380-7222
Email: beainfo@beaweb.org
http://www.beaweb.org

For broadcast education, support, and scholarship information, contact:
National Association of Broadcasters
1771 N Street, NW
Washington, D.C. 20036
Tel: 202-429-5300

Email: nab@nab.org
http://www.nab.org

For scholarship and internship information, contact:
Radio-Television News Directors Association
1600 K Street, NW, Suite 700
Washington, D.C. 20006-2838
Tel: 202-659-6510
Email: rtnda@rtnda.org
http://www.rtnda.org

REPORTERS

QUICK FACTS

School Subjects English Journalism	**Certification or Licensing** None available
Personal Skills Communication/ideas Helping/teaching	**Outlook** Little change or more slowly than the average
Work Environment Indoors and outdoors Primarily multiple locations	**DOT** 131 **GOE** 11.08.02
Minimum Education Level Bachelor's degree	**NOC** 5123
Salary Range $17,320 to $30,060 to $68,020+	**O*NET-SOC** 27-3022.00

OVERVIEW

Reporters are the foot soldiers for newspapers, magazines, and television and radio broadcast companies. They gather and analyze information about current events and write stories for publication or for broadcasting. News analysts, reporters, and correspondents hold about 78,000 jobs in the United States.

HISTORY

Newspapers are the primary disseminators of news in the United States. People read newspapers to learn about the current events that are shaping their society and societies around the world. Newspapers give public expression to opinion and criticism of government and societal issues, and, of course, provide the public with entertaining, informative reading.

Newspapers are able to fulfill these functions because of the freedom given to the press. However, this was not always the case. The first American newspaper, published in 1690, was suppressed four days after it was published. And it was not until 1704 that the first continuous newspaper appeared.

One early newspaperman who later became a famous writer was Benjamin Franklin. Franklin worked for his brother at a Boston newspaper before publishing his own paper two years later in 1723 in Philadelphia.

A number of developments in the printing industry made it possible for newspapers to be printed more cheaply. In the late 19th century, new types of presses were developed to increase production, and more importantly, the Linotype machine was invented. The Linotype mechanically set letters so that handset type was no longer necessary. This dramatically decreased the amount of prepress time needed to get a page into print. Newspapers could respond to breaking stories more quickly, and late editions with breaking stories became part of the news world.

These technological advances, along with an increasing population, factored into the rapid growth of the newspaper industry in the United States. In 1776, there were only 37 newspapers in the United States. Today there are more than 1,500 daily and nearly 7,500 weekly newspapers in the country.

As newspapers grew in size and widened the scope of their coverage, it became necessary to increase the number of employees and to assign them specialized jobs. Reporters have always been the heart of newspaper staffs. However, in today's complex world, with the public hungry for news as it occurs, reporters and correspondents are involved in all media—not only newspapers, but magazines, radio, and television as well. Today, many newspapers have an online presence in addition to the traditional print version, so reporters may work in the digital arena, as well.

THE JOB

Reporters collect information on newsworthy events and prepare stories for newspaper or magazine publication or for radio or television broadcast. The stories may simply provide information about local, state, or national events, or they may present opposing points of view on issues of current interest. In this latter capacity, the press plays an important role in monitoring the actions of public officials and others in positions of power.

Stories may originate as an assignment from an editor or as the result of a lead or a news tip. Good reporters are always on the lookout for good story ideas. To cover a story, reporters gather and verify facts by interviewing people involved in or related to the event, examining documents and public records, observing events as they happen, and researching relevant background information. Reporters generally take notes or use a tape recorder as they collect information and write their stories once they return to their offices. In order to meet a deadline, they may have to telephone the stories to *rewriters,* who write or transcribe the stories for them. After the facts have been gathered and verified, the reporters transcribe their notes, organize their material, and determine what emphasis, or angle, to give the news. The story is then written to meet prescribed standards of editorial style and format.

The basic functions of reporters are to observe events objectively and impartially, record them accurately, and explain what the news means in a larger, societal context. Within this framework, there are several types of reporters.

The most basic is the *news reporter.* This job sometimes involves covering a beat, which means that the reporter may be assigned to consistently cover news from an area such as the local courthouse, police station, or school system. It may involve receiving general assignments, such as a story about an unusual occurrence or an obituary of a community leader. Large daily papers may assign teams of reporters to investigate social, economic, or political events and conditions.

Many newspaper, wire service, and magazine reporters specialize in one type of story, either because they have a particular interest in the subject or because they have acquired the expertise to analyze and interpret news in that particular area. *Topical reporters* cover stories for a specific department, such as medicine, politics, foreign affairs, sports, consumer affairs, finance, science, business, education, labor, or religion. They sometimes write features explaining the history that has led up to certain events in the field they cover. *Feature writers* generally write longer, broader stories than news reporters, usually on more upbeat subjects, such as fashion, art, theater, travel, and social events. They may write about trends, for example, or profile local celebrities. *Editorial writers* and *syndicated news columnists* present viewpoints that, although based on a thorough knowledge, are opinions on topics of popular interest. *Columnists* write under a byline and usually specialize in a particular subject, such as politics or government activities. *Critics* review restaurants, books, works of art, movies, plays, musical performances, and other cultural events.

Specializing allows reporters to focus their efforts, talent, and knowledge on one area of expertise. It also gives them more opportunities to develop deeper relationships with contacts and sources, which is necessary to gain access to the news.

Correspondents report events in locations distant from their home offices. They may report news by mail, telephone, fax, or computer from rural areas, large cities throughout the United States, or countries. Many large newspapers, magazines, and broadcast companies have one correspondent who is responsible for covering all the news for the foreign city or country where they are based. These reporters are known as *foreign correspondents.*

Reporters on small or weekly newspapers not only cover all aspects of the news in their communities, but also may take photographs, write editorials and headlines, lay out pages, edit wire-service copy, and help with general office work. *Television reporters* may have to be photogenic as well as talented and resourceful: they may at times present live reports, filmed by a mobile camera unit at the scene where the news originates, or they may tape interviews and narration for later broadcast.

Top 10 Newspaper Companies
(by revenue)

Company	Top Media Property
1. Gannet Co.	*USA Today*
2. Tribune Co.	*Los Angeles Times*
3. Knight Ridder	*The Philadelphia Inquirer*
4. New York Times Co.	*The New York Times*
5. Advance Publications	*The Star Ledger* (Newark, NJ)
6. Dow Jones & Co.	*The Wall Street Journal*
7. Cox Enterprises	*Atlanta Journal & Constitution*
8. Hearst Corp.	*Houston Chronicle*
9. McClatchy Co.	*Star Tribune* (Minneapolis)
10. MediaNews Group	*Denver Post*

Source: Audit Bureau of Circulations (report from 3/31/02)

REQUIREMENTS

High School

High school courses that provide a firm foundation for a reporting career include English, journalism, history, social studies, communications, typing, and computer science. Speech courses will help you hone your interviewing skills, which are necessary for success as a reporter. In addition, it will be helpful to take college prep courses, such as foreign language, math, and science.

Postsecondary Training

You will need at least a bachelor's degree to become a reporter, and a graduate degree will give you a great advantage over those entering the field with lesser degrees. Most editors prefer applicants with degrees in journalism because their studies include liberal arts courses as well as professional training in journalism. Some editors consider it sufficient for a reporter to have a good general education from a liberal arts college. Others prefer applicants with an undergraduate degree in liberal arts and a master's degree in journalism. The great majority of journalism graduates hired today by newspapers, wire services, and magazines have majored specifically in news-editorial journalism.

More than 400 colleges offer programs in journalism leading to a bachelor's degree. In these schools, around three-fourths of a student's time is devoted to a liberal arts education and one-fourth to the professional study of journalism, with required courses such as introductory mass media, basic reporting and copy editing, history of journalism, and press law and ethics. Students are encouraged to select other journalism courses according to their specific interests.

Journalism courses and programs are also offered by many community and junior colleges. Graduates of these programs are prepared to go to work directly as general assignment reporters, but they may encounter difficulty when competing with graduates of four-year programs. Credit earned in community and junior colleges may be transferable to four-year programs in journalism at other colleges and universities. Journalism training may also be obtained in the armed forces. Names and addresses of newspapers and a list of journalism schools and departments are published in the annual *Editor & Publisher International Year Book: The Encyclopedia of the Newspaper Industry* (New York, Editor & Publisher, 1999), which is available for reference in most public libraries and newspaper offices.

A master's degree in journalism may be earned at approximately 120 schools, and a doctorate at about 35 schools. Graduate degrees may prepare students specifically for careers in news or as journalism teachers, researchers, and theorists, or for jobs in advertising or public relations.

A reporter's liberal arts training should include courses in English (with an emphasis on writing), sociology, political science, economics, history, psychology, business, speech, and computer science. Knowledge of foreign languages is also useful. To be a reporter in a specialized field, such as science or finance, requires concentrated course work in that area.

Other Requirements

You must be a good typist to succeed as a reporter, as you will type your stories using word processing programs. Although not essential, a knowledge of shorthand or speedwriting makes note taking easier, and an acquaintance with news photography is an asset.

You must also be inquisitive, aggressive, persistent, and detail-oriented. You should enjoy interaction with people of various races, cultures, religions, economic levels, and social statuses.

EXPLORING

You can explore a career as a reporter in a number of ways. You can talk to reporters and editors at local newspapers and radio and TV stations. You can also interview the admissions counselor at the school of journalism closest to your home.

In addition to taking courses in English, journalism, social studies, speech, computer science, and typing, high school students can acquire practical experience by working on school newspapers or on a church, synagogue, or mosque newsletter. Part-time and summer jobs on newspapers provide invaluable experience to the aspiring reporter.

College students can develop their reporting skills in the laboratory courses or workshops that are part of the journalism curriculum. College students might also accept jobs as campus correspondents for selected newspapers. People who work as part-time reporters covering news in a particular area of a community are known as *stringers* and are paid only for those stories that are printed.

More than 3,000 journalism scholarships, fellowships, and assistantships are offered by universities, newspapers, foundations, and professional organizations to college students. Many newspapers and magazines offer summer internships to journalism students to provide them with practical experience in a variety of basic reporting and editing duties. Upon graduation, students who successfully complete internships are usually placed in jobs more quickly than those without such experience.

EMPLOYERS

Of the approximately 78,000 reporters and correspondents employed in the United States, nearly 50 percent work for newspapers of all sizes. About 28 percent work in radio and television broadcasting. The rest are employed by wire services and magazines.

STARTING OUT

Jobs in this field may be obtained through college placement offices or by applying directly to the personnel departments of individual employers. If you have some practical experience, you will have an advantage; you should be prepared to present a portfolio of material you wrote as a volunteer or part-time reporter, or other writing samples.

Most journalism school graduates start out as general assignment reporters or copy editors for small publications. A few outstanding journalism graduates may be hired by large city newspapers or national magazines. They are trained on the job. But they are the exception, as large employers usually require several years' experience. As a rule, novice reporters cover routine assignments, such as reporting on civic and club meetings, writing obituaries, or summarizing speeches. As you become more skilled in reporting, you will be assigned to more important events or to a regular beat, or you may specialize in a particular field.

ADVANCEMENT

Reporters may advance by moving to larger newspapers or press services, but competition for such positions is unusually keen. Many highly qualified reporters apply for these jobs every year.

A select number of reporters eventually become columnists, correspondents, editorial writers, editors, or top executives. These important and influential positions represent the top of the field, and competition is strong for them.

Many reporters transfer the contacts and knowledge developed in newspaper reporting to related fields, such as public relations, advertising, or preparing copy for radio and television news programs.

EARNINGS

Earnings for reporters vary greatly. Salaries are related to experience, the type of employer for which the reporter works, geographic location, and whether the reporter is covered by a contract negotiated by the Newspaper Guild.

According to the *National Occupational Employment and Wage Estimates,* a salary survey by the U.S. Department of Labor, the median salary for news analysts, reporters, and correspondents was $30,060 in 2001. The lowest paid 10 percent of these workers earned $17,320 or less per year, while the highest paid 10 percent made $68,020 or more annually.

According to the Newspaper Guild, the average top minimum salary for reporters with about five years' experience was $41,400 in 2000. Salaries ranged from $20,150 to $65,528.

The U.S. Department of Labor reported that reporters and correspondents who worked in radio and television broadcasting had median annual earnings of $33,550 in 2000.

WORK ENVIRONMENT

Reporters work under a great deal of pressure in settings that differ from the typical business office. Their jobs generally require a five-day, 35- to 40-hour week, but overtime and irregular schedules are very common. Reporters employed by morning papers start work in the late afternoon and finish around midnight, while those on afternoon or evening papers start early in the morning and work until early or mid-afternoon. Foreign correspondents often work late at night to send the news to their papers in time to meet printing deadlines.

The day of the smoky, ink-stained newsroom has passed, but newspaper offices are still hectic places. Reporters have to work amid the clatter of computer keyboards and other machines, loud voices engaged in telephone conversations, and the bustle created by people hurrying about. An atmosphere of excitement prevails, especially as press deadlines approach.

Travel is often required in this occupation, and some assignments may be dangerous, such as covering wars, political uprisings, fires, floods, and other events of a volatile nature.

OUTLOOK

Employment for reporters and correspondents is expected to grow more slowly than the average for all occupations, according to the

Occupational Outlook Handbook. The U.S. Bureau of Labor Statistics projects that the number of employed reporters and correspondents will grow by 2.8 percent between 2000 and 2010. While the number of self-employed reporters and correspondents is expected to grow, newspaper jobs are expected to decrease because of mergers, consolidations, and closures in the newspaper industry.

Because of an increase in the number of small community and suburban daily and weekly newspapers, opportunities will be best for journalism graduates who are willing to relocate and accept relatively low starting salaries. With experience, reporters on these small papers can move up to editing positions or may choose to transfer to reporting jobs on larger newspapers or magazines.

Openings will be limited on big city dailies. While individual papers may enlarge their reporting staffs, little or no change is expected in the total number of these newspapers. Applicants will face strong competition for jobs on large metropolitan newspapers. Experience is a definite requirement, which rules out most new graduates unless they possess credentials in an area for which the publication has a pressing need. Occasionally, a beginner can use contacts and experience gained through internship programs and summer jobs to obtain a reporting job immediately after graduation.

A significant number of jobs will be provided by magazines and in radio and television broadcasting, but the major news magazines and larger broadcasting stations generally prefer experienced reporters. For beginning correspondents, small stations with local news broadcasts will continue to replace staff who move on to larger stations or leave the business. Network hiring has been cut drastically in the past few years and will probably continue to decline.

Stronger employment growth is expected for reporters in online newspapers and magazines.

Overall, the prospects are best for graduates who have majored in news-editorial journalism and completed an internship while in school. The top graduates in an accredited program will have a great advantage, as will talented technical and scientific writers. Small newspapers prefer to hire beginning reporters who are acquainted with the community and are willing to help with photography and other aspects of production. Without at least a bachelor's degree in journalism, applicants will find it increasingly difficult to obtain even an entry-level position.

Those with doctorates and practical reporting experience may find teaching positions at four-year colleges and universities, while highly qualified reporters with master's degrees may obtain employment in journalism departments of community and junior colleges.

Poor economic conditions do not drastically affect the employment of reporters and correspondents. Their numbers are not severely cut back even during a downturn; instead, employers forced to reduce expenditures will suspend new hiring.

FOR MORE INFORMATION

This organization provides general educational information on all areas of journalism, including newspapers, magazines, television, and radio.

**Association for Education in Journalism and Mass
 Communication**
234 Outlet Pointe Boulevard
Columbia, SC 29210-5667
Tel: 803-798-0271
Email: aejmchq@aejmc.org
http://www.aejmc.org

To receive a copy of The Journalist's Road to Success, *which lists schools offering degrees in news-editorial and financial aid to those interested in print journalism, contact:*

Dow Jones Newspaper Fund
PO Box 300
Princeton, NJ 08543-0300
Tel: 609-452-2820
Email: newsfund@wsj.dowjones.com
http://djnewspaperfund.dowjones.com

For information on careers in newspapers and industry facts and figures, contact:

Newspaper Association of America
1921 Gallows Road, Suite 600
Vienna, VA 22182-3900
Tel: 703-902-1600
Email: IRC@naa.org
http://www.naa.org

RESEARCH ASSISTANTS

QUICK FACTS

School Subjects
English
History
Journalism

Personal Skills
Communication/ideas
Following instructions

Work Environment
Primarily indoors
Primarily multiple locations

Minimum Educational Level
Bachelor's degree

Salary Range
$12,000 to $26,000 to
$74,000

Certification or Licensing
None available

Outlook
About as fast as the
average

DOT
109

GOE
11.03.03

NOC
4122

O*NET-SOC
N/A

OVERVIEW

Research assistants work to help writers, scientists, radio, film, and television producers, marketing and advertising executives, attorneys, professors, publishers, politicians, museum curators, and a wide variety of other professionals get their jobs done. They are information specialists who find the facts, data, and statistics that their employers need, leaving the employers free to pursue the larger task at hand.

HISTORY

The position of assistant is one of the oldest in the world. After all, assistants have been around for as long as people have worked: The job of research assistant was created the first time a worker sent an assistant out to gather information, whether it was to scout hunting grounds or survey land for possible dwelling places.

Although the job of the research assistant has changed little since the early days, the tools used to gather information have changed dramatically. An assistant to a doctor a hundred years ago would have had to travel to libraries and other information centers to gather data on a disease from books and then laboriously take down notes on paper. Today that same research assistant could do an Internet search and print the findings in only a few minutes. As technology becomes more advanced, research assistants will have the convenience of using new methods to complete their research, but they will also bear the burden of having to master the techniques to get the information they need.

THE JOB

Although the fields in which they work may differ greatly, all research assistants work to help their employers complete a job more easily and more thoroughly. A research assistant may work for one person, such as a university professor, or for a team of people, such as the writers of brochures, newsletters, and press releases at a large nonprofit organization. If the research assistant works for more than one person, he or she needs to follow a system to determine whose work will be done when. Sometimes the team assigning the work determines the order in which jobs should be done; other times, research assistants keep sign-up sheets and perform the research requests in the order they are listed. An urgent job often necessitates that the research assistant disregard the sheet and jump to the new task quickly. Sometimes research assistants help with clerical duties, such as transcription, word processing, and reception, or, in the case of scientific research assistants, with cleaning and maintaining laboratories and equipment.

After receiving a research assignment from the person or people they assist, research assistants must first determine how to locate the desired information. Sometimes this will be as simple as making a single phone call and requesting a brochure. Other times it may involve anywhere from hours to weeks of research in libraries, archives, museums, laboratories, and on the Internet until all of the necessary information is compiled and consolidated. Research assistants must then prepare the material for presentation to the person who requested it. If specific brochures or catalogs are requested, the research assistant need only hand them over when they arrive. More often than not, however, the research assistant has to write up notes or even a report outlining the research efforts and presenting the information they were asked to locate. These reports may include graphs, charts, statistics, and drawings or photographs. They include a listing of sources and the exact specifications of any interviews conducted, surveys taken, or experiments performed. Sometimes research assistants are asked to present this information verbally as well.

Because research assistants work in almost every field imaginable, it is impossible to list all the possible research assistant positions in this chapter. Following are some of the most common areas or situations in which research assistants work.

Research assistants work for writers in a wide variety of circumstances. They may work for commercial magazines and newspapers, where they might locate possible interview candidates, conduct surveys, scan other periodicals for relevant articles and features, or help a writer gather information for an article. For example, a writer doing an article on the history of rap music might send a research assistant to compile statistics on rap music sales from over the years or create a comprehensive list of artists signed by a specific record label. Some research assistants working for periodicals and other publications do nothing but confirm facts, such as dates, ages, and statistics. These researchers are called *fact checkers*. Research assistants who work in radio, film, or television often help locate and organize historical facts, find experts to be interviewed, or help follow up on ideas for future programs.

Many large companies, agencies, and organizations hire research assistants to help their in-house writing staff produce brochures, newsletters, and press releases. Research assistants may gather facts and statistics, retrieve applicable quotes, and conduct preliminary phone interviews.

Advertising and marketing agencies hire research assistants to help them discover consumer desires and the best ways to advertise and market products. Imagine that a small toy company is considering marketing a new toy. Research assistants for the company might be assigned to help find out how much it would cost to make the toy, whether or not there is already a similar toy on the market, who might buy the toy, and who might sell the toy. This would help the marketing department decide in what ways the toy should be marketed. In advertising, research assistants may be asked to provide executives with statistics and quotes so that the executives may determine whether a product is appealing to a certain portion of the population.

University professors hire research assistants to help them in their research in all fields. For example, a history professor working on a paper about the Italian military might send a research assistant to the library to uncover everything possible about the Italian military presence in Greece during World War II. A research assistant in microbiology will help a biologist prepare and perform experiments and record data. Often, professors hire graduate students as research assistants, either during the summer or in addition to the student's regular course load. Sometimes a research assistantship is part of a financial aid package; this ensures that the professor has help with research and gives the students an opportunity to earn money while learning more about their chosen field.

Politicians hire research assistants to help find out how a campaign is succeeding or failing, to find statistics on outcomes of past elections, and to determine the issues that are especially important to the constituents, among other things. Research assistants who work for politicians may also follow the opponent's campaign, trying to find ways to win over new supporters.

Some research assistants work for museums where they try to determine ways to add to a collection, develop signs and explanations for public education, and keep an inventory of all collection pieces. Research assistants may also do research to help curators learn more about the pieces in the museum's collection.

Again, these are only a few of the areas in which research assistants may work, and their duties may be as varied as the many fields and organizations that employ them.

REQUIREMENTS
High School

Requirements for becoming a research assistant vary depending upon the field in which you hope to work. In high school, take a wide variety of college preparatory courses, including English, history, mathematics, and the sciences. Knowledge of at least one foreign language can be extremely helpful in gaining employment as a research assistant, especially in the fields of marketing, publishing, and the arts. Since writing and presenting research are important aspects of the research assistant's work, you should take classes that strengthen these skills, such as public speaking, journalism, and statistics. Knowledge of computers and excellent library skills are absolutely vital to this profession. If you will be working in the hard sciences or engineering, laboratory skills are essential.

Postsecondary Training

In college you should begin thinking about a specific field you are interested in and take courses in that field. If you are interested in advertising research but your college does not offer an advertising degree, you should plan to major in English or psychology but take a large concentration of communications, business, and economics courses. Often, English and journalism are good majors for the research assistant career, as the work requires so much reading, researching, and writing. Some employers prefer research assistants to have a degree in library science.

Some fields require degrees beyond a bachelor's degree for research assistants. This is often true in the hard sciences, engineering, medicine, and law. Depending on the field, some employers require a master's degree, or some advanced study in the area. For instance, an insurance company that hires a research assistant may require the employee to take insurance courses in order to become more knowledgeable about the industry. Research assistants in the social sciences or arts will find more high-paying employment opportunities with a master's in library science.

Other Requirements

In order to succeed as a research assistant, you must be curious and enjoy doing research, finding and organizing facts, working with other people, and handling a variety of tasks. You should also be self-motivated, take instruction well, and be resourceful. For example, a research assistant assigned by an attorney to research marriage records at the county clerk's office should not be calling the law firm every few minutes to ask for further direction. A good research assistant must be able to take an assignment, immediately ask any questions necessary to clarify the task, and then begin retrieving the requested information.

EXPLORING

You can begin exploring this career while working on your own school assignments. Use different types of resources, such as newspapers, magazines, library catalogs, computers, the Internet, and official records and documents. If you are interested in becoming a research assistant in the sciences or medicine, pay close attention to procedures and methods in your laboratory classes.

Consider joining groups in your school devoted to research or fieldwork. Work as a reporter for your school newspaper, or volunteer to write feature articles for your yearbook. Both of these positions will provide you with experience in research and fact-finding. You can also create your own research opportunities. If you are a member of the marching band, for instance, you could research the history of the clarinet and write an article for the band newsletter.

Occasionally, small newspapers, nonprofit groups, political campaigns, and other organizations will accept student interns, volunteers, or even summer employees to help out with special projects. If you obtain such a position, you may have the opportunity to help with research, or at least, to see professionals in action, learn valuable work skills, and help support a good cause.

There are many books available describing the techniques of basic research skills. Ask a librarian or bookstore worker to help you locate them, or better yet, begin developing your research skills by tracking down materials yourself. The Internet is also full of helpful information on all subjects. To get tips on designing research surveys and analyzing data, visit http://www.hostedsurvey.com.

EMPLOYERS

All types of companies, organizations, and private individuals employ research assistants. Most college and university professors have a research assistant on staff to help them with articles and books they are writing. Newspapers and magazines use research assistants to find information for articles and verify facts. Museums employ research assistants to find information to add to museum collections, as well as to search museum archives for information requested by outside historians, scientists, writers, and other scholars. Companies in all fields need people to help find information on products, ingredients, production techniques, and competitors.

The government is a major employer of research assistants as well. Local, state, and federal government offices often hire research assistants to conduct interviews, gather statistics, compile information, and synthesize data. Research assistants for the government work for the U.S. Census Bureau, the U.S. Bureau of Labor Statistics, and the Library of Congress, among other divisions.

STARTING OUT

How you begin a career as a research assistant depends largely upon the field in which you are interested in working. In college, you may wish to pursue an assistantship with a professor. He or she can act as a mentor while you are earning your degree and offer valuable advice and feedback on your research techniques.

After receiving a bachelor's degree, you might begin by contacting agencies, firms, or companies where you'd like to work. For example, if you are interested in doing research to support writers, you might apply to newspapers, magazines, and large companies that produce their own publications. Also, some college and university career offices have listings of job openings in the research fields; occasionally these jobs are advertised in newspapers and magazines.

There may also be freelance opportunities for the beginning research assistant. Try marketing your services in the school newspaper or bulletin boards of your alma mater. You can also set up a Web page that lists your qualifications and the services you offer. Ask for referrals from professors with whom you have studied or worked. If you do a thorough, competent job on research assignments, you can use positive word-of-mouth to get more work.

ADVANCEMENT

A research assistant who gains a high skill level and demonstrates dedication to the employer and the field may earn the opportunity to lead other assistants on a special project. Some research assistants who work for writers and prove to have excellent writing skills themselves may get hired to write newsletter articles or brochures for publications. Depending on departmental needs, research assistants who work for a university while earning a degree may be offered a full-time position upon completion of their studies. Research assistants who work for clients on a freelance basis may find that they get more assignments and can command higher fees as they gain experience and a good reputation.

Advancement in this field is usually up to the individual. You will need to seek out opportunities. If you are interested in getting better assignments, you will probably need to ask for them. If you would like to supervise a newsletter or brochure project within your company, try making a proposal to your manager. With a proven track record and a solid idea of how a project can be accomplished, you will likely receive increased responsibility.

EARNINGS

Earnings vary widely, depending on field, level of education, and employer. Generally, large companies pay their research assistants more than smaller businesses and nonprofit organizations do. Research assistants with advanced degrees make more than those with bachelor's degrees only. Research assistants who work for large pharmaceutical companies or engineering laboratories and have advanced science degrees make among the highest wages in the field.

Each college and university has its own salary budget for graduate student research assistants. There are often set minimum salaries for academic year employment and for full 12-month employment. Most student research assistants work part-time and receive a percentage of these minimums based on the number of hours they work (usually 50 percent, 25 percent, or 33 percent). Some schools have an hourly rate that averages about $10 to $15. Annual salaries for university research assistants can range from $12,000 to $42,000.

According to *The Scientist* and Abbott, Langer & Associates, Inc., senior researchers in the life sciences who work in academia earn from $30,000 to $74,000 annually, and postdoctoral researchers earn from $26,000 to $39,000. In industry, senior researchers earn from $30,000 to $72,000, and junior/postdoctoral researchers earn from $26,000 to $44,000.

Self-employed research assistants are paid by the hour or by assignment. Depending on the experience of the research assistant, the complexity of the assignment, and the location of the job, pay rates may be anywhere from $7 to $25 per hour, although $10 to $12 is the norm.

Benefits such as health insurance, vacation, and sick leave vary by field and employer. Universities generally provide health care coverage, paid vacations, sick time, and a pension plan for full-time employees. Research assistants employed full-time by a private company are also eligible for similar benefits; some companies may provide benefits to part-time or contract workers. Freelancers must provide their own benefits.

Research assistants who work in some fields may receive additional bonuses. A person working on a research project about movies, for instance, may receive free passes to a local theater. A woman's magazine may send research assistants cosmetics samples so they can test different lipsticks for staying power. Research assistants charged with finding information about another country's economy may even be sent abroad. All of these perks, of course, vary depending on the needs of the employer and the experience of the researcher.

WORK ENVIRONMENT

Most research assistants work indoors in clean, climate-controlled, pleasant facilities. Many spend most of their time at the business that employs them, checking facts over the phone, finding data on a computer, searching the company's records, writing up reports, or conducting laboratory research. Others spend a great deal of time in libraries, government offices, courthouses, museums, archives, and even in such unlikely places as shopping malls and supermarkets. In short, research assistants go wherever they can to obtain the information requested.

Most assignments require that research assistants do their work on their own, with little direct supervision. Research assistants need to be very self-motivated in order to get the work done since they often do not have someone readily available to support them. It is important for research assistants who leave their offices for work to remember that they are representatives of their company or employer and to act and dress according to the employer's standards.

Full-time research assistants work 35 to 40 hours a week. They may have to work overtime or on weekends right before deadlines or when involved in special projects. Some research assistants, especially those who work for smaller organizations or for professors or private employers, work only part-time. They may work as little as 10 hours a week. These research assistants are usually graduate students or freelancers who have a second job in a related field.

OUTLOOK

The outlook for the research assistant career generally depends upon the outlook for the field in which the researcher works. That is, a field that is growing quickly will usually need many new researchers, whereas a field with little growth will not. A researcher with a good background in many fields will be in higher demand, as will a researcher with specialized knowledge and research techniques specific to a field.

Although definite statistical data as to the present and future of all researchers is sketchy at best, as technology becomes more advanced and the amount of information available through newer media like the Internet increases, knowledgeable research assistants will be essential to find, sort, compile, present, and analyze this information. As a result of technological advancements, a new career niche has developed for *information brokers*, who compile information from online databases and services.

Since many people take research assistant positions as stepping-stones to positions with more responsibility or stability, positions are often available to beginning researchers. Research assistants with good experience, excellent work ethics, and the drive to succeed will rarely find themselves out of work. Jobs will be available, but it may take some creative fact-finding for research assistants to locate positions that best meet their needs and interests.

FOR MORE INFORMATION

To find out about health care research projects and opportunities with the U.S. Department of Health and Human Services, contact:

Agency for Healthcare Research and Quality
2101 East Jefferson Street, Suite 501
Rockville, MD 20852
Tel: 301-594-1364
Email: info@ahrq.gov
http://www.ahcpr.gov

For a list of research opportunities and student internships with National Institutes of Health, contact:

National Institutes of Health
Office of Human Resources Management
6100 Executive Boulevard, Room 3E01 MSC 7509
Bethesda, MD 20892-7509
http://ohrm.cc.nih.gov

For information on research assistant positions with the U.S. Census Bureau, contact:

U.S. Census Bureau
Washington, DC 20233
Tel: 301-457-4608
Email: recruiter@ccmail.census.gov
http://www.census.gov

For a national list of research opportunities in physics, contact:

The University of Pennsylvania School for Arts and Sciences
http://dept.physics.upenn.edu/undergraduate/lablist.html

SCIENCE AND MEDICAL WRITERS

QUICK FACTS

School Subjects Biology English Journalism **Personal Skills** Communication/ideas Technical/scientific **Work Environment** Primarily indoors Primarily multiple locations **Minimum Education Level** Bachelor's degree **Salary Range** $20,570 to $42,450 to $83,180+	**Certification or Licensing** Voluntary **Outlook** Faster than the average **DOT** 131 **GOE** 11.08.02 **NOC** 5121 **O*NET-SOC** 27-3042.00, 27-3043.00

OVERVIEW

Science and medical writers translate technical medical and scientific information so it can be disseminated to the general public and professionals in the field. Science and medical writers research, interpret, write, and edit scientific and medical information. Their work often appears in books, technical studies and reports, magazine and trade journal articles, newspapers, company newsletters, and on websites, and it may be used for radio and television broadcasts.

HISTORY

The skill of writing has existed for thousands of years. Papyrus fragments with writing by ancient Egyptians date from about 3000 B.C., and archaeological findings show that the Chinese had developed books by about 1300 B.C. A number of technical obstacles had to be overcome before printing and the writing profession progressed.

The modern publishing age began in the 18th century. Printing became mechanized, and the novel, magazine, and newspaper developed. Developments in the printing trades, photoengraving, retailing, and the availability of capital produced a boom in newspapers and magazines in the 19th century. Further mechanization in the printing field, such as the use of the Linotype machine, high-speed rotary presses, and special color reproduction processes, set the stage for further growth in the book, newspaper, and magazine industries.

In addition to print media, the broadcasting industry has contributed to the development of the professional writer. Film, radio, and television are sources of entertainment, information, and education that provide employment for thousands of writers. Today, the computer industry and the Internet and its proliferation of websites have also created the need for more writers.

As our world becomes more complex and people seek even more information, professional writers have become increasingly important. As medicine and science continue to make discoveries that impact our lives, skilled science and medical writers are needed to document these changes and disseminate the information to the general public and more specialized audiences.

THE JOB

Science and medical writers usually write about subjects related to these fields. Because the medical and scientific subject areas may sometimes overlap, writers often find that they do science writing as well as medical writing. For instance, a medical writer might write about a scientific study that has an impact on the medical field.

Medical and science writing may be targeted for the printed page, broadcast media, or the Web. It can be specific to one product and one type of writing, such as writing medical information and consumer publications for a specific drug line produced by a pharmaceutical company. Research facilities hire writers to edit reports or write about their scientific or medical studies. Writers who are *public information officers* write press releases that inform the public about the latest scientific or medical research findings. Educational publishers use writers to edit or write educational materials for the medical profession. Science and medical writers also write online articles or interactive courses that are distributed over the Internet.

According to Barbara Gastel, M.D., coordinator of the Master of Science Program in Science and Technology Journalism at Texas A&M University, many science and technology-related industries are using specialized writers to communicate complex subjects to the public. "In addition," she says, "opportunities exist in the popular media. Newspapers, radio, TV, and the Web have writers who specialize in covering medical and scientific subjects."

Science and medical writers usually write for the general public. They translate high-tech information into articles and reports that can be understood by the general public and the media. Good writers who cover the subjects thoroughly have inquisitive minds and enjoy looking for additional information that might add to their articles. They research the topic to gain a thorough understanding of the subject matter. This may require hours of research on the Internet, or in corporate, university, or public libraries. Writers always need good background information regarding a subject before they can write about it.

In order to get the information required, writers may interview professionals such as doctors, pharmacists, scientists, engineers, managers, and others who are familiar with the subject. Writers must know how to present the information so it can be understood, which requires a solid knowledge of the target audience. For example, an article for a specific audience may need graphs, photos, or historical facts to be effective. Writers sometimes enlist the help of technical or medical illustrators or engineers in order to add a visual dimension to their work.

For example, if reporting on a new heart surgery procedure that will soon be available to the public, writers may need to illustrate how that surgery is performed and what areas of the heart are affected. They may give a basic overview of how the healthy heart works, show a diseased heart in comparison, and report on how this surgery can help the patient. The public will also want to know how many people are affected by this disease, what the symptoms are, how many procedures have been done successfully, where they were performed, what the recovery time is, and if there are any complications. In addition, interviews with doctors and patients add a personal touch to the story.

Broadcast media need short, precise articles that can be transmitted in a specific time allotment. Writers usually need to work quickly because news-related stores are often deadline-oriented. Because science and medicine can be so complex, science and medical writers also need to help the audience understand and evaluate the information. Writing for the Web encompasses most journalistic guidelines including time constraints and sometimes space constraints.

Some science and medical writers specialize in their subject matter. For instance, a medical writer may write only about heart disease and earn a reputation as the best writer in that subject area. Science writers may limit their writing or research to environmental science subjects, or may be even more specific and focus only on air pollution issues.

According to Jeanie Davis, president of the Southeast Chapter of the American Medical Writers Association, "Medical writing can take several different avenues. You may be a consumer medical writer, write technical medical research, or write about health care issues. Some choose to be medical editors and edit reports written by researchers. Sometimes this medical research must be translated into reports and news releases that the public can understand. Today many writers write for the Web." Davis adds, "It is a very dynamic profession, always changing."

Dr. Gastel says, "This career can have various appeals. People can combine their interest in science or medicine with their love of writing. It is a good field for a generalist who likes science and doesn't want to be tied to research in one area. Plus," she adds, "it is always fun to get things published."

Some writers may choose to be freelance writers either on a full- or part-time basis, or to supplement other jobs. Freelance science and medical writers are self-employed writers who work with small and large companies, health care organizations, research institutions, or publishing firms on a contract or hourly basis. They may specialize in writing about a specific scientific or medical subject for one or two clients, or they may write about a broad range of subjects for a number of different clients. Many freelance writers write articles, papers, or reports and then attempt to get them published in newspapers, trade, or consumer publications.

REQUIREMENTS
High School

If you are considering a career as a writer, you should take English, journalism, and communication courses in high school. Computer classes will also be helpful. If you know in high school that you want to do scientific or medical writing, it would be to your advantage to take biology, physiology, chemistry, physics, math, health, psychology, and other science-related courses. If your school offers journalism courses and you have the chance to work on the school newspaper or yearbook, you should take advantage of these opportunities.

Part-time employment at health care facilities, newspapers, publishing companies, or scientific research facilities can also provide experience and insight regarding this career. Volunteer opportunities are usually available in hospitals and nursing homes as well.

Postsecondary Training

Although not all writers are college educated, today's jobs almost always require a bachelor's degree. Many writers earn an undergraduate degree in English, journalism, or liberal arts and then obtain a master's degree in a communications field such as medical or science writing. A good liberal arts education is important since you are often required to write about many subject areas. Science and medical-related courses are highly recommended. You should investigate internship programs that give you experience in the communications department of a corporation, medical institution, or research facility. Some newspapers, magazines, or public relations firms also have internships that give you the opportunity to write.

Some people find that after working as a writer, their interests are strong in the medical or science fields and they evolve into that writing specialty. They may return to school and enter a master's degree program or take some additional courses related specifically to science and medical writing. Similarly, science majors or people in the medical fields may find that they like the writing aspect of their jobs and return to school to pursue a career as a medical or science writer.

Certification or Licensing

Certification is not mandatory; however, certification programs are available from various organizations and institutions. The American Medical Writers Association Education Program offers an extensive continuing education and certification program.

Other Requirements

If you are considering a career as a medical or science writer, you should enjoy writing, be able to write well, and be able to express your ideas and those of others clearly. You should have an excellent knowledge of the English language and have superb grammar and spelling skills. You should be skilled in research techniques and be computer literate and familiar with software programs related to writing and publishing. You should be curious, enjoy learning about new things, and have an interest in science or medicine. You need to be detail-oriented since many of your writing assignments will require that you obtain and relay accurate and detailed information. Interpersonal skills are also important because many jobs require that you interact with and interview professional people such as scientists, engineers, researchers, and medical personnel. You must be able to meet deadlines and work under pressure.

EXPLORING

As a high school or college student, you can test your interest and aptitude in the field of writing by serving as a reporter or writer on school newspapers, yearbooks, and literary magazines. Attending writing workshops and taking writing classes will give you the opportunity to practice and sharpen your skills.

Community newspapers and local radio stations often welcome contributions from outside sources, although they may not have the resources to pay for them. Jobs in bookstores, magazine shops, libraries, and even newsstands offer a chance to become familiar with various publications. If you are interested in science writing, try to get a part-time job in a research laboratory, interview science writers, and read good science writing in major newspapers such as the *New York Times* or the *Wall Street Journal*. Similarly, if your interest is medical writing, work or volunteer in a health care facility, visit with people who do medical writing, and read medical articles in those newspapers previously listed. You may also find it helpful to read publications such as the *American Medical Writers Association Journal* (http://www.amwa.org/publications/journal.html).

Information on writing as a career may also be obtained by visiting local newspapers, publishing houses, or radio and television stations and interviewing some of the writers who work there. Career conferences and other guidance programs frequently include speakers from local or national organizations who can provide information on communication careers.

Some professional organizations such as the Society for Technical Communication welcome students as members and have special student membership rates and career information. In addition, participation in professional organizations gives you the opportunity to meet and visit with people in this career field.

EMPLOYERS

Pharmaceutical and drug companies, medical research institutions, government organizations, insurance companies, health care facilities, nonprofit organizations, medical publishers, medical associations, and other medical-related industries employ medical writers.

Science writers may also be employed by medical-related industries. In addition, they are employed by scientific research companies, government research facilities, federal, state, and local agencies, manufacturing companies, research and development departments of corporations, and the chemical industries. Large universities and hospitals often employ science writers, as do large technology-based corporations and industrial research groups.

Many science and medical writers are employed, often on a freelance basis, by newspapers, magazines, and the broadcast industries as well. Internet publishing is a growing field that hires science and medical writers. Corporations that deal with the medical or science industries also hire specialty writers as their public information officers or to head up communications departments within their facilities.

STARTING OUT

A fair amount of experience is required to gain a high-level position in this field. Most writers start out in entry-level positions. These jobs may be listed with college placement offices, or you may apply directly to the employment departments of corporations, institutions, universities, research facilities, nonprofit organizations, and government facilities that hire science and medical writers. Many firms now hire writers directly upon application or recommendation of college professors and placement offices. Want ads in newspapers and trade journals are another source for jobs. Serving an internship in college can give you the advantage of knowing people who can give you personal recommendations.

Internships are also excellent ways to build your portfolio. Employers in the communications field are usually interested in seeing samples of your published writing assembled in an organized portfolio or scrapbook. Working on your college's magazine or newspaper staff can help you build a portfolio. Sometimes small, regional magazines will also buy articles or assign short pieces for you to write. You should attempt to build your portfolio with good writing samples. Be sure to include the type of writing you are interested in doing, if possible.

You may need to begin your career as a junior writer or editor and work your way up. This usually involves library research, preparation of rough drafts for part or all of a report, cataloging, and other related writing tasks. These are generally carried on under the supervision of a senior writer.

Many science and medical writers enter the field after working in public relations departments, the medical profession, or science-related industries. They may use their skills to transfer to specialized writing positions or they may take additional courses or graduate work that focuses on writing or documentation skills.

ADVANCEMENT

Writers with only an undergraduate degree may choose to get a graduate degree in science or medical writing, corporate communications, document design, or a related program. An advanced degree may open doors to more progressive career options.

Many experienced science and medical writers are often promoted to head writing, documentation, or public relations departments within corporations or institutions. Some may become recognized experts in their field and their writings may be in demand by trade journals, newspapers, magazines, and the broadcast industry.

As freelance writers prove themselves and work successfully with clients, they may be able to demand increased contract fees or hourly rates.

EARNINGS

Although there are no specific salary studies for science and medical writers, salary information for all writers is available. The U.S. Department of Labor reports that the median annual salary for writers in 2001 was $42,450. Salaries ranged from less than $20,570 to more than $83,180. Median annual earnings for technical writers were $49,370 in 2001. The lowest 10 percent earned less than $29,750, while the highest 10 percent earned more than $77,330.

The Society for Technical Communication's 2001 salary survey of its membership reported that the mean salary of its members was $55,360. The entry-level salary was reported to be $36,210, with senior-level supervisors earning $75,180.

Freelance writers' earnings can vary depending on their expertise, reputation, and the articles they are contracted to write.

Most full-time writing positions offer the usual benefits such as insurance, sick leave, and paid vacation. Some jobs also provide tuition reimbursement and retirement benefits. Freelance writers must pay for their own insurance. However, there are professional associations that may offer group insurance rates for its members.

WORK ENVIRONMENT

Work environment depends on the type of science or medical writing and the employer. Generally, writers work in an office or research environment. Writers for the news media sometimes work in noisy surroundings. Some writers travel to research information and conduct interviews while other employers may confine research to local libraries or the Internet. In addition, some employers require writers to conduct research interviews over the phone, rather than in person.

Although the workweek usually runs 35 to 40 hours in a normal office setting, many writers may have to work overtime to cover a story, interview people, meet deadlines, or to disseminate information in a timely manner. The newspaper and broadcasting industries deliver the news 24 hours a day, seven days a week. Writers often work nights and weekends to meet press deadlines or to cover a late-developing story.

Each day may bring new and interesting situations. Some stories may even take writers to exotic locations with a chance to interview famous people and write about timely topics. Other assignments may be boring or they may take place in less than desirable settings where interview subjects may be rude and unwilling to talk. One of the most difficult elements for writers may be meeting deadlines or gathering information. People who are the most content as writers work well with deadline pressure.

OUTLOOK

According to the U.S. Department of Labor, there is a lot of competition for writing and editing jobs; however, the demand for writers and editors is expected to grow faster than the average over the next several years due to the growing numbers of publications, both print and online.

The Society for Technical Communication also states that there is a growing demand for technical communicators. They report that it is one of the fastest growing professions and that this growth has created a variety of career options.

FOR MORE INFORMATION

For information on careers as science and medical writers, contact the following organizations:

American Medical Writers Association
40 West Gude Drive, Suite 101
Rockville, MD 20850-1192
Tel: 301-294-5303
Email: info@amwa.org
http://www.amwa.org

National Association of Science Writers, Inc.
PO Box 890
Hedgesville, WV 25427
Tel: 304-754-5077
http://www.nasw.org

For information on scholarships and student memberships aimed at those preparing for a career in technical communication, contact:
Society for Technical Communication
901 North Stuart Street, Suite 904
Arlington, VA 22203-1822
Tel: 703-522-4114
Email: stc@src.org
http://www.stc.org

SPEECH TEACHERS

QUICK FACTS

School Subjects
English
Speech

Personal Skills
Communication/ideas
Helping/teaching

Work Environment
Primarily indoors
Primarily one location

Minimum Education Level
Bachelor's degree (elementary
and secondary teachers)
Master's degree (college
professors)

Salary Range
$27,000 to $41,080 to
$64,280+ (elementary
teachers)
$27,980 to $43,280 to
$67,940+ (secondary
teachers)
$35,790 to $60,000 to
$78,912 (college professors)

Certification or Licensing
Required by all states
(elementary and secondary
teachers)
None available (college
professors)

Outlook
About as fast as the average
(elementary and secondary
teachers)
Faster than the average
(college professors)

DOT
090, 091, 092

GOE
11.02.01

NOC
4121, 4141, 4142

O*NET-SOC
25-1122.00,
25-2021.00

OVERVIEW

Speech teachers instruct students of all ages, from kindergarten through the graduate level, how to communicate clearly and effectively with others. They develop teaching outlines and lesson plans, give lectures, facilitate discussions and activities, keep class attendance records, assign homework, and evaluate student progress.

HISTORY

The ability to communicate has always been recognized as a sign of intelligence. Early history labeled the study of communication "rhetoric," and it was studied and analyzed by the ancient Greeks and Romans. The National Communication Association reports that the study of communication has been a part of U.S. formal education since Harvard's founding in 1636.

In the last century, the field of speech has grow exponentially to include communication in areas such as the workplace, the media, and advertising. Today, speech teachers are concerned with how students communicate as individuals, in society, and between various cultures.

THE JOB

Speech teachers who work in elementary schools teach grades one through six or eight. In smaller schools, grades may be combined. In most cases, teachers instruct approximately 20–30 children of the same grade. Those working in the first and second grades cover basic communication skills, helping young students with their pronunciation as they read aloud from books or tell stories. With older students, speech teachers may assign oral reports, which work on both the students' researching and public speaking skills. To capture attention and teach new concepts, teachers might incorporate group presentations, workbooks, music, and other interactive teaching methods.

Like those working in elementary schools, speech teachers working in secondary schools must also rely on a variety of teaching methods. They spend a great deal of time lecturing, but they also facilitate student discussion and develop projects and activities to interest students, such as oral reports and class debates. They may show films and videos, use computers and the Internet, and bring in guest speakers. They assign essays, presentations, and other projects. Some speech teachers also have the opportunity for extracurricular activities.

Speech teachers also work at the college or university level. At four-year institutions, most faculty members are *assistant professors, associate professors,* or *full professors.* These three types of professorships differ in regards to status, job responsibilities, and salary.

Speech professors work with students at all levels, from college freshmen to graduate students. They may head several classes a semester or only a few a year. Some of their classes will have large enrollment, while graduate seminars may consist of only 12 or fewer students.

Though speech professors may spend fewer than 10 hours a week in the actual classroom, they spend many hours preparing lectures and lesson plans, grading papers and presentations, and preparing grade reports. They also schedule office hours during the week to be available to students outside of the classroom, and they meet with students individually throughout the semester.

In addition to teaching, most college faculty members conduct research and write publications. Speech professors publish their research findings in various scholarly journals. They also write books based on their research or on their own knowledge and experience in the field. Publishing a significant amount of work has been the traditional standard by which assistant professors prove themselves worthy of becoming permanent, tenured faculty.

The *junior college speech instructor* has many of the same kinds of responsibilities as the speech teacher in a four-year college or university. Because junior colleges offer only a two-year program, speech instructors working in these schools teach only undergraduates.

REQUIREMENTS
High School
To prepare for a career in speech education, follow your school's college preparatory program and take advanced courses in English and speech. Composition, journalism, and communications classes are important for developing your writing and speaking skills.

Postsecondary Training
Your college training will depend on the level at which you plan to teach. All 50 states and the District of Columbia require public elementary education teachers to have a bachelor's degree in either education or in the subject they teach. Prospective teachers must also complete an approved training program, which combines subject and educational classes with work experience in the classroom, called student teaching.

If you want to teach speech at the high school level, you may choose to major in speech while taking required education courses, or you may major in secondary education with a concentration in speech. Similar to prospective elementary teachers, you will need to student teach in an actual classroom environment.

Prospective speech professors need at least one advanced degree in speech communications. The master's degree is considered the minimum standard, and graduate work beyond the master's is usually desirable. If you hope to advance in academic rank above speech instructor, most institutions require a doctorate degree. Your graduate school program will be similar to a life of teaching—in addition to attending seminars, you'll research, prepare articles for publication, and teach undergraduate courses.

Certification or Licensing

Elementary and secondary speech teachers who work in public schools must be licensed under regulations established by the state in which they teach. If moving, teachers have to comply with any other regulations in their new state to be able to teach, though many states have reciprocity agreements that make it easier for teachers to change locations.

Licensure examinations test prospective teachers for competency in speech communications and related subjects such as English and composition. In addition, many states are moving towards a performance-based evaluation for licensing. In this case, after passing the teaching examination, prospective speech teachers are given provisional licenses. Only after proving themselves capable in the classroom are they eligible for a full license.

Another growing trend spurred by recent teacher shortages in elementary and high schools is alternative licensure arrangements. For those who have a bachelor's degree but lack formal education courses and training in the classroom, states can issue a provisional license. These workers immediately begin teaching under the supervision of a licensed educator for one to two years and take education classes outside of their working hours. Once they have completed the required coursework and gained experience in the classroom, they are granted a full teaching license.

Other Requirements

Many consider the desire to teach a calling. This calling is based on a love of learning. Teachers of young children and young adults must respect students as individuals, with personalities, strengths, and weaknesses of their own. They must also be patient and self-disciplined to manage a large group independently. Because they work with students who are at very impressionable ages, they should serve as good role models. Elementary and secondary speech teachers should also be well organized, as you'll have to keep track of the work and progress of many students.

If you aim to teach speech at the college level, you should enjoy reading, writing, and researching. Not only will you spend many years studying in school, but your whole career will be based on communicating your thoughts and ideas. People skills are important because you'll be dealing directly with students, administrators, and other faculty members on a daily basis. You should feel comfortable in a role of authority and possess self-confidence.

EXPLORING

To explore a career in speech education, become involved in your own high school speech and/or debate teams. Talk to your speech instructors or debate advisors about their jobs and how they got into the field. If your school has a television or radio station, get experience speaking on air.

If you are interested in teaching younger students, you need to become accustomed to working with children and young adults. You might find summer work as a counselor in a summer camp, as a leader of a scout troop, or as an assistant in a public park or community center. You could also volunteer for a peer-tutoring program.

If you are interested in becoming a college speech communications professor, spend some time on a college campus to get a sense of the environment. Write to colleges for their admissions brochures and course catalogs (or check them out online); read about speech departments, individual faculty members, and the courses they teach. Before visiting college campuses, make arrangements to speak to professors who teach speech and debate. These professors may allow you to sit in on their classes and observe.

EMPLOYERS

Elementary and secondary school speech teachers are employed in public and private institutions, day care centers, juvenile detention centers, and vocational schools. Although rural areas maintain schools, more teaching positions are available in urban or suburban areas. Teachers are also finding opportunities in charter schools, which are smaller, deregulated schools that receive public funding.

College and university speech professors hold over 18,000 jobs. With a doctorate, a number of publication credits, and a record of good teaching, speech professors should find opportunities in universities all across the country.

STARTING OUT

Elementary and secondary school speech teachers can use their college placement offices and state departments of education to find job openings. Many local schools advertise teaching positions in newspapers. Another option is to directly contact the schools in which you'd like to work.

Prospective college speech professors should start the process of finding a teaching position while in graduate school. You will need to develop a curriculum vitae (a detailed, academic resume), work on your academic writing, assist with research, attend conferences, and gain teaching experience and recommendations. Because of the competition for tenure-track positions, you may have to work for a few years in temporary positions. Some professional speech and communication associations maintain lists of teaching opportunities in their areas. They may also make lists of applicants available to college administrators looking to fill an available position.

ADVANCEMENT

As elementary and secondary speech teachers acquire experience or additional education, they can expect higher wages and more responsibilities. Teachers with leadership skills and an interest in administrative work may advance to serve as principals or supervisors, though the number of these positions is limited and competition is fierce. Another move may be into higher education, teaching speech classes at a college or university. For most of these positions, additional education is required. Other common career transitions are into related fields. With additional preparation, speech teachers can become drama teachers, public relations specialists, or political or business communications consultants, to name a few positions.

At the college level, the normal pattern of advancement is from instructor to assistant professor, to associate professor, to full professor. All four academic ranks are concerned primarily with teaching and research. College faculty members who have an interest in and a talent for administration may be advanced to chair of a department or to dean of their college. A few become college or university presidents or other types of administrators.

EARNINGS

According to the Bureau of Labor Statistics, the median annual salary for all elementary school teachers was $41,080 in 2001. The lowest 10 percent earned $27,000 or less; the highest 10 percent earned $64,280 or more. The median annual salary for all secondary school teachers was $43,280 in 2001. The lowest 10 percent earned $27,980; the highest 10 percent earned $67,940 or more.

The American Federation of Teachers reports that the average salary for beginning teachers with a bachelor's degree was $28,986 in 2001. The estimated average salary of all public elementary and secondary school teachers was $43,250.

College professors' earnings vary depending on their academic department, the size of the school, the type of school (public, private, women's only), and by the level of position the professor holds. The American Association of University Professors (AAUP) reported the average yearly income for all full-time faculty was $60,000 in 2001. The AAUP also reports that professors averaged the following salaries by rank: full professors, $78,912; associate professors, $57,380; assistant professors, $47,358; and instructors, $35,790.

WORK ENVIRONMENT

Most speech teachers are contracted to work 10 months out of the year, with a two-month vacation during the summer. During their summer break, many continue their education to renew or upgrade their teaching licenses and earn higher salaries. Teachers in schools that operate year-round work eight-week sessions with one-week breaks in between and a five-week vacation in the winter.

Speech teachers work in generally pleasant conditions, although some older schools may have poor heating or electrical systems. The work can seem confining, requiring them to remain in the classroom throughout most of the day. Speech teachers who work with younger (and usually more busy) children all day, may find the work tiring and trying.

Elementary and high school hours are generally 8 A.M. to 3 P.M., but speech teachers work more than 40 hours a week teaching, preparing for classes, grading work, and directing extracurricular activities such as drama productions or speech teams.

Similarly, most college speech teachers work more than 40 hours each week. Although they may teach only two or three classes a semester, they spend many hours preparing for lectures, examining student work, and conducting research.

OUTLOOK

According to the *Occupational Outlook Handbook (OOH)*, employment opportunities for all teachers in grades K–12 are expected to grow as fast as the average for all occupations over the next several years. The need to replace retiring teachers will provide many opportunities nationwide. The demand varies widely depending on geographic area. Inner-city schools characterized by poor working conditions and low salaries often suffer a shortage of teachers.

The *OOH* predicts faster-than-average employment growth for all college and university professors over the next several years. College enrollment is projected to grow due to an increased number of 18- to 24-year-olds, an increased number of adults returning to college, and an increased number of foreign-born students who need specialized assistance in their speech communication skills. Retirement of current faculty members will also provide job openings. However, competition for full-time, tenure-track positions at four-year schools will be very strong.

FOR MORE INFORMATION

For information about careers, education, and union membership, contact the following organizations:

American Association of University Professors
1012 14th Street, NW, Suite 500
Washington, DC 20005
Tel: 202-737-5900
http://www.aaup.org

American Federation of Teachers
555 New Jersey Avenue, NW
Washington, D.C. 20001
Tel: 202-879-4400
Email: online@aft.org
http://www.aft.org

National Communication Association
1765 N Street, NW
Washington, D.C. 20036
Tel: 202-464-4622
Web: http://www.natcom.org

National Council for Accreditation of Teacher Education
2010 Massachusetts Avenue, NW, Suite 500
Washington, DC 20036
Tel: 202-466-7496
Email: ncate@ncate.org
http://www.ncate.org

National Education Association
1201 16th Street, NW
Washington, DC 20036
Tel: 202-833-4000
http://www.nea.org

SPORTS BROADCASTERS AND ANNOUNCERS

QUICK FACTS

School Subjects English Journalism Speech **Personal Skills** Communication/ideas Leadership/management **Work Environment** Indoors and outdoors Primarily multiple locations **Minimum Education Level** Some postsecondary training **Salary Range** $20,000 to $53,300 to $2,000,000+	**Certification or Licensing** None available **Outlook** Little change or more slowly than the average **DOT** 159 **GOE** 01.03.03 **NOC** 5231 **O*NET-SOC** 27-3011.00

OVERVIEW

Sports broadcasters, or *sportscasters,* for radio and television stations select, write, and deliver footage of current sports news for the sports segment of radio and television news broadcasts or for specific sports events, channels, or shows. They may provide pre- and postgame coverage of sports events, including interviews with coaches and athletes, as well as play-by-play coverage during the game or event.

Sports announcers are the official voices of the teams. At home games it is the sports announcer who makes pre-game announcements, introduces the players in the starting lineups, and keeps the spectators in the stadium or arena abreast of the details of the game by announcing such things as fouls, substitutions, and goals, and who is making them.

HISTORY

In the early days of radio broadcasts, anyone who operated the station would read, usually verbatim, news stories from the day's paper. Quickly, station managers realized that the station's "voice" needed as much charisma and flair as possible. Announcers and journalists with good speaking voices were hired. With the arrival of television, many of those who worked in radio broadcasting moved to this new medium.

Corporate-sponsored radio stations weren't long in coming; Westinghouse Corporation and American Telephone and Telegraph (AT&T) raced to enter the market. Westinghouse engineer Frank Conrad received a license for what is viewed as the first modern radio station, KDKA, in Pittsburgh, Pennsylvania. KDKA broadcast music programs, the 1920 presidential election, and sports events. The next year, Westinghouse began to sell radio sets for as little as $25. By 1924, the radio-listening public numbered 20 million.

Meanwhile, as early as 1929, Vladimir Kosma Zworykin, a Soviet immigrant employed by Westinghouse, was experimenting with visual images to create an all-electronic television system. By 1939 the system was demonstrated at the New York's World Fair with none other than President Franklin D. Roosevelt speaking before the camera. World War II and battles over government regulation and AM and FM frequencies interrupted the introduction of television to the American public, but by 1944, the government had determined specific frequencies for both FM radio and television.

In 1946, the number of television sets in use was 6,000; by 1951, the number had risen to an astonishing 12 million sets. Unknowingly, the stage had been set for a battle between radio and television. In the ensuing years, expert after expert predicted the demise of radio. The popularity of television, its soap operas, family dramas, and game shows, was believed by nearly everyone to be too strong a competitor for the old-fashioned, sound-only aspect of radio. The experts proved wrong; radio flourished well into the 1990s, when the industry experienced some cutbacks in the number of stations and broadcast hours because of recession.

The national radio networks of the early days are gone, but satellites allow local stations to broadcast network shows anywhere with the equipment to receive the satellite link. The development of filmed and videotaped television, cable and satellite transmissions, broadcasting deregulation, and an international market through direct broadcast satellite systems has drastically changed the face and future of both radio and television.

Today's sports broadcasters in radio and television have all these technological tools and more at their fingertips. Want to see an instant replay of the game-winning three-point shot by Kobe Bryant? As the sportscaster describes it, a technician is playing it back for the viewing public. Have to travel to Costa Rica for a business trip, but hate to miss that Yankees game? No problem. A sportscaster is giving the play-by-play to an AM network station that is, in turn, sending it via satellite to a Costa Rican client-station.

THE JOB

One of the primary jobs of most sportscasters for both radio and television stations is to determine what sports news to carry during a news segment. The sportscaster begins working on the first broadcast by reading the sports-related clippings that come in over the various news wire services, such as Associated Press and United Press International. To follow up on one of these stories, the sportscaster might telephone several contacts, such as a coach, scout, or athlete, to see if he can get a comment or more information. The sportscaster also might want to prepare a list of upcoming games, matches, and other sports events. Athletes often make public appearances for charity events and the sportscaster might want to include a mention of the charity and the participating athlete or athletes.

After deciding which stories to cover and the lineup of the stories that will be featured in the first of the day's broadcasts, sportscasters then review any audio or video clips that will accompany the various stories. Sportscasters working for radio stations choose audio clips, usually interviews, that augment the piece of news they will read. Sportscasters working for television stations look for video footage—the best 10 seconds of this game or that play—to demonstrate why a certain team lost or won. Sometimes sportscasters choose footage that is humorous or poignant to illustrate the point of the news item.

After they decide which audio or video segments to use, sportscasters then work with sound or video editors to edit the data into a reel or video, or they edit the footage into a tape themselves. In either case, the finished product will be handed over to the news director or producer with a script detailing when it should play. The news producer or director will make certain that the reel or video comes in on cue during the broadcast.

Frequently, a sportscaster will make brief appearances at local sports events to interview coaches and players before and after the game, and sometimes during breaks in the action. These interviews, as well as any footage of the game that the station's camera crews obtain, are then added to the stock from which sportscasters choose for their segments.

Usually, the main broadcast for both radio and television sportscasters is the late evening broadcast following the evening's scheduled programming. This is when most of the major league sports events have concluded, the statistics for the game are released, and final, official scores are reported. Any changes that have occurred since the day's first sports broadcast are updated and new footage or sound bites are added. The final newscast for a television sportscaster will most likely include highlights from the day's sports events, especially dramatic shots of the most impressive or winning points scored.

Increasingly, in televised sports news the emphasis is on image. Often sportscasters, like other newscasters, are only on camera for several seconds at a time, but their voices continue over the videotape that highlights unique moments in different games.

For many sportscasters who work in television, preparing the daily sportscasts is their main job and takes up most of their time. For others, especially sportscasters who work in radio, delivering a play-by-play broadcast of particular sports events is the main focus of their job. These men and women use their knowledge of the game or sport to create with words a visual picture of the game, as it is happening, for radio listeners. The most common sports for which sportscasters deliver play-by-play broadcasts are baseball, basketball, football, and hockey. A few sportscasters broadcast horse races from the race track and sometimes these broadcasts are carried by off-track betting facilities.

Sportscasters who give the play-by-play for a basketball game, for example, usually arrive an hour or so before the start of the game. Often, they have a pregame show that features interviews with, and a statistical review of, the competing teams and athletes. To broadcast a basketball game, sportscasters sit courtside in a special media section so that they can see the action up close. During football, baseball, and hockey games sportscasters usually sit in one of the nearby media boxes. Throughout the game sportscasters narrate each play for radio listeners using rapid, precise, and lively descriptions. During time-outs, half-times, or other breaks in play, sportscasters might deliver their own running commentaries of the game, the players' performances, and the coaching.

Although some skills are advantageous to both aspects of the job, the sportscaster who specializes in play-by-play broadcasts needs to have an excellent mastery of the rules, players, and statistics of a sport, as well as the hand signals used by officials to regulate the flow of a game. Some sportscasters provide play-by-play broadcasts for several different teams or sports, from college to professional levels, requiring them to know more than one sport or team well.

Some sportscasters, often former athletes or established sports personalities, combine the two aspects of the job. They act as anchors or co-anchors for sports shows and give some play-by-play commentary while also providing their television or radio audience with statistics and general updates.

Sports announcers provide spectators with public address announcements before and during a sports event. For this job, announcers must remain utterly neutral, simply delivering the facts—goals scored, numbers of fouls, or a time-out taken. Sports announcers may be sportscasters or they may be professional announcers or emcees who make their living recording voice-overs for radio and television commercials and for large corporations or department stores.

Sports announcers usually give the lineups for games, provide player names and numbers during specific times in a contest, make public announcements during time-outs and pauses in play, and generally keep the crowd involved in the event (especially in baseball). Baseball announcers may try to rally the crowd or start the crowd singing or doing the wave.

REQUIREMENTS
High School
Graduating from high school is an important first step on the road to becoming a sports broadcaster or announcer. While in school, take classes that will allow you to work on your speaking and writing skills. Classes in speech, English, journalism, and foreign languages, such as Spanish and French, will be helpful. You may also find it helpful to take courses in drama and computer science.

Postsecondary Training
Educational requirements for sportscasting positions vary, depending on the position. Competition for radio and television sports broadcasting positions is especially fierce, so any added edge can make the difference.

Top 50 Television Markets
(in number of viewers)

1. New York, NY
2. Los Angeles, CA
3. Chicago, IL
4. Philadelphia, PA
5. San Francisco–Oakland–San Jose, CA
6. Boston (Manchester), MA
7. Dallas–Ft. Worth, TX
8. Washington, DC (Hagerstown, MD)
9. Atlanta, GA
10. Detroit, MI
11. Houston, TX
12. Seattle-Tacoma, WA
13. Tampa–St. Petersburg (Sarasota), FL
14. Minneapolis–St. Paul, MN
15. Cleveland-Akron (Canton), OH
16. Phoenix, AZ
17. Miami–Ft. Lauderdale, FL
18. Denver, CO
19. Sacramento–Stockton–Modesto, CA
20. Orlando–Daytona Beach–Melbourne, FL
21. Pittsburgh, PA
22. St. Louis, MO
23. Portland, OR
24. Baltimore, MD
25. Indianapolis, IN
26. San Diego, CA
27. Hartford & New Haven, CT
28. Charlotte, NC
29. Raleigh–Durham (Fayetteville), NC
30. Nashville, TN
31. Milwaukee, WI
32. Cincinnati, OH
33. Kansas City
34. Columbus, OH
35. Greenville–Sparta–Asheville–Andrews, NC
36. Salt Lake City, UT
37. San Antonio, TX
38. Grand Rapids, Kalamazoo, Battle Creek, MI
39. West Palm Beach–Ft. Pierce
40. Birmingham (Ann and Tusc), AL
41. Norfolk-Portsmouth-Newport News, VA
42. New Orleans, LA
43. Memphis, TN
44. Buffalo, NY
45. Oklahoma City, OK
46. Greensboro–High Point–Winston-Salem, NC
47. Harrisburg–Lancaster–Lebanon-York, PA
48. Providence–New Bedford, RI
49. Albuquerque–Santa Fe, NM
50. Louisville, KY

Source: Nielsen Media Research Local Universe Estimates

Television sportscasters who deliver the news in sports usually have bachelor's degrees in communications or journalism, although personality, charisma, and overall on-camera appearance is so important to ratings that station executives often pay closer attention to the taped auditions they receive from prospective sportscasters than to the items on resumes. If you are interested in pursuing a career in sports broadcasting, keep in mind that the industry is finicky and subjective about looks and charisma,; thus,you should continue to prepare yourself for the job by learning a sport inside and out, developing valuable contacts in the field through internships and part-time or volunteer jobs, and earning a degree in journalism or communications.

It isn't as crucial for sportscasters who deliver play-by-play broadcasts for radio stations to have the journalistic skills that a television sportscaster has, although good interviewing skills are essential. Instead, they need excellent verbal skills, a daunting command of the sport or sports they will be broadcasting, and a familiarity with the competing players, coaches, and team histories. To draw a complete picture for their listeners, sportscasters often reach back into history for an interesting detail or statistic, so a good memory for statistics and trivia and a knowledge of sports history is helpful, too.

Other Requirements

A nice speaking voice, excellent verbal and interviewing skills, a pleasant appearance, a solid command of sports in general, as well as in-depth knowledge of the most popular sports (football, basketball, baseball, and hockey), and an outgoing personality are all necessary for a successful career in sportscasting.

In addition, you need to have a strong voice, excellent grammar and English usage, and the ability to ad-lib if and when it is necessary.

EXPLORING

High school and college students have many opportunities to investigate this career choice, but the most obvious way is to participate in a sport. By learning a sport inside and out, you can gain valuable insight into the movements and techniques that, as a sportscaster, you will be describing. In addition, firsthand experience and a love of the sport itself makes it easier to remember interesting trivia related to the sport as well as the names and numbers of the pros who play it.

If you do not have the coordination or skill for the sport itself, you can volunteer to help out with the team by shagging balls, running drills, or keeping statistics. The latter is perhaps the best way to learn the percentages and personal athletic histories of athletes.

An excellent way to develop the necessary communications skills is to take a journalism course, join the school's speech or debate team, deliver the morning announcements, deejay on the school radio station, or volunteer at a local radio station or cable television station.

John Earnhardt from the National Association of Broadcasters has this advice: "Write about your school's sports teams for your school newspaper or hometown newspaper and read, read, read about sports. Knowledge about the area you are interested in reporting about is the best tool for success. It is also necessary to be able to express yourself well through the spoken word. Speaking before an audience can be the best practice for speaking before the camera or on a microphone."

Finally, you can hone your sportscasting skills on your own while watching your favorite sports event by turning down the sound on your television and tape-recording your own play-by-play deliveries.

EMPLOYERS

Most sports broadcasters work for television networks or radio stations. The large sports networks also employ many broadcasters. John Earnhardt says, "The main employers of sports broadcasters are sports networks that own the rights to broadcast sporting events and the broadcast stations themselves." Radio sportscasters are hired by radio stations of all sizes.

Sports announcers work for professional sports arenas, sports teams, minor league and major league ball teams, colleges, universities, and high schools.

Because sports are popular all over the country, there are opportunities everywhere, although the smaller the town the fewer the opportunities. "Larger cities generally have more opportunities because of the number of stations and the number of sports teams that need to be covered," Earnhardt says.

STARTING OUT

Although an exceptional audition tape might land you an on-camera or on-air job, most sportscasters get their start by writing copy, answering phones, operating cameras or equipment, or assisting the sportscaster with other jobs. Internships or part-time jobs will give you the opportunity to grow comfortable in front of a camera or behind a microphone. Of course, contacts within the industry come in handy. In many cases, it is simply an individual's devotion to the sport and the job that makes the difference—that and being in the right place at the right time. John Earnhardt adds that knowledge is key as well. "It obviously helps to know the sport you are reporting on—first, one needs to study the sport and know the sport's rules, history, and participants better than anyone," he advises.

Don't forget to put together an audio tape (if you are applying for a radio job or an announcer position) or a video tape (for television jobs) that showcases your abilities. On the tape, give your real-live account of the sports events that took place on a certain day.

ADVANCEMENT

In the early stages of their careers, sportscasters might advance from a sports copywriter to actual broadcaster. Later in their careers, sportscasters advance by moving to larger and larger markets, beginning with local television stations and advancing to one of the major networks.

Sportscasters who work in radio may begin in a similar way; advancement for these individuals might come in the form of a better time slot for a sports show, or the chance to give more commentary.

Sports announcers advance by adding to the number of teams for whom they provide public address announcements. Some sports announcers also may start out working for colleges and minor leagues and then move up to major league work.

EARNINGS

Salaries in sportscasting vary, depending on the medium (radio or television), the market (large or small, commercial or public), and whether the sportscaster is a former athlete or recognized sports celebrity, as opposed to a newcomer trying to carve out a niche.

According to the *Occupational Outlook Handbook*, the average salaries of television sportscasters range from $68,900 for weekday anchors to $37,200 for weekend sportscasters.

Sportscasting jobs in radio tend to pay less than those in television. Beginners will find jobs more easily in smaller stations, but the pay will be correspondingly lower than it is in larger markets. The average salary for a radio sportscaster, according to a 2001 survey by the National Association of Broadcasters and the Broadcast Cable Financial Management Association, was $53,300.

Salaries are usually higher for former athletes and recognized sports personalities or celebrities, such as ex-coaches like John Madden. These individuals already have an established personality within the sports community and may thus have an easier time getting athletes and coaches to talk to them. Salaries for such recognizable personalities can be $2 million or more per year.

WORK ENVIRONMENT

Sportscasters usually work in clean, well-lighted booths or sets in radio or television studios, or in special soundproof media rooms at the sports facility that hosts sports events.

Time constraints and deadlines can create havoc and add stress to an already stressful job; often a sportscaster has to race back to the studio to make the final evening broadcast. Sportscasters who deliver play-by-play commentary for radio listeners have the very stressful job of describing everything going on in a game as it happens. They can't take their eyes off the ball and the players while the clock is running and this can be nerve-wracking and stressful.

On the other hand, sportscasters are usually on a first-name basis with some of the most famous people in the world, namely, professional athletes. They quickly lose the star-struck quality that usually afflicts most spectators and must learn to ask well-developed, concise, and sometimes difficult questions of coaches and athletes.

Sports announcers usually sit in press boxes near the action so they can have a clear view of players and their numbers when announcing. Depending on the type of sport, this may be an enclosed area or out in the open air. Sports announcers start announcing before the event begins and close the event with more announcements, but then are able to end their work day. Because sporting events are scheduled at many different times of the day, announcers sometimes must be available at odd hours.

OUTLOOK

Competition for jobs in sportscasting will continue to be fierce, with the better paying, larger market jobs going to experienced sportscasters who have proven they can keep ratings high. Sportscasters who can easily substitute for other on-camera newscasters or anchors may be more employable.

The projected employment outlook is one of slower-than-average growth, as not that many new radio and television stations are expected to enter the market. Most of the job openings will come as sportscasters leave the market to retire, relocate, or enter other professions. In general, employment in this field is not affected by economic recessions or declines; in the event of cutbacks, the on-camera sports broadcasters and announcers are the last to go.

FOR MORE INFORMATION

For a list of schools that offer programs and courses in broadcasting, contact:

Broadcast Education Association
1771 N Street, NW
Washington, DC 20036-2891
Tel: 202-429-5355
Email: beainfo@beaweb.org
http://www.beaweb.org

For information on FCC licenses, contact:

Federal Communications Commission (FCC)
445 12th Street, SW
Washington, DC 20554
Tel: 888-225-5322
Email: fccinfo@fcc.gov
http://www.fcc.gov

To get general information about broadcasting, contact:

National Association of Broadcasters
1771 N Street, NW
Washington, DC 20036-2891
Tel: 202-429-5300
Email: nab@nab.org
http://www.nab.org

For career information and helpful Internet links, contact:

Radio-Television News Directors Association
1600 K Street, NW, Suite 700
Washington, DC 20006-2838
Tel: 202-659-6510
Email: rtnda@rtnda.org
http://www.rtnda.org

SPORTS PUBLICISTS

QUICK FACTS

School Subjects
English
Journalism
Speech

Personal Skills
Communication/ideas
Leadership/management

Work Environment
Primarily indoors
One location with some
travel

Minimum Education Level
Bachelor's degree

Salary Range
$20,000 to $40,000 to
$250,000+

Certification or Licensing
Voluntary

Outlook
About as fast as the
average

DOT
N/A

GOE
N/A

NOC
5124

O*NET-SOC
N/A

OVERVIEW

There are two types of *sports publicists*: those who work for professional and amateur teams and those who work for individual professional athletes. *Sports team publicists* handle the daily press operations for the organization. They handle the media relations, set up interviews with players, ensure that the correct information is distributed to the press, and write press releases. Sports publicists who work for individual players try to enhance their client's image by casting them in a positive light via newspaper, magazine, and television stories. Sports publicists are sometimes called *sports information directors, press agents, public relations (PR) directors, marketing directors,* or *directors of communication.*

HISTORY

The sports industry has matured into one of our nation's largest industries. Professional teams are the most widely recognized industry segment in sports. Professional teams include all of the various sports teams, leagues, and governing bodies for which individuals get paid for their performance. Some of the most notable areas include the National Football League, National Basketball League, National Hockey League, and Major League Baseball. These are commonly known as the four majors. During recent decades, more professional leagues have started, such as the Women's National Basketball League, Arena Football, and Major League Soccer. There are also many minor league and collegiate organizations.

Promoting sports has become a huge industry. There may be as many as 1.5 million marketing and 300,000 media front office personnel positions in professional and amateur sports, according to the article "Sports Information: The Most Coveted, Ignored Profession," by Nick Neupauer (*Public Relations Strategist*).

THE JOB

Sports publicists are responsible for all of the team's publications, including media guides, programs for all home games, schedule cards, mail order brochures, recruiting kits, annual reports, and booster club newsletters. They also handle all of the team's publicity, which includes news and feature releases, news conferences and background information, photography, media interviews, and media tours.

Publicity people also deal with game management, which includes PA announcers, scoreboard operations, telephone hookups, scorers, officiating facilities, press box seating and credentials, broadcast facilities, video facilities, and travel and lodging. They also are in charge of generating crowd participation by developing promotions, giveaways, half-time exhibitions, and music. Publicists also help design the team's uniform insignia and team banners.

Sports information directors might have other responsibilities, such as creating and placing advertising, attending league meetings, conventions, and workshops, coordinating booster club activities, fundraising, fan surveys, budgets, equipment negotiations, licensing, and merchandising.

Collegiate publicists might not be affiliated with the college or university's public relations department, but instead might be housed under the athletic department. Unlike other public relations practitioners, most sports information directors promote their competition as well as the team they work for. The better the opposition, the better the fan interest and ticket sales.

Publicists that work for athletes can be viewed as spin doctors, constantly creating angles and news events to get their clients into the spotlight. Many publicists try to show their clients in a positive light by having the athletes participate in goodwill appearances or work with organizations like the United Way. Maintaining that positive image increases the athletes' potential income and market value.

REQUIREMENTS
High School

As a sports publicist, you are the voice of the person or team that you represent, so it is very important that you are an effective communicator. Take classes in English and journalism to hone your writing skills, and take speech classes to help you learn how to compose your ideas and thoughts and convey them to an audience. You should also take other college preparatory classes, such as math, science, and foreign language. Since you will be dealing with the public, a general knowledge of history, sociology, psychology, and current events will be especially important.

Postsecondary Training

Most publicists working in the sports industry are college graduates with degrees in public relations, marketing, communications, journalism, or sports administration. A college degree is essential, according to the Public Relations Society of America.

Certification or Licensing

The Public Relations Society of America offers voluntary certification to public relations specialists. While this certification is not sports-related, it will help show prospective employers that you possess a high level of knowledge and experience. Candidates who pass a written and oral examination may use the designation "Accredited in Public Relations."

Other Requirements

In order to be a successful sports publicist, you should be outgoing and able to get along with many different types of people. Participate in sports or be a team manager in high school or college so that you become familiar with the lifestyle of an athlete and you can relate to it. You should also be organized and able to work well under stress, since you will likely be dealing with big-name clients.

EXPLORING

Ask your teacher or counselor to set up an informational interview with a publicist. Volunteer to handle various public relations-type duties for your high school sports teams or clubs. Run for student council or another leadership position at school to gain experience with public speaking and management. Read publications such as *Sports Illustrated* (http://www.si.com) and *Sports Business Journal* (http://www.sportsbusinessjournal.com), and attend sporting events so that you stay current on sports knowledge. It is also a good idea to volunteer to assist your school's athletic department (in high school or college); you may be able to have a hand in developing a team's media guide or programs. Cover sports for your college newspaper so that you will have some clips to show employers.

EMPLOYERS

Sports publicists work in one of three areas. Some work for public relations firms that handle athletes or sports-oriented events. Others work directly for sports teams in their front offices. Some are self-employed, working directly with clients.

STARTING OUT

The best way to enter the professional sports public relations level is by gaining experience at the collegiate ranks. There are many internships available at this level, and getting one is the best way to get your foot in the door. As an intern, you may be asked to contribute to publications and write and prepare press releases. This will give you a great opportunity not only to learn how to generate all of this material, but also to begin collecting samples of your writing and to develop your clip file. Every interviewer you will meet will ask you for your clip file, since they provide proof of your journalistic and PR writing skills.

There are also training programs within established PR companies. They might be hard to obtain, but they can be had.

ADVANCEMENT

"Like baseball players, front office staff generally look to advance to higher levels, from single-A to double-A or triple-A onto the majors," says Gary Radke, former marketing director of the Wisconsin Timber Rattlers minor league baseball team. "Within the given organizations, there really isn't much in the way of advancement because everyone is basically at the same level. Upper-management positions are the general manager and assistant general manager."

EARNINGS

Sports publicists can earn anywhere from $20,000 to more than $250,000 per year. People just starting out might make less, while those with proven track records command higher salaries. Publicists who work for individual athletes can earn more money.

"Minor league marketing directors make anywhere from $21,000 up to $60,000," says Gary Radke. "I received health insurance, 10 sick days, two personal days, apparel discounts, health club memberships, and free soda at the games."

WORK ENVIRONMENT

During the season, sports publicists may work 12- to 20-hour days, seven days a week. Since most sporting events take place in the evening or on weekends, and half are played on the road, sports publicists spend a lot of time on the job. Some publicists travel with their teams, while others do not. Either way, this job is very time-consuming.

OUTLOOK

The field of sports publicity is very competitive, and even though it is expanding as more teams and leagues form, it is still difficult to land a job. The U.S. Department of Labor predicts that employment of public relations specialists in general is expected to increase much faster than average for all occupations over the next several years, but the number of applicants with degrees in the communications fields (journalism, public relations, and advertising) is expected to exceed the number of job openings.

FOR MORE INFORMATION

For information on careers and certification in public relations, contact:

The Public Relations Society of America
33 Irving Place
New York, NY 10003-2376
Tel: 212-995-2230
Email: hq@prsa.org
http://www.prsa.org

SPORTSWRITERS

QUICK FACTS

School Subjects
English
Journalism
Physical education

Personal Skills
Communication/ideas

Work Environment
Indoors and outdoors
Primarily multiple locations

Minimum Education Level
Bachelor's degree

Salary Range
$20,290 to $42,270 to
$81,370+

Certification or Licensing
None available

Outlook
Little change or more
slowly than the average

DOT
131

GOE
11.08.03

NOC
5231

O*NET-SOC
27-3043.02

OVERVIEW

Sportswriters cover the news in sports for newspapers and magazines. They research original ideas or follow up on breaking stories by contacting coaches, athletes, and team owners and managers for comments or more information. Sometimes a sportswriter is fortunate enough to get his or her own column, in which the sportswriter editorializes on current news or developments in sports.

HISTORY

Throughout the world there are some 7,200 daily newspapers and far more semiweeklies, biweeklies, and weeklies, circulating at least 500 million copies on a regular basis. In the international context, the average newspaper is crude, poorly printed, heavy with sensational news, light on serious criticism, and burdened by all types of problems (especially economic). Outside Western Europe and North America there are very few "elite," or ultra serious, newspapers. Although most of the world's newspapers are privately owned, some degree of government control of newspapers is evident in many countries.

Magazine journalism has been a potent force in the United States (and throughout the world), appealing mainly to the elite, the well educated, and the opinion leaders. (This is especially true in regard to "journalistic" magazines.) Generally more incisive, more articulate, more interpretive, and certainly more comprehensive than newspapers, magazines have supplied an important intellectual dimension to news-oriented journalism. Whereas the main function of newspaper journalism is to inform or summarize in brief fashion, the aim of most magazine journalism is to fill gaps—to explain, interpret, criticize, and comment. In short, magazine journalism in its many types and styles supplements newspapers and fleshes out the bare bones of newspaper journalism.

Most magazines and newspapers have sections that focus on sports; others, such as *Sports Illustrated* and *ESPN the Magazine,* focus entirely on sports reporting. In either case, sportswriters are needed to write articles about athletes, teams, and sports competitions. Sportswriters are employed by both newspapers and magazines.

THE JOB

The sportswriter's primary job is to report the outcomes of the sports events that occurred that day. Since one newspaper can't employ enough reporters to cover, in-person, every single high school, college, and professional sports event that happens on any given day, let alone sports events happening in other cities and countries, sportswriters use the wire news services to get the details. Major national and international wire services include Reuters, AP, UPI, Agence France-Presse, and ITAR-Tass. The entire body of statistics for tennis matches, hockey games, and track-and-field events, for example, can be sent over the wire service so that sportswriters can include the general story and the vital statistics in as condensed or lengthy a form as space allows.

A sportswriter begins work each day by reviewing the local, national, and international news that comes in over the wire news services. He or she then begins researching the top or lead stories to try to flesh out the details, perhaps by providing a local perspective, or to come up with a completely new angle or spin. Examples of a lead story might be the comeback of a professional tennis star, the underdog victory of a third-rate, much-maligned football team, the incredible pitching record of a high school athlete, or the details about a football running back who blew out his knee in a crucial last-minute play. The sportswriter then performs in-person or telephone interviews with coaches, athletes, scouts, agents, promoters, and sometimes, in the case of an athletic injury, a physician or team of physicians.

Depending on the edition of the newspaper or magazine, the sportswriter might report events that happened anywhere from the day before to events that took place within that week or month. For example, a sportswriter who writes for a magazine such as *Sports Illustrated* probably won't write articles with the same degree of detail per game. Instead, he or she writes articles, commonly called *features,* that explore an entire season for a team or an athlete. The magazine sportswriter might take the same story of the running back with the damaged knee ligaments and follow that athlete through his surgery and rehabilitation, interviewing not only the running back, but his wife, doctors, coaches, and agent. This information-gathering stage is the same for both newspaper and magazine sportswriters; the only difference is the timeline. A newspaper sportswriter may have only a few hours to conduct research and call around for comments, while the sportswriter for a magazine may have anywhere from several weeks to several months to compose the story.

Regardless of whether the sportswriter works for a newspaper or magazine, the next step for the sportswriter is to write the story. The method will vary, again, depending on the medium. Most sportswriters for newspapers are subject to the constraints of space, and these limits can change in a matter of minutes. On a dull day, up until the hour before the paper is published or "put to bed," the sportswriter might have a quarter of a page to fill with local sports news. At the last minute, however, an entire Super Bowl team could come down with food poisoning, in which case the sports editor would probably want to cover this larger, breaking story. To accommodate the new articles about the poisoning, the effect on team morale, whether or not the Super Bowl might be postponed for the first time in history, the local sports coverage would either have to shrink considerably or be completely cut. To manage this, sportswriters, like other reporters who write for daily newspapers, compose their stories with the most crucial facts contained within the first one or two paragraphs of the story. They may write a 10-paragraph story, but if it had to be shortened, the pertinent information would be easily retained.

Sportswriters for magazines, on the other hand, seldom need to worry about their stories being cut down at the last minute. Rather, their stories are subject to more careful editing. Magazines usually have story meetings weeks or months in advance of the relevant issue, giving sportswriters ample time to plan, research, and write their articles. As a result of the different timetable, the presentation of the story will change. The sportswriter will not cram all the essential facts into an opening paragraph or two. Instead, he or she is allowed much greater leeway with the introduction and the rest of the article. The sportswriter, in this case, will want to set a mood in the introduction, developing the characters of the individuals being interviewed—literally, telling a story about the story. In short, details can hinder a newspaper sports story from accomplishing its goal of getting across the facts in a concise form, while in a magazine sports article, those extraneous, revealing details actually become part of the story.

Even with the help of news services, sportswriters still couldn't have all the sports news at their fingertips without the help of other reporters and writers, known in the world of reporting as *stringers.* A stringer covers an event that would probably not be covered by the wire services, events such as high school sports events, as well as games in professional sports that are occurring simultaneously with other major sports events. The stringer attends the sports event and phones in scores, or emails or faxes in a complete report.

While the sportswriters for magazines don't necessarily specialize in one area of sports, but instead, routinely write features on a wide variety of sports and athletes, sportswriters for newspapers do specialize. Many only cover a particular sport, such as baseball. Others are assigned a beat, or specific area, and like other reporters must cover all the events that fall into that beat. For example, a sportswriter assigned to the high school football beat for a newspaper in Los Angeles, California, would be expected to cover all the area high school football games. Since football is seasonal, he or she might be assigned to the high school basketball beat during the winter season. On the other hand, the sportswriter working in Lexington, Kentucky, might be assigned coverage of all the high school sports in the area, not simply one sport. Much of the way in which assignments are given depends on experience as well as budget and staffing constraints.

REQUIREMENTS
High School

English, journalism, and speech are the most important classes for you to take in high school. You will need to master the art of writing in order to convey your ideas concisely, yet creatively, to your readers. Speech classes will help you become comfortable interacting with others. Be sure to take physical education classes and participate in organized sports, be it as a competitor, a team manager, or an assistant. You also should join the staff of your school paper or yearbook. This will give you a chance to cover and write about your school's sports teams or other school activities.

Postsecondary Training

You will need at least a bachelor's degree to become a sportswriter, although many sportswriters go on to study journalism at the graduate level. Most sportswriters concentrate on journalism while in college, either by attending a program in journalism or by taking whatever courses are available outside of a specialized program. This isn't to say that you can't become a sportswriter without a degree in journalism, but competition for sportswriting jobs is incredibly fierce. After all, not only do sportswriters spend their time writing about one of their favorite topics, but they also get great seats at sporting events and have the credentials to meet and interview sports celebrities. Increasingly, a specialized education is becoming the means by which sports editors and managers sift through the stacks of resumes from prospective sportswriters. Sportswriters may have degrees in communications or English, among other majors.

Other Requirements

Clearly, the ability to write well and concisely is another requirement for the job of the sportswriter. In addition, you must have a solid understanding of the rules and play of many different sports. If you hope to specialize in the coverage of one particular sport, your knowledge of that sport has to be equal to that of anyone coaching or playing it at the professional level.

Finally, you must be able to elicit information from a variety of sources, as well as to determine when information being leaked is closer to promotional spin than to fact. There will be more times when a coach or agent will not want to comment on a story than the times when they will want to make an on-the-record comment, so the sportswriter must be assertive in pressing the source for more information.

EXPLORING

You can learn on-the-job skills by working for your high school and college papers. The experience can be related to sports, of course, but any journalistic experience will help you develop the basic skills useful to any reporter, regardless of the area about which you are writing.

You can increase your chances and success in the field by applying to colleges or universities with renowned academic programs in journalism. Most accredited programs have a required period of training in which you will intern with a major newspaper somewhere in the United States; student-interns are responsible for covering a beat.

You may also find it helpful to read publications that are related to this field, such as *Sports Illustrated* (http://www.si.com) and *Sports Business Journal* (http://www.sportsbusinessjournal.com), and visit websites such as the Associated Press Sports Edition (http://apse.dallasnews.com).

EMPLOYERS

Sportswriters are employed by newspapers and magazines throughout the world. They may cover professional teams based in large cities or high school teams located in tiny towns. Sportswriters also work as freelance writers.

STARTING OUT

You may have to begin your career as a sportswriter by covering the games or matches that no else wants to or can cover. As a stringer, you won't earn much money, you'll probably have a second or even third job, but eventually it may lead to covering bigger and better games and teams. Some sportswriters make a living out of covering sports for very small towns, others only work at those jobs until they have gained the experience to move on.

Most journalists start their careers by working in small markets— little towns and cities with local papers. You may work for a newspaper for a year or two and then apply for positions with larger papers in bigger towns and cities. Sportswriters for newspapers follow the same routine, and more than a few eventually pursue areas other than sports because the job openings in sports are limited. The lucky few who hang on to a small sports beat can often parlay the experience into a better position by sticking with the job and demonstrating a devotion to the sport, even cultivating a following of loyal fans. This could lead to a full-time column.

Most likely, as a sportswriter, you will take advantage of opportunities to learn more about athletes and sports in general. Becoming an expert on a little-known but rapidly growing sport may be one way for you to do this. For example, if you were to learn all that you can about mountain biking, you might be able to land a job with one of the magazines specializing in the sport of mountain biking.

Competition for full-time jobs with magazines as a sportswriter is just as keen as it is for major newspapers. Often, a sportswriter will write articles and try to sell them to one of the major magazines, hoping that when an opening comes, he or she will have first crack at it. Still, most sportswriters move into the world of sports magazines after they've proven themselves in newspaper sportswriting. It is possible to get a job with a sports magazine straight from college or graduate school, but chances are you'll have to work your way up.

The placement centers of colleges or universities with accredited undergraduate and graduate programs in journalism can be extremely helpful in beginning your job search. In fact, many graduates of these programs are not only highly sought after by newspapers and magazines, but these graduates are often offered jobs by the newspapers and magazines with whom they had an internship during school.

ADVANCEMENT

The constraints of budget, staffing, and time—which make a sportswriters' job difficult—are also often what can help a sportswriter rise through the ranks. For example, the writer asked to cover all the sports in a small area may have to hustle to cover the beat alone, but that writer also won't have any competition when covering the big events. Thus, he or she can gain valuable experience and bylines writing for a small paper, whereas in a larger market, the same sportswriter would have to wait much longer to be assigned an event that might result in a coveted byline.

Sportswriters advance by gaining the top assignments, covering the major sports in feature articles, as opposed to the bare bones summaries of events. They also advance by moving to larger and larger papers, by getting columns, and finally, by getting a syndicated column—that is, a column carried by many papers around the country or even around the world.

Sportswriters for magazines advance by moving up the publishing ladder, from editorial assistant to associate editor to writer. Often, an editorial assistant might be assigned to research a story for a sports brief—a quirky or short look at an element of the game. For example, *Sports Illustrated* might have a page devoted to new advances in sports equipment for the amateur athlete. The editorial assistant might be given the idea and asked to research it, or specific items. A writer might eventually write it up, using the editorial assistant's notes. Advancement, then, comes in being actually listed as the author of the piece.

In the publishing worlds of both newspapers and magazines, sportswriters can advance by becoming editors of a newspaper's sports page or of a sports magazine. There are also *sports publicists* and *sports information directors* who work for the publicity and promotions arms of colleges, universities, and professional sports teams. These individuals release statements, write and disseminate to the press articles on the organizations' teams and athletes, and arrange press opportunities for coaches and athletes.

EARNINGS
According the *Occupational Outlook Handbook*, writers earned median annual earnings of $42,270 in 2000. The lowest 10 percent earned less than $20,290, while the highest 10 percent earned over $81,370. The median annual salary (for all writers) in the newspaper industry was $26,470.

Sportswriters who cover the major sports events, who have their own column, or who have a syndicated column can expect to earn more than the salaries above. Sportswriters who write for major magazines can also expect to earn more, sometimes per article, depending on their reputations and the contracts worked out by themselves or their agents.

WORK ENVIRONMENT
Like other journalists, sportswriters work in a variety of conditions, from the air-conditioned offices of a newsroom or magazine publisher to the sweaty, humid locker room of a professional basketball team, to the arid and dusty field where a baseball team's spring training is held. Sportswriters work irregular hours, putting in as much or as little time as the story requires, often traveling to small towns and out-of-the-way locales to cover a team's away games.

For individuals who love sports, the job offers the chance to cover sports events every day, to immerse themselves in the statistics and injury lists and bidding wars of professional and amateur sports, to speak, sometimes one-on-one, with the greatest athletes of yesterday, today, and tomorrow.

OUTLOOK

The turnover rate for top sportswriters with major newspapers and magazines isn't very high, which means that job openings occur as sportswriters retire, die, are fired, or move into other markets. While the publishing industry may have room in it for yet another magazine devoted to a particular sports specialty, competition for sportswriting jobs will continue to be strong over the next several years and beyond.

FOR MORE INFORMATION

Career information, including a pamphlet called Facts about Newspapers, is available from:

Newspaper Association of America
1921 Gallows Road, Suite 600
Vienna, VA 22182-3900
Tel: 703-902-1600
http://www.naa.org

For information on careers and salaries in the newspaper industry, contact:

The Newspaper Guild
501 Third Street, NW, Suite 250
Washington, DC 20001
Tel: 202-434-7177
Email: guild@cwa-union.org
http://www.newsguild.org

TECHNICAL WRITERS AND EDITORS

QUICK FACTS

School Subjects
Business
English

Personal Skills
Communication/ideas
Technical/scientific

Work Environment
Primarily indoors
Primarily one location

Minimum Education Level
Bachelor's degree

Salary Range
$23,090 to $50,000 to
$77,330+

Certification or Licensing
None available

Outlook
Faster than the average

DOT
131 (writers), 132 (editors)

GOE
11.08.02 (writers), 11.08.01
(editors)

NOC
5121

O*NET-SOC
27-3041.00, 27-3042.00,
27-3043.00

OVERVIEW

Technical writers, sometimes called *technical communicators,* express technical and scientific ideas in easy-to-understand language. *Technical editors* revise written text to correct any errors and make it more readable. They also may coordinate the activities of technical writers, technical illustrators, and other staff in preparing material for publication and oversee the document development and production processes. Technical writers hold about 57,000 jobs in the United States.

HISTORY

Humans have used writing as a means to communicate information for over 5,500 years. Technical writing, though, did not emerge as a specific profession in the United States until the early years of the 20th century. Before that time, engineers, scientists, and researchers did any necessary writing themselves.

During the early 1900s, technology expanded rapidly. The use of machines to manufacture and mass-produce a wide number of products paved the way for more complex and technical products. Scientists and researchers were discovering new technologies and applications for technology, particularly in electronics, medicine, and engineering. The need to record studies and research and report them to others grew. Also, as products became more complex, there was a greater need to document their components, show how they were assembled, and explain how to install, use, and repair them. By the mid-1920s, writers were being used to help engineers and scientists document their work and prepare technical information for nontechnical audiences.

Editors had been used for many years to work with printers and authors. They often checked copies of a printed document to correct any errors made during printing, to rewrite unclear passages, and to correct errors in spelling, grammar, and punctuation. As the need for technical writers grew, so too did the need for technical editors. Editors became more involved with documents before the printing stage, and they worked closely with writers as they prepared their materials. Today, many editors coordinate the activities of all the people involved in preparing technical communications and manage the document development and production processes.

The need for technical writers grew still more with the growth of the computer industry in the 1960s. Originally, many computer companies used computer programmers to write user manuals and other documentation. It was widely assumed that the material was so complex that only those who were involved with creating computer programs would be able to write about them. Although computer programmers had the technical knowledge, many were not able to write clear, easy-to-use manuals. Complaints about the difficulty of using and understanding manuals were common. By the 1970s, computer companies began to hire technical writers to write computer manuals and documents. Today, this is one of the largest areas of technical writing .

The need for technical marketing writers also grew as a result of expanding computer technology. Many copywriters who worked for advertising agencies and marketing firms did not have the technical background to describe the features of the technical products that were coming to market. Thus writers who could combine an ability to promote products with an ability to communicate technical information were much sought after.

The nature of technical writers' and technical editors' jobs continues to change with emerging technologies. Today, the ability to store, transmit, and receive information through computers and electronic means is changing the very nature of documents. Traditional books and paper documents are being replaced by floppy disks, CD-ROMs, interactive multimedia documents, and material accessed through bulletin board systems, faxes, the World Wide Web, and the Internet.

THE JOB

Technical writers and editors prepare a wide variety of documents and materials. The most common types of documents they produce are manuals, technical reports, specifications, and proposals. Some technical writers also write scripts for videos and audiovisual presentations and text for multimedia programs. Technical writers and editors prepare manuals that give instructions and detailed information on how to install, assemble, use, service, or repair a product or equipment. They may write and edit manuals as simple as a two-page leaflet that gives instructions on how to assemble a bicycle, or as complex as a 500-page document that tells service technicians how to repair machinery, medical equipment, or a climate-control system. One of the most common types of manuals is the computer software manual, which informs users on how to load software on their computers, explains how to use the program, and gives information on different features.

Technical writers and editors also prepare technical reports on a multitude of subjects. These reports include documents that give the results of research and laboratory tests and documents that describe the progress of a project. They also write and edit sales proposals, product specifications, quality standards, journal articles, in-house style manuals, and newsletters.

The work of a technical writer begins when he or she is assigned to prepare a document. The writer meets with members of an account or technical team to learn the requirements for the document, the intended purpose or objectives, and the audience. During the planning stage, the writer learns when the document needs to be completed, approximately how long it should be, whether artwork or illustrations are to be included, who the other team members are, and any other production or printing requirements. A schedule is created that defines the different stages of development and determines when the writer needs to have certain parts of the document ready.

The next step in document development is the research, or information-gathering, phase. During this stage, technical writers gather all the available information about the product or subject, read and review it, and determine what other information is needed. They may research the topic by reading technical publications, but in most cases they will need to gather information directly from the people working on the product. Writers meet with and interview people who are sources of information, such as scientists, engineers, software developers, computer programmers, managers, and project managers. They ask questions, listen, and take notes or tape record interviews. They gather any available notes, drawings, or diagrams that may be useful.

After writers gather all the necessary information, they sort it out and organize it. They plan how they are going to present the information and prepare an outline for the document. They may decide how the document will look and prepare the design, format, and layout of the pages. In some cases an editor, rather than the author, may do this. If illustrations, diagrams, or photographs are going to be included, either the editor or writer makes arrangements for an illustrator, photographer, or art researcher to produce or obtain them.

Then, the writer starts writing and prepares a rough draft of the document. If the document is very large, a writer may prepare it in segments. Once the rough draft is completed, it is submitted to a designated person or group for technical review. Copies of the draft are distributed to managers, engineers, or subject-matter experts who can easily determine if any technical information is inaccurate or missing. These reviewers read the document and suggest changes.

The rough draft is also given to technical editors to review a variety of factors. The editors check that the material is organized well, that each section flows with the section before and after it, and that the language is appropriate for the intended audience. They also check for correct use of grammar, spelling, and punctuation. They ensure that names of parts or objects are consistent throughout the document and that references are accurate. They also check the labeling of graphs and captions for accuracy. Technical editors use special symbols, called proofreader's marks, to indicate the types of changes needed.

The editor and reviewers return their copies of the document to the technical writer. The writer incorporates the appropriate suggestions and revisions and prepares the final draft. The final draft is once again submitted to a designated reviewer or team of reviewers.

In some cases, the technical reviewer may do a quick check to make sure that the requested changes were made. In other cases, the technical reviewer may examine the document in depth to ensure technical accuracy and correctness. A walkthrough, or test of the document, may be done for certain types of documents. For example, a walkthrough may be done for a document that explains how to assemble a product. A tester assembles the product by following the instructions given in the document. The tester makes a note of all sections that are unclear or inaccurate, and the document is returned to the writer for any necessary revisions.

For some types of documents, a legal review may also be done. For example, a pharmaceutical company that is preparing a training manual to teach its sales representatives about a newly released drug needs to ensure that all materials are in compliance with Food and Drug Administration (FDA) requirements. A member of the legal department who is familiar with these requirements will review the document to make sure that all information in the document conforms to FDA rules.

Once the final draft has been approved, the document is submitted to the technical editor, who makes a comprehensive and detailed check of the document. In addition to checking that the language is clear and reads smoothly, the editor makes sure the table of contents matches the different sections or chapters of a document, all illustrations and diagrams are correctly placed, all captions are matched to the correct picture, consistent terminology is used, and correct references are used in the bibliography and text.

The editor returns the document to either the writer or a word processor, who makes any necessary corrections. This copy is then checked by a *proofreader*. The proofreader compares the final copy against the editor's marked-up copy and makes sure that all changes were made. The document is then prepared for printing. In some cases, the writer is responsible for preparing camera-ready copy or electronic files for printing purposes, and in other cases, a print production coordinator prepares all material to submit to a printer.

Some technical writers specialize in a specific type of material. *Technical marketing writers* create promotional and marketing materials for technological products. They may write the copy for an advertisement for a technical product, such as a computer workstation or software, or they may write press releases about the product. They also write sales literature, product flyers, Web pages, and multimedia presentations.

Other technical writers prepare scripts for videotapes and films about technical subjects. These writers, called *scriptwriters,* need to have an understanding of film and video production techniques.

Some technical writers and editors prepare articles for scientific, medical, computer, or engineering trade journals. These articles may report the results of research conducted by doctors, scientists, or engineers or report on technological advances in a particular field. Some technical writers and editors also develop textbooks. They may receive articles written by engineers or scientists and edit and revise them to make them more suitable for the intended audience.

Technical writers and editors may create documents for a variety of media. Electronic media, such as compact discs and online services, are increasingly being used in place of books and paper documents. Technical writers may create materials that are accessed through bulletin board systems and the Internet or create computer-based resources, such as help menus on computer programs. They also create interactive, multimedia documents that are distributed on compact discs or floppy disks. Some of these media require knowledge of special computer programs that allow material to be hyperlinked, or electronically cross-referenced.

REQUIREMENTS
High School

In high school, you should take composition, grammar, literature, creative writing, journalism, social studies, math, statistics, engineering, computer science, and as many science classes as possible. Business courses are also useful as they explain the organizational structure of companies and how they operate.

Postsecondary Training

Most employers prefer to hire technical writers and editors who have bachelor's or advanced degrees. Many technical editors graduate with degrees in the humanities, especially English or journalism. Technical writers typically need to have a strong foundation in engineering, computers, or science. Many technical writers graduate with degrees in engineering or science and take classes in technical writing.

Many different types of college programs are available that prepare people to become technical writers and editors. A growing number of colleges are offering degrees in technical writing. Schools without a technical writing program may offer degrees in journalism or English. Programs are offered through English, communications, and journalism departments. Classes vary based on the type of program. In general, classes for technical writers include a core curriculum in writing and classes in algebra, statistics, logic, science, engineering, and computer programming languages. Useful classes for editors include technical writing, project management, grammar, proofreading, copyediting, and print production.

Many technical writers and editors earn master's degrees. In these programs, they study technical writing in depth and may specialize in a certain area, such as scriptwriting, instructional design, or multimedia applications. In addition, many nondegree writing programs are offered to technical writers and editors to hone their skills. Offered as extension courses or continuing education courses, these programs include courses on indexing, editing medical materials, writing for trade journals, and other related subjects.

Technical writers, and occasionally technical editors, are often asked to present samples of their work. College students should build a portfolio during their college years in which they collect their best samples from work that they may have done for a literary magazine, newsletter, or yearbook.

Technical writers and editors should be willing to pursue learning throughout their careers. As technology changes, technical writers and editors may need to take classes to update their knowledge. Changes in electronic printing and computer technology will also change the way technical writers and editors do their jobs and writers and editors may need to take courses to learn new skills or new technologies.

Other Requirements

Technical writers need to have good communications skills, science and technical aptitudes, and the ability to think analytically. Technical editors also need to have good communications skills and judgment, as well as the ability to identify and correct errors in written material. They need to be diplomatic, assertive, and able to explain tactfully what needs to be corrected to writers, engineers, and other people involved with a document. Technical editors should be able to understand technical information easily, but they need less scientific and technical backgrounds than writers. Both technical writers and editors need to be able to work as part of a team and collaborate with others on a project. They need to be highly self-motivated, well organized, and able to work under pressure.

EXPLORING

If you enjoy writing and are considering a career in technical writing or editing, you should make writing a daily activity. Writing is a skill that develops over time and through practice. You can keep journals, join writing clubs, and practice different types of writing, such as scriptwriting and informative reports. Sharing writing with others and asking them to critique it is especially helpful. Comments from readers on what they enjoyed about a piece of writing or difficulty they had in understanding certain sections provides valuable feedback that helps to improve your writing style.

Reading a variety of materials is also helpful. Reading exposes you to both good and bad writing styles and techniques and helps you to identify why one approach works better than another.

You may also gain experience by working on a literary magazine, student newspaper, or yearbook (or starting one of your own if one is not available). Both writing and editing articles and managing production give you the opportunity to learn new skills and to see what is involved in preparing documents and other materials.

Students may also be able to get internships, cooperative education assignments, or summer or part-time jobs as proofreaders or editorial assistants that may include writing responsibilities.

EMPLOYERS

There are approximately 57,000 technical writers currently employed in the United States. Editors of all types (including technical editors) hold 122,000 jobs.

Employment may be found in many different types of places, such as in the fields of aerospace, computers, engineering, pharmaceuticals, and research and development, or with the nuclear industry, medical publishers, government agencies or contractors, and colleges and universities. The aerospace, engineering, medical, and computer industries hire significant numbers of technical writers and editors. The federal government, particularly the Departments of Defense and Agriculture, the National Aeronautics and Space Administration, and the Atomic Energy Commission, also hire many writers and editors with technical knowledge.

STARTING OUT

Many technical writers start their careers as scientists, engineers, technicians, or research assistants and move into writing after several years of experience in those positions. Technical writers with a bachelor's degree in a technical subject such as engineering may be able to find work as a technical writer immediately upon graduating from college, but many employers prefer to hire writers with some work experience.

Technical editors who graduate with a bachelor's degree in English or journalism may find entry-level work as editorial assistants, copy editors, or proofreaders. From these positions they are able to move into technical editing positions. Or beginning workers may find jobs as technical editors in small companies or those with a small technical communications department.

If you plan to work for the federal government, you need to pass an examination. Information about examinations and job openings is available at federal employment centers.

You may learn about job openings through your college's job placement services and want ads in newspapers and professional magazines. You may also research companies that hire technical writers and editors and apply directly to them. Many libraries provide useful job resource guides and directories that provide information about companies that hire in specific areas.

ADVANCEMENT

As technical writers and editors gain experience, they move into more challenging and responsible positions. At first, they may work on simple documents or are assigned to work on sections of a document. As they demonstrate their proficiency and skills, they are given more complex assignments and are responsible for more activities.

Technical writers and editors with several years of experience may move into project management positions. As project managers, they are responsible for the entire document development and production processes. They schedule and budget resources and assign writers, editors, illustrators, and other workers to a project. They monitor the schedule, supervise workers, and ensure that costs remain in budget.

Technical writers and editors who show good project management skills, leadership abilities, and good interpersonal skills may become supervisors or managers. Both technical writers and editors can move into senior writer and senior editor positions. These positions involve increased responsibilities and may include supervising other workers.

Many technical writers and editors seek to develop and perfect their skills rather than move into management or supervisory positions. As they gain a reputation for their quality of work, they may be able to select choice assignments. They may learn new skills as a means of being able to work in new areas. For example, a technical writer may learn a new desktop program in order to become more proficient in designing. Or a technical writer may learn a hypermedia or hypertext computer program in order to be able to create a multimedia program. Technical writers and editors who broaden their skill base and capabilities can move to higher paying positions within their own company or at another company. They also may work as freelancers or set up their own communications companies.

EARNINGS

Median annual earnings for salaried technical writers were $49,370 in 2001, according to the Bureau of Labor Statistics. Salaries ranged from less than $29,750 to more than $77,330. Editors of all types earned a median salary of $39,960. The lowest 10 percent earned $23,090 or less and the highest 10 percent earned $73,460 or more.

The Society for Technical Communication's 2001 salary survey of its membership reports that the mean salary of its members was $55,360. The entry-level salary was reported to be $36,210, with senior-level supervisors earning $75,180.

Most companies offer benefits that include paid holidays and vacations, medical insurance, and 401-K plans. They may also offer profit sharing, pension plans, and tuition assistance programs.

WORK ENVIRONMENT

Technical writers and editors usually work in an office environment, with well-lit and quiet surroundings. They may have their own offices or share work space with other writers and editors. Most writers and editors have computers. They may be able to utilize the services of support staff who can word-process revisions, run off copies, fax material, and perform other administrative functions or they may have to perform all of these tasks themselves.

Some technical writers and editors work out of home offices and use computer modems and networks to send and receive materials electronically. They may go in to the office only on occasion for meetings and gathering information. Freelancers and contract workers may work at a company's premises or at home.

Although the standard workweek is 40 hours, many technical writers and editors frequently work 50 or 60 hours a week. Job interruptions, meetings, and conferences can prevent writers from having long periods of time to write. Therefore, many writers work after hours or bring work home. Both writers and editors frequently work in the evening or on weekends in order to meet a deadline.

In many companies there is pressure to produce documents as quickly as possible. Both technical writers and editors may feel at times that they are compromising the quality of their work due to the need to conform to time and budget constraints. In some companies, technical writers and editors may have increased workloads due to company reorganizations or downsizing. They may need to do the work that was formerly done by more than one person. Technical writers and editors also are increasingly assuming roles and responsibilities formerly performed by other people and this can increase work pressures and stress.

Despite these pressures, most technical writers and editors gain immense satisfaction from their work and the roles that they perform in producing technical communications.

OUTLOOK

The writing and editing field is generally very competitive. Each year, there are more people trying to enter this field than there are available openings. The field of technical writing and editing, though, offers more opportunities than other areas of writing and editing, such as book publishing or journalism. Employment opportunities for technical writers and editors are expected to grow faster than the average over the next several years. Demand is growing for technical writers who can produce well-written computer manuals. In addition to the computer industry, the pharmaceutical industry is showing an increased need for technical writers. Rapid growth in the high technology and electronics industries and the Internet will create a continuing demand for people to write users' guides, instruction manuals, and training materials. Technical writers will be needed to produce copy that describes developments and discoveries in the law, science, and technology for a more general audience.

Writers may find positions that include duties in addition to writing. A growing trend is for companies to use writers to run a department, supervise other writers, and manage freelance writers and outside contractors. In addition, many writers are acquiring responsibilities that include desktop publishing and print production coordination.

The demand for technical writers and editors is significantly affected by the economy. During recessionary times, technical writers and editors are often among the first to be let go. Many companies that are downsizing or reducing their number of employees are reluctant to keep writers on staff. Such companies prefer to hire writers and editors on a temporary contract basis, using them only as long as it takes to complete an assigned document. Technical writers and editors who work on a temporary or freelance basis need to market their services and continually look for new assignments. They also do not have the security or benefits offered by full-time employment.

FOR MORE INFORMATION

For information on writing and editing careers in the field of communications, contact:

National Association of Science Writers
PO Box 890
Hedgesville, WV 25427
Tel: 304-754-5077
http://www.nasw.org

For information on careers, contact:

Society for Technical Communication
901 North Stuart Street, Suite 904
Arlington, VA 22203-1822
Tel: 703-522-4114
Email: stc@stc.org
http://www.stc.org

TELEVISION DIRECTORS

QUICK FACTS

School Subjects
English
Theater/dance

Personal Skills
Communication/ideas
Leadership/management

Work Environment
Primarily indoors
Primarily one location

Minimum Education Level
Bachelor's degree

Salary Range
$18,000 to $64,000 to
$250,000

Certification or Licensing
None available

Outlook
Faster than the average

DOT
159

GOE
01.03.01

NOC
5131

O*NET-SOC
27-2012.02

OVERVIEW

Television directors have ultimate control over the decisions that shape a TV production. The director is an artist who coordinates the elements of a television show and is responsible for its overall style and quality. Television directors work on a variety of productions. For example, they may work on local news programs, cover national sporting events, or tape commercials for businesses. And with the development of "narrowcasting" (broadcasting meant for limited viewing, such as for classrooms, hospitals, or corporations), some directors create programming for very small audiences. Directors are well known for their part in guiding actors and other TV professionals, but they are involved in much more, such as casting, costuming, cinematography, editing, and sound recording. Every television project, no matter how short or how small the intended audience, requires a director.

HISTORY

Drama developed in societies all over the world and dates back thousands of years. Playwrights and actors strove to impress, educate, and influence audiences with their dramatic interpretations of stories. From these ancient beginnings until the early half of the 19th century, actors directed themselves in productions. Until that time it had been common practice for one of the actors involved in a production to be responsible not only for his or her own performance but also for conducting rehearsals and coordinating the tasks involved in putting on a play. Usually the most experienced and respected troupe member would guide the other actors, providing advice on speech, movement, and interaction.

A British actress and opera singer named Madame Vestris (1797–1856) is considered to have been the first professional director. In the 1830s Vestris leased a theater in London and staged productions in which she herself did not perform. She displayed a new, creative approach to directing, making bold decisions about changing the traditional dress code for actors and allowing them to express their own interpretations of their roles. Vestris coordinated rehearsals, advised on lighting and sound effects, and chose nontraditional set decorations; she introduced props, such as actual windows and doors, that were more realistic than the usual painted panoramas.

By the turn of the century, theater directors such as David Belasco (1859–1931) and Konstantin Stanislavsky (1863–1938) had influenced the way in which performances were given, provoking actors and actresses to strive to identify with the characters they revealed so that audiences would be passionately and genuinely affected. By the early 1900s, Stanislavsky's method of directing performers had made an overwhelming mark on drama. His method (now often referred to as "the Method"), as well as his famous criticism, "I do not believe you," continue to influence performers to this day.

By the early 20th century, the film industry had also begun its rapid growth, and directors joined the teams of professionals who contributed to the production of movies. Commercial television, first available in the mid-1940s, provided yet another medium for directors, actors, and other professionals to work with. As a variety of television shows developed—dramas, newscasts, talk shows, for example—and the number of television stations multiplied, new opportunities opened up for television directors. Today, some TV directors work on a freelance basis, completing different projects for various production companies; others work for special interest cable channels, such as ESPN or MTV; still others work for network affiliates across the country. No matter what the project, however, all directors have one thing in common: they direct the talents and skills of a number of professionals, bringing together all the pieces to create a complete program.

THE JOB

The television director's responsibilities are varied and often depend on the project. For example, the director of a TV movie, documentary, or an episode of a series will have more control over the final production than the director of a news broadcast or a live event. The TV director working on a movie will use a script, go through rehearsals with actors, and shoot and reshoot scenes from many perspectives. To achieve the intended mood of the piece—such as dark and gloomy for a mystery—the director carefully orchestrates the work of lighting and sound technicians, camera operators, and editors. With such a production, the director can take the time to polish the final product that the audience will see.

A director covering a live event, such as a football game, has much less control over the outcome. In this case, the director only gets one shot at broadcasting the game. The director's responsibilities may include working with announcers to make sure their equipment is functioning properly, stationing camera operators so that they are positioned correctly to cover any possible play the teams might make, and being ready to introduce graphics, such as charts with player statistics. The director has little room for error when covering a live event.

Richard Perry, a director/editor for WWAY TV-3 in Wilmington, North Carolina, directs the 5:30 P.M. newscast. News directors may need to combine working from a script and arranged order of stories with the unpredictability of covering a live event. In addition, the news director's job isn't limited to the actual broadcast; he or she must also direct promotional segments, news updates, and some videotaped segments to accompany the live reports later. Although Perry directs the evening news, he reports to work at 5 A.M. to help prepare for the daily morning show as well as to direct the various updates and promotions to be broadcast throughout the day.

One of the first things Perry does every morning is to make the graphics for the morning news and, as he says, "I prep the 'supers'." Supers are superimposed words that run across the TV screen and provide information such as the names of interview subjects. The newsroom sends a printed list of these supers to Perry. He then types the names and titles into the chryon (the character generator), making sure everything is spelled correctly and in the right order. From 6 to 7 A.M., Perry runs the chryon for the morning show. This involves hitting the control for running the words across the screen at the right time. From 7 to 8:30 A.M., Perry directs the local weather and news cut-ins for broadcasting during *Good Morning, America*.

After his morning work, Perry is usually able to take a break. He returns to the station mid-afternoon and often spends a couple of hours working on commercial production, then he begins preproduction for the evening news. "We make graphics for over-the-shoulder shots," he explains, "and put boards on tape for the news editors to put in their stories." Boards are graphics and lists of information. These boards are videotaped, then edited by the reporter directly into news packages (or self-contained stories on tape, consisting of the reporter's audio and edited video). In the half hour before the evening news, Perry goes over the script, which has information about the order stories will be shown and who is covering them.

During the broadcast, the director typically sits in the control room and wears a headset through which he or she can communicate with the producer and TV crew. The director gives orders to keep the broadcast running smoothly and on time. Large TV stations have both a director and a technical director—a member of the technical crew who works directly with the cameras and other equipment and may make adjustments on the control board. But in a smaller station, like Perry's, directors take on many responsibilities. "I sit in front of the switcher," Perry says, "and tell everyone what to do and push all the right buttons at the right time so the show looks smooth." He tells the camera people what to shoot next and calls for tapes to be played (or "rolled") during the broadcast.

Freelance directors may work on live or taped productions. In addition to their responsibilities as directors—coordinating the work of crews, deciding on shots, overseeing editing—they may also need to take on many other elements involved in production. For example, they may need to work on getting funding for a project, hiring writers and assistants, or setting up locations for filming. They may even be involved in publicizing the project and entering it in festivals or competitions. In addition to all these responsibilities, freelance directors must also continually promote themselves and look for new projects to work on. The workflow for a freelance director can be unpredictable. They often take on a variety of projects, covering anything from sporting events to beauty pageants, in order to maintain a steady work schedule.

Top 10 Broadcast TV Companies
(by revenue)

Company	Top Media Property
1. Viacom	CBS-TV Network
2. NBC-TV (General Electric Co.)	NBC-TV Network
3. Walt Disney Co.	ABC-TV Network
4. News Corp.	Fox-TV Network
5. Tribune Co.	WPIX-TV (WB), New York
6. Univision Communications	Univision Network
7. Gannett Co.	WXIA-TV (NBC), Atlanta
8. Sinclair Broadcast Group	KOVR-TV (CBS), Sacramento
9. Hearst Corp.	WCVB-TV (ABC), Boston
10. Belo	WFAA-TV (ABC), Dallas/ Fort Worth

Source: *Advertising Age* (http://www.adage.com)

REQUIREMENTS
High School
The sooner you can get to know a camera and how to set up interesting shots, the better. If your high school offers courses about media or television production, be sure to take them. You should also consider taking photography classes that will teach you about the composition of an image. Take English and journalism classes to hone your communication skills and give you a feeling for completing assignments on deadline. Computer classes that teach you how to work with graphics programs will also be beneficial. If you are considering working as a freelancer, take mathematics, business, or accounting classes to help you manage your business. If you're interested in live directing and working with actors and story scripts, take drama classes to gain experience in this area.

Postsecondary Training
Although a college degree isn't necessarily required of a TV director, it does give you an edge in the workplace. Also, many colleges have

internship programs and career services that can help you get your foot in the door of the professional world. If you're interested in working for a TV news station, you should apply to the broadcast departments of journalism schools.

If you're interested in directing dramas or sitcoms for network and cable TV, you may want to enroll in a drama school to develop a theater background and experience working with scripts and actors. A number of universities and colleges also offer film studies programs or courses on television broadcast production. Your guidance counselor should be able to help you locate these. Also, do research on your own by checking out school websites and reading books such as *The Complete Guide to American Film Schools and Cinema and Television Courses* by Ernest Pintoff.

No matter what college program you enroll in, however, one of your top goals should be to gain practical hands-on experience through an internship at a TV station. You will probably not be paid for your work, but you may be able to get course credit. Some schools offer internship opportunities.

Organizations may also be a source of information on internships. The Radio-Television News Directors Association, for example, offers a limited number of scholarships and internships. The Directors Guild of America sponsors several training programs. One of these, the New York Assistant Director Training Program, lasts two years and the participants gain experience shooting on locations primarily in the New York City area. Competition for these programs is extremely fierce. A summer fellowship at the International Radio and Television Society offers an all-expense paid program, which includes career-planning advice and practical experience at a New York-based corporation. They also offer a minority career workshop, which brings college students to New York for orientation in electronic media.

Other Requirements

Those who want to be television directors should be strong leaders. "You have to be in order to pull together so many people to this one common goal: getting the show on the air cleanly," says Richard Perry. Directors also must be able to concentrate in a hectic environment. Perry notes, "I have an ability to focus on whatever is before me and to block out everything else that is unnecessary."

A director also needs self-confidence as well as the ability to work with other people. Personality conflicts sometimes arise between producers and directors or other members of the production team. The director needs to be able to mediate differences and bring people together. As a director, you might need to join a union. Directors working at network stations and for major markets typically have union membership.

EXPLORING

Join your high school newspaper staff to become familiar with reporting and editing. Volunteer as a staff photographer. If your high school has its own TV station, join the production crew. You might be able to videotape school events or work on the school newscast. Also, consider getting involved with the drama club. You may not want to be the star of the school play, but you can be involved in production work and may be able to videotape the play for the drama archives.

Contact a local TV station and ask for a tour of the facilities. Explain that you are interested in working as a director and ask to meet with one during your tour. Or set up a separate appointment for an informational interview with a director. Go to the interview prepared to ask questions about the work and the director's experience. People are often happy to talk about their work if you show a genuine interest.

EMPLOYERS

Television directors may work as salaried full-time employees for network or network-affiliated stations, cable stations, businesses, or agencies, or they may work as freelancers. Freelancers are not full-time employees of a particular company. Instead, freelancers work on a project-by-project basis for different employers, for example doing one project for a network and another for an advertising agency.

STARTING OUT

The position of director is not an entry-level job. You will need to work your way up through the ranks, gaining experience and knowledge along the way. Internships provide the best way to enter this competitive field. The internship gives you hands-on experience and the opportunity to make contacts within the industry. Richard Perry's internship as a production assistant during college led to his permanent position with WWAY-TV. "I gradually worked my way up through prompter, camera, tapes, audio, and finally I was a director." Perry also worked part time for the station for three-and-a-half years before being hired full time.

Other starting-out possibilities include working as an assistant for a freelance director or video production company. Be prepared to take any position that will give you hands-on experience with cameras and production, even if it's only on a part-time or temporary basis.

ADVANCEMENT

Advancement for television directors depends somewhat on their individual goals. One director might consider it an advancement to move from general TV programming to special interest programming. Another might feel that becoming a full-time freelancer is an advancement. Those who work at small stations tend to advance by relocating and working for larger stations. "If I want to move up as a director," Richard Perry says, "I'll have to move up to a larger market, maybe Charlotte or Raleigh." Such a move would mean receiving a larger salary and overseeing a bigger staff.

EARNINGS

Salaries vary greatly for TV directors and are determined by a number of factors. A director of a newscast at a small TV station will probably be at the low end of the scale, while a director working on a hit series for a network may earn hundreds of thousands of dollars a year. A freelance director working project-to-project may earn a great deal one year and much less the following year.

According to the Bureau of Labor Statistics, the median yearly income for all producers and directors was $45,090 in 2001. The lowest 10 percent earned less than $22,810; the highest 10 percent earned more than $140,070. A 2001 salary survey by the Radio-Television News Directors Association found that television news directors had salaries that ranged from $18,000 to $250,000. Their median annual salary was $64,000. Assistant news directors earned between $19,000 to $150,000. The median salary was $57,000.

Directors who work full time for stations or other organizations generally receive benefits such as health insurance and paid vacation and sick days.

WORK ENVIRONMENT

A TV station is a busy and exciting place where no two days are exactly alike. If the director is working on a live event, the atmosphere may be stressful and somewhat chaotic as he or she makes snap decisions, calls up the correct graphics, and keeps the show within the time limits. A director working on a taped project that will air at a later date may feel somewhat less "on air" stress; however, this director must also constantly pay attention to numerous production details, staying on budget and resolving problems among the staff. Because the director is responsible for clarifying what everyone's responsibilities for a project are, he or she may need to mediate in a tense situation. "Nine-to-five" definitely does not describe a day in the life of a director; 12-hour days (and more) are not uncommon. Because directors are ultimately responsible for so much, schedules often dictate that they become immersed in their work around the clock, from preproduction to final cut. Nonetheless, those able to make it in the industry find their work to be extremely enjoyable and satisfying.

OUTLOOK

The U.S. Department of Labor predicts that employment growth for actors, producers, and directors will increase at a rate faster than the average over the next several years. On a cautionary note, those wanting to become directors should realize that many see the television industry as a glamorous field, and there will be stiff competition for jobs.

More TV programs are produced now than ever before, and this number should continue to grow. New technology will allow cable stations to offer hundreds of additional channels and therefore need more original programming. Also, as more businesses and organizations recognize that TV and video productions can educate the public about their work as well as train employees, they will need directors' services to complete new projects.

Newsrooms provide TV stations with healthy profits every year, and this is not expected to change. Therefore, directors will continue to be in demand to direct newscasts. Directors of traditionally less recognized forms, such as commercials and music videos, are beginning to receive more attention. In 1997, the Emmy Awards program introduced nominations for the best TV commercials of the year. Also, directors of music videos are now listed along with the performer and record company at the beginning of all videos aired on MTV.

In the future, the number of TV directors who work freelance will likely increase. As productions become more costly and as smaller networks produce original programming, hiring directors on a project-to-project basis is becoming more economical.

FOR MORE INFORMATION

To learn more about the industry and DGA-sponsored training programs and to read selected articles from DGA Magazine, *contact:*

Directors Guild of America (DGA)
7920 Sunset Boulevard
Los Angeles, CA 90046
Tel: 310-289-2000
http://www.dga.org

For more information on fellowships, contact:

International Radio and Television Society
420 Lexington Avenue, Suite 1601
New York, NY 10170
Tel: 212-867-6650
http://www.irts.org

This organization for electronic media news professionals has information on internships, scholarships, and the news industry. The website has a "bookstore" featuring titles of interest to students and professionals involved in the industry.

Radio-Television News Directors Association
1600 K Street, NW, Suite 700
Washington, DC 20006-2838
Tel: 202-659-6510
Email: rtnda@rtnda.org
http://www.rtnda.org

This website contains links to numerous television-related sites and lists colleges and universities worldwide that offer training in television broadcast production.

CineMedia
http://www.cinemedia.org

TELEVISION EDITORS

QUICK FACTS

School Subjects Art English	**Certification or Licensing** None available
Personal Skills Artistic Communication/ideas	**Outlook** Faster than the average **DOT** 132
Work Environment Primarily indoors Primarily one location	**GOE** 11.08.01
Minimum Education Level Some postsecondary training	**NOC** 5225
Salary Range $19,430 to $36,900 to $100,000+	**O*NET-SOC** 27-4032.00

OVERVIEW

Television editors perform an essential role in the television industry. They take an unedited draft of videotape and use specialized equipment to improve the draft until it is ready for viewing. It is the responsibility of the television editor to create the most effective product possible. Television editors may also be employed in the film industry. There are approximately 16,000 film, video, and television editors employed in the United States.

HISTORY

The television industry has experienced substantial growth in the last few years in the United States. The effect of this growth is a steady demand for the essential skills that television editors provide. With recent innovations in computer technology, much of the work that these editors perform is accomplished using sophisticated computer programs. All of these factors have enabled many television editors to find steady work as salaried employees of television production companies and as independent contractors who provide their services on a per-job basis.

In the early days of the industry, editing was sometimes done by directors, studio technicians, or others for whom this work was not a specialty. Now every videotape, including the most brief television advertisement, has an assigned editor who is responsible for the continuity and clarity of the project.

THE JOB

Television editors work closely with producers and directors throughout an entire project. These editors assist in the earliest phase, called preproduction, and during the production phase, when actual filming occurs. Their skills are in the greatest demand during post-production, the completion of primary filming. During preproduction, in meetings with producers, editors learn about the objectives of the film or video. If the project is a television commercial, for example, the editor must be familiar with the product the commercial will attempt to sell. If the project is a feature-length motion picture, the editor must understand the story line. The producer may explain the larger scope of the project so that the editor knows the best way to approach the work when it is time to edit the film. In consultation with the director, editors may discuss the best way to accurately present the screenplay or script. They may discuss different settings, scenes, or camera angles even before filming or taping begins. With this kind of preparation, film and television editors are ready to practice their craft as soon as the production phase is complete.

Feature-length films, of course, take much more time to edit than television commercials. Therefore, film editors may spend months on one project, while others may be working on several shorter projects simultaneously.

Steve Swersky owns his own editorial company in Santa Monica, California, and he has done editing for commercials, films, and TV. In addition to editing many Jeep commercials and coming-attractions trailers for such movies as *Titanic, Fargo,* and *The Usual Suspects,* Swersky has worked on 12 films. Though commercials can be edited quickly, a film project can possibly take six to nine months to edit. Swersky's work involves taking the film that has been developed in labs and transferring it to videotape for him to watch. He uses "nonlinear" computer editing for his projects, as opposed to traditional "linear" systems involving many video players and screens. "The difference between linear and nonlinear editing," he says, "is like the difference between typing and using a word processor. When you want to change a written page, you have to retype it; with word processing you can just cut and paste." Swersky uses the Lightworks nonlinear editing system. With this system, he converts the film footage to a digital format. The computer has a database that tracks individual frames and puts all the scenes together in a folder of information. This information is stored on a hard drive and can instantly be brought up on a screen, allowing an editor to access scenes and frames with the click of a mouse.

Editors are usually the final decision-makers when it comes to choosing which segments will stay in as they are, which segments will be cut, or which may need to be redone. Editors look at the quality of the segment, its dramatic value, and its relationship to other segments. They then arrange the segments in an order that creates the most effective finished product. "I assemble the scenes," Swersky says, "choosing what is the best, what conveys the most emotion. I bring the film to life, in a way." He relies on the script and notes from the director, along with his natural sense of how a scene should progress, in putting together the film, commercial, or show. He looks for the best shots, camera angles, line deliveries, and continuity.

Some editors specialize in certain areas of television or film. *Sound editors* work on the soundtracks of television programs or motion pictures. They often keep libraries of sounds that they reuse for various projects. These include natural sounds such as thunder or raindrops, animal noises, motor sounds, or musical interludes. Some sound editors specialize in music and may have training in music theory or performance. Others work with sound effects. They may use unusual objects, machines, or computer-generated noisemakers to create a desired sound for a film or TV show.

REQUIREMENTS
High School
Broadcast journalism and other media and communications courses may provide you with practical experience in video editing. Because television editing requires a creative perspective along with technical skills, you should take English, speech, theater, and other courses that will allow you to develop writing skills. Art and photography classes will involve you with visual media. If you're lucky enough to attend a high school that offers film classes, either in film history or in production, be sure to take those courses. Finally, don't forget to take computer classes. Editing work constantly makes use of new

technology, and you should become familiar and comfortable with computers as soon as possible.

Postsecondary Training

Some studios require a bachelor's degree for those seeking positions as television editors. However, actual on-the-job experience is the best guarantee of securing lasting employment. Degrees in communications or liberal arts fields are preferred, but courses in cinematography and audiovisual techniques help editors get started in their work. You may choose to pursue a degree in such subjects as English, journalism, theater, or film. Community and two-year colleges often offer courses in the study of film as literature. Some of these colleges also teach video and film editing. Universities with departments of broadcast journalism offer courses in video and film editing and also may have contacts at local television stations.

Training as a television editor takes from four to 10 years. Many editors learn much of their work on the job as an assistant or apprentice at larger studios that offer these positions. During an apprenticeship, the apprentice has the opportunity to see the work of the editor up close. The editor may eventually assign some of his or her minor duties to the apprentice, while the editor makes the larger decisions. After a few years, the apprentice may be promoted to editor or may apply for a position as a television editor at other studios.

Training in video and film editing is also available in the military, including the Air Force, Marine Corps, Coast Guard, and Navy. You can also participate in an educational conference that will teach you some of the basics and recent developments in editing technology. The Digital Media Educational Center offers an annual conference for editors and student editors. See http://www.filmcamp.com for more details.

Other Requirements

You should be able to work cooperatively with other creative people when editing a project. You should remain open to suggestions and guidance, while also maintaining your confidence in the presence of other professionals. A successful editor has an understanding of the history of television and a feel for the narrative form in general. Computer skills are also important and will help you to learn new technology in the field. You may be required to join a union to do this work, depending on the studio. "You should have a good visual understanding," Steve Swersky says. "You need to be able to tell a story, and be aware of everything that's going on in a frame."

EXPLORING

Many high schools have film clubs, and some have cable television stations affiliated with the school district. Often school-run television channels give students the opportunity to actually create and edit short programs. Check out what's available at your school.

Another good way to prepare for a career as a television editor is to read as much as you can. Reading literature will help develop your understanding of the different ways in which stories can be presented.

You should be familiar with all different kinds of television and film projects, including documentaries, short films, feature films, TV shows, and commercials. See as many different projects as you can and study them, paying close attention to the decisions the editors made in piecing together the scenes.

Large television stations occasionally have volunteers or student interns. Most people in the industry start out doing minor tasks helping with production. These production assistants get the opportunity to see all of the professionals at work. By working closely with an editor, a production assistant can learn television operations as well as specific editing techniques.

EMPLOYERS

Some television editors work primarily with news programs, documentaries, or special features. They may develop ongoing working relationships with directors or producers who hire them from one project to another. Many editors who have worked for a studio or postproduction company for several years often become independent contractors. They offer their services on a per-job basis to producers of commercials and films, negotiating their own fees, and typically have purchased or leased their own editing equipment.

STARTING OUT

Because of the glamour associated with television work, this is a popular field that can be very difficult to break into. With a minimum of a high school diploma or a degree from a two-year college, you can apply for entry-level jobs in many television studios, but these jobs won't be editing positions. Most studios will not consider people for television editor positions without a bachelor's degree or several years of on-the-job experience.

One way to get on-the-job experience is to complete an apprenticeship in editing. However, in some cases, you won't be eligible for an apprenticeship unless you are a current employee of the studio.

Therefore, start out by applying to as many television studios as possible and take an entry-level position, even if it's not in the editing department. Once you start work, let people know that you are interested in an editor apprenticeship so that you'll be considered the next time one becomes available.

Those who have completed bachelor's or master's degrees have typically gained hands-on experience through school projects. Another benefit of going to school is that contacts that you make while in school, both through your school's placement office and alumni, can be a valuable resource when you look for your first job. Your school's placement office may also have listings of job openings. Some studio work is union regulated. Therefore you may also want to contact union locals to find out about job requirements and openings.

ADVANCEMENT

Once television editors have secured employment in their field, their advancement comes with further experience and greater recognition. Some editors develop good working relationships with directors or producers. These editors may be willing to leave the security of a studio job for the possibility of working one-on-one with the director or producer on a project. These opportunities often provide editors with the autonomy they may not get in their regular jobs. Some are willing to take a pay cut to work on a project they feel is important.

Some editors choose to stay at their studios and advance through seniority to editing positions with higher salaries. They may be able to negotiate better benefits packages or to choose the projects they will work on. They may also choose which directors they wish to work with. In larger studios, they may train and supervise staffs of less experienced or apprentice editors.

Some sound or sound-effects editors may wish to broaden their skills by working as general editors. Some television editors may, on the other hand, choose to specialize in sound effects, music, or some other editorial area. Some editors who work in television may move to motion pictures or may move from working on commercials or television series to television movies.

EARNINGS

Television editors are not as highly paid as others working in their industry. They have less clout than directors or producers, but they have more authority in the production of a project than many other film technicians. According to the Bureau of Labor Statistics, the median annual wage for television, film, and video editors was $36,900 in 2001. A small percentage of editors earn less than $19,430 a year, while others earn over $72,480. The most experienced and sought after television and film editors can command much higher salaries, even more than $100,000 a year.

WORK ENVIRONMENT

Most of the work done by editors is done in television studios or at postproduction companies using editing equipment. The working environment is often a small, cramped studio office. Working hours vary widely depending on the project. During the filming of a commercial, for instance, editors may be required to work overtime, at night, or on weekends to finish the project by an assigned date. "As stressful as the work can be," Steve Swersky says, "we joke around that it's not like having a real job. Every day is a fun day."

During filming, editors may be asked to be on hand at the filming location. Locations may be outdoors or in other cities, and travel is occasionally required. More often, however, the television or film editor edits in the studio, and that is where the bulk of the editor's time is spent.

Disadvantages of the job involve the editor's low rank on the totem pole of television industry jobs. However, most editors feel that this is outweighed by the advantages. Television editors can view the projects on which they have worked and be proud of their role in creating them.

OUTLOOK

The outlook for television editors is very good. In fact, the U.S. Department of Labor predicts faster-than-average employment growth for television and film editors over the next several years. The growth of cable television and an increase in the number of independent film studios will translate into greater demand for editors. This will also force the largest studios to offer more competitive salaries in order to attract the best television and film editors.

The developments of companies such as Avid Technology, which engineered and introduced many of the digital editing tools used today, will continue to greatly affect the editing process. Editors will work much more closely with special effects houses in putting together projects. When using more effects, television and film editors will have to edit scenes with an eye towards special effects to be added later. Digital editing systems are also available for home computers. Users can feed their own digital video into their computers, then edit the material, and add their own special effects and titles. This technology may allow some prospective editors more direct routes into the industry, but the majority of editors will have to follow traditional routes, obtaining years of hands-on experience.

FOR MORE INFORMATION

The ACE features career and education information for film and television editors on its website, along with information about internship opportunities and sample articles from Cinemeditor Magazine.

American Cinema Editors (ACE)
100 Universal City Plaza
Building 2282, Room 234
Universal City, CA 91608
Tel: 818-777-2900
Email: amercinema@earthlink.net
http://www.ace-filmeditors.org

This union counts film and television production workers among its craft members. For education and training information as well as links to film commissions and production companies, check out the IATSE website's Craft page: Film and Television Production.

International Alliance of Theatrical Stage Employees, Moving Picture Technicians, Artists and Allied Crafts of the United States and Canada (IATSE)
1430 Broadway, 20th Floor
New York, NY 10018
Tel: 212-730-1770
http://www.iatse.lm.com

For information on NATAS scholarships and to read articles from Television Quarterly, the organization's official journal, visit the NATAS website.

National Academy of Television Arts and Sciences (NATAS)
111 West 57th Street, Suite 600
New York, NY 10019
Tel: 212-586-8424
http://www.emmyonline.org

TELEVISION PRODUCERS

QUICK FACTS

School Subjects
Business
English

Personal Skills
Communication/ideas
Leadership/management

Work Environment
Primarily indoors
Primarily one location

Minimum Education Level
Bachelor's degree

Salary Range
$15,000 to $45,090 to
$140,070+

Certification or Licensing
None available

Outlook
Faster than the average

DOT
159

GOE
01.03.01

NOC
5131

O*NET-SOC
27-2012

OVERVIEW

Television producers are behind-the-scenes professionals who are involved with budgeting and financing, working out a production timeline, casting appropriate actors, or even hiring the crew for a TV project. Producers oversee the production of newscasts, sporting events, dramas, comedies, documentaries, holiday specials, and the many other programs that make up network and cable broadcasting. Because of the varied nature of television programming, a producer's role may also change from project to project. A producer on one project, for example, may only be involved in arranging financial backing and putting together the creative team of directors and actors. A producer on another project may oversee practically every detail of the production, including arranging for equipment and scheduling personnel.

HISTORY

The position of television producer has its roots in two older forms of visual arts: drama and film. Drama has existed in cultures around the world for thousands of years. As drama and theaters developed, the roles of actors, writers, directors, and producers became clearly defined. The motion picture industry, which experienced rapid growth during the early 20th century, provided a new medium for artistic professionals to work in, and many positions, such as producer, were copied from the theater world.

In 1945, following World War II, commercial television broadcasting became available in the United States. The television industry experienced phenomenal growth through increasingly better equipment, more TV stations, and larger audiences. By 1949, for example, the inauguration of President Truman was seen on television by nearly 10 million people.

Naturally, professionals were needed to create, perform, and produce programming for this ever-growing new media. This new opportunity drew producers from the film world and others who simply wanted to work with television. The producer became an essential member of production teams at small stations across the country as well as at large network stations. Today, with such factors as increasingly sophisticated equipment (for example, computers that can generate images), enormous salaries for popular TV stars (Helen Hunt, for example, made $22 million for her last season of *Mad About You*), and a growing number of networks showing specialized programming (such as Oxygen and VH1), the job of the producer has become more complex. The producer must have a depth of technical knowledge, the ability to manage large financial sums, and an instinct for choosing projects that will draw large audiences.

THE JOB

Producers oversee television projects, from the idea stage to the final taped or aired version. Their responsibilities, however, vary depending on both the producer's employer and the project. One of the primary responsibilities of independent producers, those with their own production companies, may be to raise money for projects. A producer employed by a television station, on the other hand, may be given a budget to work with. In either case, though, the producer is responsible for keeping an eye on costs and making sure the project stays within budget. This also requires time-management skills, because the producer must schedule just the right amount of time for different phases of production. If the producer underestimates the time needed for filming on location, for example, the producer's company will need to pay the expenses for extra time on location, causing the project to go over budget.

A producer's responsibilities are also affected by what type of project he or she works on. For example, *newscast producers,* along with reporters, determine what stories are worth broadcasting. Newscast producers assign stories, review taped reports, and may even help edit the material. Often these producers must deal with late-breaking developments and must quickly assign reporters and TV crews to cover a story, then weave the new report into the broadcast while staying within the broadcast's time requirements. The newscast is a combination of live and taped segments, and the producer often needs to make decisions quickly while the show is on the air.

Documentary producers are also very actively involved in their productions, but they typically have days, rather than hours, to complete projects. They may be involved in deciding on a concept for the documentary; hiring writers, directors, and the crew; and scouting out locations and finding interview subjects. Once interviews and other segments are taped, they may review the material, select the best footage, and edit it into a program of predetermined length.

Whereas newscast and documentary producers rely on their news judgment, *drama* and *comedy producers* rely on their understanding of the entertainment world. These producers come up with ideas for shows, hire writers, directors, and actors, and review the final product for its tone and content.

Freddy James is an associate producer for Home and Garden Television (HGTV). He works on producing specials for this cable network, and his work often takes him away from the station for periods of time. One project he worked on focused on the Habitat for Humanity program, which recruits volunteers to build homes for families in need. James's work began long before the filming took place. "We pre-interviewed 10 families who were to receive homes and selected three [to focus on]," he says. "We centered the show around them and around the volunteers who came from all over the world to help them build these homes in one week."

With other members of the production, James planned the shoot. They set up all the hotel and crew arrangements, as well as researched the Habitat for Humanity program. They scheduled interviews with officials of Habitat for Humanity. "And we went to the families' old homes and interviewed them about the project and how they felt about being a part of it," James explains. During the four-day shoot, the production team got footage of the houses going up, and they talked to officials and volunteers. The on-air talent then arrived for a day to shoot his commentary.

Once all the filming was done, the producers returned to the station with all the footage and reviewed the material. "We select our bites," James says, "and start writing the show. Our executive producers proof our scripts, then we set up a voice-over session for our talent, and he voices the script." After selecting video for a program, the producers have it digitized for editing on the computer. On this project, the producers also worked with musicians who composed music for the show and graphic artists who created design work.

No matter what type of programming producers work on, they must be organized team leaders, able to communicate their ideas about a project from concept to conclusion.

REQUIREMENTS
High School

Does working as a producer sound interesting to you? If so, there are a number of classes you can take in high school to help you get ready for this work. It will be very important for you to take composition, speech, and English classes to help you develop your research, writing, and speaking skills. These communication skills will be essential to have in your career. In addition, take mathematics, business, or accounting classes since you will be managing budgets. Consider taking psychology classes that may give you an understanding of people and their interests. Take computer classes so that you can develop a familiarity with current technology. If your high school offers any classes on the history of broadcast media or the use of broadcast media, be sure to take those. If you are specifically interested in producing entertainment shows, consider taking drama classes that will give you an understanding of scripts and working with actors.

Postsecondary Training

While there are no formal educational requirements for becoming a television producer, many producers do have college degrees. The degree you get may depend on the area of television that you are interested in. For example, if you are interested in news broadcasting, you may want to consider attending a journalism school to receive a broadcast journalism degree. Make sure that you get a broad-based education, however. Anyone working in the news industry will need an understanding of history, geography, and political science, so take classes that cover these subjects as well.

If you are interested in producing a television series, you may want to attend a drama or film school. Programs at these schools will help you hone your understanding of story lines and audiences and markets. A number of universities and colleges also offer film studies programs or courses on television broadcast production. Ask your school guidance counselor to help you locate these programs.

In addition, do your own research. Check out the websites of schools you are interested in and read books on the topic, such as *The Complete Guide to American Film Schools and Cinema and Television Courses* by Ernest Pintoff. A number of producers have rounded out their education by taking business courses or even by completing a business degree along with their broadcast studies to prepare them for this career.

Perhaps the most important thing to consider when selecting a school is the internship opportunities that will be available to you. Some schools have their own broadcasting stations where you can work; others require students to complete an internship that they locate on their own; and still others may offer internships through local participating network affiliates. No matter what the arrangements, you should be sure the school you choose will provide you with a way to gain practical hands-on experience working at a TV station. Competition for internships is high, and most positions are unpaid. In some cases, though, you may be able to get course credit for your work.

A number of organizations provide information on internships or sponsor internship programs. The Radio-Television News Directors Association, for example, offers several scholarships and internships for college students involved with electronic journalism. The Institute on Political Journalism offers a seven-week summer program during which college students combine classroom work at Georgetown University with work at a Washington, D.C. media organization. The Directors Guild of America sponsors a Los Angeles-based training program for a limited number of college graduates. The trainees in this program are paid and work on television series projects. See the end of this article for contact information to learn more about these opportunities.

Other Requirements

The successful producer is an organized individual who can deal quickly and effectively with problems that may cause a change in production plans. Producers need to have a good sense of what stories, news, or other items will interest viewers. They also need salesmanship qualities since they may have to "sell" a station on a project idea or convince an actor to take a role. Producers work with teams of professionals and must be able to bring people together to work on the single goal of completing a project.

While working in the television world may seem glamorous, you should realize that as a producer your work will take place behind the scenes. Although people recognize stars of sitcoms and news anchors when they are in public, few are able to spot a producer in a crowd. You must be self-confident and be comfortable with this anonymity if you are to enjoy this work.

EXPLORING

Consider joining the staff of your high school newspaper. This will give you experience in completing projects on a deadline and, if you are involved in selling ad space, you will get a taste of what it is like to work with budgets and financing. If your school has a radio or TV station, volunteer to be part of the staff. Become involved in the production work and learn how to use the cameras, control sound, or edit pieces. If your school doesn't have these facilities, consider joining the drama club. You will be able to do production work for a play and may also gain experience with advertising and financing the production.

To meet professionals in the field, ask your media department teacher or guidance counselor to arrange for a producer from a local TV station to come talk to interested students. Another option is to call the local TV station and request a tour of the facility. Explain that you are interested in becoming a producer and ask to meet a producer during your tour. You may also be able to set up an informational interview with the producer. Come to this interview prepared to ask questions. What type of educational background does this producer have? What is the hardest part of the job? What is the most enjoyable part? Does the producer have any advice for you? People are often happy to talk about their work when you have specific questions to ask and show a true interest. You may even find that you can develop a mentor relationship through this contact.

EMPLOYERS

Producers may be salaried employees of television stations or networks, or they may work independently, running their own production company. Independent producers may take on projects for networks as well as other organizations. Producers who work on newscasts are employed across the country at large as well as medium-sized and small stations. Producers who work on television series typically live in Los Angeles, where many network headquarters are located. However, some producers live in New York.

STARTING OUT

The job of producer is not an entry-level position. You will need to "pay your dues" by gaining experience working with different equipment and people. Internships are often the best way to break into the business. Interns are frequently offered paid positions after they graduate from school. If your internship doesn't lead to employment, make yourself visible in the field and take any job that allows you to work as a member of the production team.

Freddy James got his first job his junior year of college after a tour of a TV station. "I made sure the executive producer knew who I was when I left that day," he says. While most of the other students were interested in anchoring, James stressed his interest in producing. "And I sent a follow-up letter to the executive producer. The next thing I knew, they called wanting to know if I wanted to run a studio camera for minimum wage." The station was number one in the city, and James took the job knowing it would be an excellent opportunity to get a start in the field.

ADVANCEMENT

Advancement for producers depends to an extent on their individual goals. They may change stations, moving from smaller stations to larger ones where they oversee a larger staff and have increased pay. Some producers may decide to specialize, working in an area that interests them such as live broadcasts or music videos. Most consider it an advancement to work on their own projects. At some stations, an executive producer will oversee the work of one or more producers. Independent producers may advance by increasing their clientele and working on large-budget projects.

EARNINGS

Although producers who work for their own production companies or for the larger television networks can make well over $100,000 a year, most producers make considerably less. Bringing in the big paychecks as a producer for television comes from years of hard work, good luck, and well-established connections. But good producers don't generally enter the field with big money in mind—they love the work. Producers who don't make a great deal of money benefit in other ways: they often call all the shots and have control of a project.

Salaries for producers depend on such factors as the station's size and location, the type of programming the producer works on, and the producer's experience. The Bureau of Labor statistics reports that the median annual salary for all producers and directors was $45,090 in 2001. The lower 10 percent earned $22,810 or less, while the higher 10 percent earned $140,070 or more.

According to a 2001 salary survey by the Radio-Television News Directors Association, executive producers earned a median salary of $47,000, with earnings ranging from as low as $18,000 to as high as $115,000. New producers earned a median salary of $27,000, with a low of $15,000 to a high of $100,000.

Producers who are full-time, salaried employees of stations or networks typically receive benefits such as health insurance and paid vacation and sick days. Independent producers must provide these extras for themselves.

WORK ENVIRONMENT

TV stations are generally clean, comfortable places equipped with up-to-date, sophisticated broadcasting equipment. The atmosphere is busy and exciting, with numerous professionals concentrating on completing their specific jobs. Some producers, such as Freddy James, may need to travel and work on location. The conditions for those working on location vary. For example, the producer may have to stand in the rain for hours with the crew attempting to get the right shot.

The work of a producer is stressful, both for those who work on live programming and those who work on taped programming. The producer needs to be a creative and fast-acting problem solver because production difficulties arise almost every day. A lot of people are needed to put on a television show, and personalities sometimes clash, which can lead to tension on the set. The producer must be able to work successfully in this atmosphere.

A producer's schedule will depend on the projects he or she is working on. A producer of a morning news show, for example, may need to be at the station by 4 A.M. A producer working on a television movie, on the other hand, might not need to be at the shoot until midday but work until late in the night. No matter what the project, though, long workdays (10 to 12 hours) are common.

OUTLOOK

According to the U.S. Department of Labor, the employment of actors, directors, and producers is expected to increase faster than the average over the next several years. New cable networks needing original programming are developing at a rapid rate. Freelance opportunities are also expected to increase as networks look to independent production companies for more programming. Producers will also be in demand to put together newscasts: newsrooms provide TV stations with healthy profits every year. Because many consider this exciting and glamorous work, however, competition for jobs will be high. TV producers (and those just starting out in the business) who have a thorough knowledge of new technologies will be in the best position to get jobs. Producers will not only need to understand various computer-assisted techniques, but as broadcasting becomes more closely involved with the Internet and interactive television, producers will also need to know how to work with these technologies.

FOR MORE INFORMATION

For more information on the industry and training programs, contact:

Directors Guild of America
7920 Sunset Boulevard
Los Angeles, CA 90046
Tel: 800-421-4173
http://www.dga.org

For information on summer internships, contact:

Institute of Political Journalism
The Fund for American Studies
1706 New Hampshire Avenue, NW
Washington, DC 20009
Tel: 800-741-6964
http://www.dcinternships.org/ipj

For more industry news and career information, contact:

Producers Guild of America
8530 Wilshire Boulevard, Suite 450
Beverly Hills, CA 90211
Tel: 310-358-9020
Email: info@producersguild.org
http://www.producersguild.org

RTNDA, an organization for electronic media news professionals, has information on internships, scholarships, and the news industry.
 Radio-Television News Directors Association (RTNDA)
 1600 K Street, NW, Suite 700
 Washington, DC 20006-2838
 Tel: 202-659-6510
 Email: rtnda@rtnda.org
 http://www.rtnda.org

To read television news online, check out this website:
 The Hollywood Reporter.com
 http://www.hollywoodreporter.com

TELEVISION PROGRAM DIRECTORS

QUICK FACTS

School Subjects Business Journalism	**Certification or Licensing** None available
Personal Skills Communication/ideas Leadership/management	**Outlook** Little change or more slowly than the average
Work Environment Primarily indoors Primarily one location	**DOT** 184 **GOE** 11.05.02
Minimum Education Level Bachelor's degree	**NOC** 2263
Salary Range $10,000 to $66,165 to $250,000	**O*NET-SOC** 27-2012.02, 27-2012.03

OVERVIEW

Television program directors are responsible for scheduling programs on television networks. They plan and arrange news broadcasts, comedy shows, drama series, and other program materials. The program director may work alone or supervise a large programming staff.

HISTORY

The first public demonstration of television in the United States came in 1939 at the opening of the New York World's Fair. Further development was limited during World War II, but by 1953 there were about 120 stations. According to the Federal Communications Commission (FCC), there were 1,719 commercial, public, and cable television stations in the United States in 2002. The National Cable Television Association reports that between 1996 and 2002, the number of cable networks increased by 98 percent, from 145 to 287 channels.

THE JOB

Television program directors must evaluate all their programming options, from educational shows to nightly news to commercial announcements, and decide when to broadcast shows to tap into the largest potential audience. To plan the schedule, program directors must consider many factors, such as the channel's budget, the target audience for each show, station policies on programming content, and the advertisers most appropriate for the program. They consult with other staff to develop shows or purchase programs from outside producers. In addition, program directors set staff schedules, audition and hire news anchors and other television personalities, and help negotiate advertising contracts.

At smaller television stations, one program director may handle all these duties. At larger television stations, the program director usually has a programming staff that includes film editors, sound experts, and script writers. Some networks employ *public service directors*, who schedule shorter television programs or "spots" covering education, religion, and civic and government affairs. Larger networks also may employ *broadcast operations directors*, who coordinate scheduling personnel, review program schedules, issue daily corrections, and advise affiliated stations on their schedules.

Top 10 Cable Companies
(by revenue)

Company	Top Media Property
1. AOL Time Warner	Time Warner Cable
2. AT&T Broadband	AT&T Broadband
3. Comcast Corp.	Comcast
4. Walt Disney Co.	ESPN
5. Viacom	Nickelodeon, Nick at Nite
6. Cox Enterprises	Cox Cable
7. Charter Communications	Charter
8. Cablevision Systems Corp.	Cablevision Systems
9. Adelphia Communications Corp.	Adelphia
10. News Corp.	Fox Sports Networks

Source: Paul Kagan Associates

Production managers, operations directors, news directors, and sports directors are other managing personnel that work with the program directors to run the station. Keep in mind that the job of program directors is not the same as the job of *television directors.* The latter are responsible for more of the creative decisions within one or more shows, not the entire programming lineup.

REQUIREMENTS
High School
While in high school, take classes to develop your communication skills, such as English, speech, and debate. Take computer science classes to develop your computer skills; program directors use computers in almost everything they do, from filing reports, to maintaining schedules, to planning future programming projects. You will also need management skills as a programming director, so take business and economic classes. Finally, since the creative arts are the backbone of many television stations, classes in drama, music, and art will also be beneficial.

Postsecondary Training
Because of the high level of competition for programming director positions, a college degree is recommended. Possible majors include radio and television production, broadcasting, business administration, communications, or a degree in a liberal arts field. You may also want to consider a degree (or at least some training) in engineering to be comfortable with the more technical side of broadcasting.

Other Requirements
As a program director, you should be able to juggle many tasks and people at one time, be flexible and adapt to sudden changes (such as program availability or budget constraints), and always be open to new ideas that may strike a chord with the viewing audience. In order to handle their managing duties, you also need to be confident in your decision making, be attentive to costs and deadlines, and work well with others.

EXPLORING
The best way to get a sense of this job is to work at a school or local television station. Though you may not be responsible for the station's programming, just the experience and ability to meet with professionals in the industry will give you a sense of how a television station is run and perhaps give you a good contact when look-

ing for job leads in the future. If a part-time or summer position is not a possibility, plan to visit a station and talk with one of the staff members about his or her job and how best to get into television.

EMPLOYERS

According to the FCC, there were 1,719 broadcast television stations in the United States at the start of 2003. Cable television stations add another option for employment.

Large conglomerates own some stations, while other networks are owned individually. Job opportunities will be concentrated in the nation's largest markets. According to the National Association of Broadcasting, the five largest television markets (in rank order) are New York, Los Angeles, Chicago, San Francisco, Philadelphia, and Dallas-Fort Worth.

STARTING OUT

Keep in mind that most program directors work in other positions, gaining television experience and contacts, before advancing to programming jobs. Besides a college degree, you will need technical and on-air experience. While you are in college, internships are key for getting your start in the industry and learning some of the basics of running a station. Your college placement offices should give you some assistance, possibly setting up an interview or providing contacts. However, you can also send resumes to radio and television stations directly or travel to local stations and apply in person.

The more willing you are to relocate, the better your chances are of finding a position. If possible, look at working in smaller cities or rural areas. Smaller stations may be more willing to give an inexperienced television hopeful a job, and because of the small staff, you should be able to learn a variety of skills.

ADVANCEMENT

Advancement depends on the career goals of program directors. They may choose to move from a smaller station to a larger one, moving to a different city with a larger market, or stay at their current station and become the head station manager.

EARNINGS

According to the 2002 *Radio and Television Salary Survey* by the Radio-Television News Directors Association, television news directors earned a median of $64,000, with salaries ranging from $18,000 to $250,000. The U.S. Bureau of Labor Statistics reports that the median annual earnings of general and operations managers in television broadcasting were $66,165 in 2001.

Salaries will vary depending on whether the television station is commercial or public, the market size and location of the station, and the program director's level of experience. In addition to their salary, television program directors may receive performance bonuses and generally receive health insurance packages.

WORK ENVIRONMENT

It is not uncommon for a television program director to work evenings, late at night, and weekends, especially if he or she works for a smaller station. Those working for larger stations, with programming staffs, have a better chance of working a normal workweek.

The job of programming director can be stressful at times, since they have to manage employees, strive for high viewer ratings, and please paying advertisers all at the same time. However, despite these many demands, program directors usually enjoy working and interacting with a variety of people.

OUTLOOK

The U.S. Department of Labor reports that employment in television broadcasting is expected to grow slower than the average rate for other industries, increasing by only 10 percent through 2010. This is due to many factors, such as the increased use of prepared programming, competition from other forms of media, and industry consolidation. In addition, the competition for all jobs in television is fierce. Most stations, especially those in large cities, hire only experienced workers.

However, all television stations need a program director or some form of programming staff. The popularity and growth of cable networks should create additional openings. In the end, jobs will go to those who have worked a long time in the industry and who have the education and skills to meet the high demands of the job.

FOR MORE INFORMATION

For a list of schools offering degrees in broadcasting, contact:
Broadcast Education Association
1771 N Street, NW
Washington, DC 20036-2891
Tel: 888-380-7222
Email: beainfo@beaweb.org
http://www.beaweb.org

For broadcast education, support, and scholarship information, contact:
National Association of Broadcasters
1771 N Street, NW
Washington, DC 20036
Tel: 202-429-5300
Email: nab@nab.org
http://www.nab.org

For a booklet on careers in cable, contact:
National Cable Television Association
1724 Massachusetts Avenue, NW
Washington, DC 20036
Tel: 202-775-3550
http://www.ncta.com

For scholarship and internship information, contact:
Radio-Television News Directors Association
1600 K Street, NW, Suite 700
Washington, DC 20006-2838
Tel: 202-659-6510
Email: rtnda@rtnda.org
http://www.rtnda.org

TRAVEL AGENTS

QUICK FACTS

School Subjects Business Computer science Geography	**Certification or Licensing** Required by certain states
Personal Skills Communication/ideas Helping/teaching	**Outlook** Little change or more slowly than the average
Work Environment Indoors and outdoors One location with some travel	**DOT** 252 **GOE** 08.02.06
Minimum Education Level High school diploma	**NOC** 6431 **O*NET-SOC** 41-3041.00
Salary Range $15,830 to $25,580 to $45,000+	

OVERVIEW

Travel agents help plan the itineraries for individuals or groups who will be traveling, which involved making transportation, hotel, and tour reservations, obtaining or preparing tickets, and performing related services. There are over 135,000 travel agents employed in the United States.

HISTORY

The first travel agency in the United States was established in 1872. Before this time, travel as an activity was not widespread, due to wars and international barriers, inadequate transportation and hotels, lack of leisure, the threat of contagious disease, and lower standards of living. Despite the glamour attached to such early travelers as Marco Polo (ca. 1254–1324), people of the Middle Ages and the 17th and 18th centuries were not accustomed to traveling for pleasure.

The manufacturing operations that started in the Industrial Revolution caused international trade to expand greatly. Commercial traffic between countries stimulated both business and personal travel. Yet until the 20th century, travel was arduous, and most areas were unprepared for tourists.

The travel business began with Thomas Cook, an Englishman who first popularized the guided tour. In 1841, Cook arranged his first excursion—a special Midland Counties Railroad Company train to carry passengers from Leicester to a temperance meeting in Loughborough. His business grew rapidly. He made arrangements for 165,000 visitors to attend the Great Exhibition of 1851 in London. The following year, he organized the first "Cook's Tour." Earnest groups of English tourists were soon seen traveling by camel to view the Pyramids and the Sphinx, gliding past historic castles on the Rhine, and riding by carriage to view the wonders of Paris. The "Grand Tour" of Europe soon became an integral part of a young person's education among the privileged classes.

In the next hundred years, the development of the railroads, the replacement of sailing ships with faster steamships, the advent of the automobile and the bus, and the invention of the airplane provided an improved quality of transportation that encouraged people to travel for relaxation and personal enrichment. At the same time, cities, regions, and countries began to appreciate the economic aspects of travel. Promotional campaigns were organized to attract and accommodate tourists. Formal organization of the travel industry was reflected in the establishment in 1931 of the American Society of Travel Agents.

In recent years, travel agents have accommodated a great increase in family travel. This increase is in part a result of greater leisure time. As long as leisure time continues to grow and the nation's standard of living increases, there will be a need for travel agents to help people in planning their vacations wisely.

THE JOB

The travel agent may work as a salesperson, travel consultant, tour organizer, travel guide, bookkeeper, or small business executive. If the agent operates a one-person office, he or she usually performs all of these functions. Other travel agents work in offices with dozens of employees, which allows them to specialize in certain areas. In such offices, one staff member may become an authority on sea cruises, another may work on trips to the Far East, and a third may develop an extensive knowledge of either low-budget or luxury trips. In some cases, travel agents are employed by national or international firms and can draw upon very extensive resources.

As salespeople, travel agents must be able to motivate people to take advantage of their services. Travel agents study their customers' interests, learn where they have traveled, appraise their financial resources and available time, and present a selection of travel options. Customers are then able to choose how and where they want to travel with a minimum of effort.

Travel agents consult a variety of published and computer-based sources for information on air transportation departure and arrival times, air fares, and hotel ratings and accommodations. They often base their recommendations on their own travel experiences or those of colleagues or clients. Travel agents may visit hotels, resorts, and restaurants to rate their comfort, cleanliness, and quality of food and service.

As travel consultants, agents give their clients suggestions regarding travel plans and itineraries, information on transportation alternatives, and advice on the available accommodations and rates of hotels and motels. They also explain and help with passport and visa regulations, foreign currency and exchange, climate and wardrobe, health requirements, customs regulations, baggage and accident insurance, traveler's checks or letters of credit, car rentals, tourist attractions, and welcome or escort services.

Many travel agents only sell tours that are developed by other organizations. The most skilled agents, however, often organize tours on a wholesale basis. This involves developing an itinerary, contracting a knowledgeable person to lead the tour, making tentative reservations for transportation, hotels, and side trips, publicizing the tour through descriptive brochures, advertisements, and other travel agents, scheduling reservations, and handling last-minute problems. Sometimes tours are arranged at the specific request of a group or to meet a client's particular needs.

In addition to other duties, travel agents may serve as *tour guides*, leading trips ranging from one week to six months to locations around the world. Agents often find tour leadership a useful way to gain personal travel experience. It also gives them the chance to become thoroughly acquainted with the people in the tour group, who may then use the agent to arrange future trips or recommend the agent to friends and relatives. Tour leaders are usually reimbursed for all their expenses or receive complimentary transportation and lodging. Most travel agents, however, arrange for someone to cover for them at work during their absence, which may make tour leadership prohibitive for self-employed agents.

Agents serve as bookkeepers to handle the complex pattern of transportation and hotel reservations that each trip entails. They work directly with airline, steamship, railroad, bus, and car rental companies. They make direct contact with hotels and sightseeing organizations or work indirectly through a receptive operator in the city involved. These arrangements require a great deal of accuracy because mistakes could result in a client being left stranded in a foreign or remote area. After reservations are made, agents write up or obtain tickets, write out itineraries, and send out bills for the reservations involved. They also send out confirmations to airlines, hotels, and other companies.

Travel agents must promote their services. They present slides or movies to social and special interest groups, arrange advertising displays, and suggest company-sponsored trips to business managers.

REQUIREMENTS
High School

A high school diploma is the minimum requirement for becoming a travel agent. If you are interested in pursuing a career as an agent, be certain to include some computer courses, as well as typing or keyboarding courses, in your class schedule. Since much of your work as a travel agent will involve computerized reservation systems, you should acquire basic keyboarding skills and be comfortable working with computers.

Because being able to communicate clearly with clients is central to this job, any high school course that enhances communication skills, such as English or speech, is a good choice. Proficiency in a foreign language, while not a requirement, might be helpful in many cases, such as when you are working with international travelers. Finally, geography, social studies, and business mathematics are classes that may also help prepare you for various aspects of the travel agent's work.

You can also begin learning about being a travel agent while still in high school by getting a summer or part-time job in travel and tourism. D. G. Elmore, president of Gant Travel, a national chain of corporate travel agencies, suggests that interested high school students find a job in a travel agency, doing whatever they can do. "I would advise them to get a job doing anything from tearing down tickets to delivering tickets. Anything that brings them in contact with the business will go a long way toward getting them a job," he says. "If they did that their senior year in high school in a major city, they'd have a job by the end of the summer, almost certainly." If finding a part-time or summer job in a travel agency proves impossible, you might consider looking for a job as a reservation agent for an airline, rental car agency, or hotel.

Postsecondary Training

Travel courses are available from certain colleges, private vocational schools, and adult education programs in public high schools. Some colleges and universities grant bachelor's and master's degrees in travel and tourism. Although college training is not required for work as a travel agent, it can be very helpful and is expected to become increasingly important. It is predicted that in the future most agents will be college graduates. Travel schools provide basic reservation training and other training related to travel agents' functions, which is helpful but not required.

A liberal arts or business administration background is recommended for a career in this field. Useful liberal arts courses include foreign languages, geography, English, communications, history, anthropology, political science, art and music appreciation, and literature. Pertinent business courses include transportation, business law, hotel management, marketing, office management, and accounting. As in many other fields, computer skills are increasingly important.

Certification or Licensing

To be able to sell passage on various types of transportation, you must be approved by the conferences of carriers involved. These are the Airlines Reporting Corporation, the International Air Transport Association, Cruise Lines International Association, and the Rail Travel Promotion Agency. To sell tickets for these individual conferences, you must be clearly established in the travel business and have a good personal and business background. Not all travel agents are authorized to sell passage by all of the above conferences. Naturally, if you wish to sell the widest range of services, you should seek affiliation with all four.

Currently, travel agents are not required to be federally licensed. The following states require some form of registration or licensing: California, Florida, Hawaii, Illinois, Iowa, Ohio, Oregon, Rhode Island, and Washington.

Travel agents may choose to become certified by the Institute of Certified Travel Agents (ICTA). The ICTA offers certification programs leading to the designations of Certified Travel Associate (CTA) and Certified Travel Counselor (CTC). In order to become a CTA, you must have 18 months of experience as a travel agent, complete a 12-course program, and pass a written test. In order to become a CTC, you must have five years of experience, have attained CTA status, take a 12-course program, and pass a final exam. While not a requirement, certification by ICTA will help you progress in your career.

The ICTA also offers travel agents a number of other programs such as sales skills development courses and destination specialist courses, which provide a detailed knowledge of various geographic regions of the world.

Other Requirements

The primary requisite for success in the travel field is a sincere interest in travel. Your knowledge of and travel experiences with major tourist centers, various hotels, and local customs and points of interest make you a more effective and convincing source of assistance. Yet the work of travel agents is not one long vacation. They operate in a highly competitive industry.

As a travel agent, you must be able to make quick and accurate use of transportation schedules and tariffs. You must be able to handle addition and subtraction quickly. Almost all agents make use of computers to get the very latest information on rates and schedules and to make reservations.

You will work with a wide range of personalities as a travel agent, so skills in psychology and diplomacy will be important for you to have. You must also be able to generate enthusiasm among your customers and be resourceful in solving any problems that might arise. A knowledge of foreign languages is useful because many customers come from other countries, and you will be in frequent contact with foreign hotels and travel agencies.

EXPLORING

Any type of part-time experience with a travel agency will be helpful if you're interested in pursuing this career. A small agency may welcome help during peak travel seasons or when an agent is away from the office. If your high school or college arranges career conferences, you may be able to invite a speaker from the travel industry. Visits to local travel agents will also provide you with helpful information.

If you are already pursuing a travel or hospitality career in college, you might also consider joining the Future Travel Professionals Club, organized by the American Society of Travel Agents (ASTA). Membership allows you to network with professional members of the ASTA, attend chapter meetings, be eligible for scholarships, and receive two newsletters. For more information contact the ASTA (see sources at the end of this article).

EMPLOYERS

There are about 135,000 travel agents employed in the United States. Agents may work for commercial travel agents, work in the corporate travel department of a large company, or be self-employed. Travel agencies employ more than 8 out of 10 salaried agents.

In addition to the regular travel business, a number of travel jobs are available with oil companies, automobile clubs, and transportation companies. Some jobs in travel are on the staffs of state and local governments seeking to encourage tourism.

STARTING OUT

As you start searching for a career in the travel field, you may begin by working for a company involved with transportation and tourism. Fortunately, a number of positions exist that are particularly appropriate if you are young and have limited work experience. Airlines, for example, hire flight attendants, reservation agents, and ticket clerks. Railroads and cruise line companies also have clerical positions; the rise in their popularity in recent years has resulted in more job opportunities. Those with travel experience may secure positions as tour guides. Organizations and companies with extensive travel operations may hire employees whose main responsibility is making travel arrangements.

Since travel agencies tend to have relatively small staffs, most openings are filled as a result of direct application and personal contact. While evaluating the merits of various travel agencies, you may wish to note whether the agency's owner belongs to ASTA. This trade group may also help in several other ways. It sponsors adult night school courses in travel agency operation in some metropolitan areas. It also offers a 15-lesson travel agency correspondence course. Also available, for a modest charge, is a travel agency management kit containing information that is particularly helpful to if you are considering setting up your own agency. ASTA's publication *Travel News* includes a classified advertising section listing available positions and agencies for sale.

ADVANCEMENT

Advancement opportunities within the travel field are limited to growth in terms of business volume or extent of specialization. Successful agents, for example, may hire additional employees or set up branch offices. A travel agency worker who has held his or her position for a while may be promoted to a *travel assistant*. Travel assistants are responsible for answering general questions about transportation, providing current costs of hotel accommodations, and providing other valid information.

Travel agents may also advance to work as a *corporate travel manager*. Corporate travel managers work for companies, not travel agencies. They book all business travel for a company's employees.

Travel bureau employees may decide to go into business for themselves. Agents may show their professional status by belonging to ASTA, which requires its members to have three years of satisfactory travel agent experience and approval by at least two carrier conferences.

EARNINGS

Travel agency income comes from commissions paid by airlines, hotels, car rental companies, cruise lines, and tour operators. Although many suppliers pay a standard rate (for example, the airline industry pays travel agents a flat commission of $20 per domestic flight they book) of the total cost to the customer, commissions do vary somewhat. Cruise lines, for example, pay commissions on a sliding scale depending on the season.

Travel agents typically earn a straight salary. Although less common, some agents are paid a salary plus commission or entirely on a commission basis. Salaries of travel agents ranged from $15,830 to $40,420, with an average of $25,580, according to the U.S. Department of Labor's *2001 National Occupational Employment and Wage Estimates*. Managers with 10 years of experience may earn more than $45,000 annually. In addition to experience level, the location of the firm is also a factor in how much travel agents earn. Agents working in larger metropolitan areas tend to earn more than their counterparts in smaller cities.

A 1998 survey by the Institute of Certified Travel Counselors reports that 77 percent of travel agency employers offered their employees health insurance, 49 percent offered life insurance, and 48 percent offered a dental plan.

Small travel agencies provide a smaller-than-average number of fringe benefits such as retirement, medical, and life insurance plans.

Self-employed agents tend to earn more than those who work for others, although the business risk is greater.

Those who own their own businesses may experience large fluctuations in income because the travel business is extremely sensitive to swings in the economy.

One of the benefits of working as a travel agent is the chance to travel at a discounted price. Major airlines offer special agent fares, which are often only 25 percent of regular cost. Hotels, car rental companies, cruise lines, and tour operators also offer reduced rates for travel agents. Agents also get the opportunity to take free or low-cost group tours sponsored by transportation carriers, tour operators, and cruise lines. These trips, called "fam" trips, are designed to familiarize agents with locations and accommodations so that agents can better market them to their clients.

WORK ENVIRONMENT

While this is an interesting and appealing occupation, the job of the travel agent is not as simple or glamorous as might be expected. Travel is a highly competitive field. Since almost every travel agent can offer the client the same service, agents must depend on repeat customers for much of their business. Their reliability, courtesy, and effectiveness in past transactions will determine whether they will get repeat business.

Travel agents also work in an atmosphere of keen competition for referrals. They must resist direct pressure or indirect pressure from travel-related companies that have provided favors in the past (free trips, for example) and book all trips based only on the best interests of clients.

Most agents work a 40-hour week, although this frequently includes working a half-day on Saturday or an occasional evening. During busy seasons (typically from January through June), overtime may be necessary. Agents may receive additional salary for this work or be given compensatory time off.

As they gain experience, agents become more effective. One study revealed that 98 percent of all agents had more than three years' experience in some form of the travel field. Almost half had 20 years or more in this area.

OUTLOOK

Although future prospects in the travel field will depend to some degree on the state of the economy and the perceived level of travel safety in the wake of the terrorist attacks of September 2001, the travel industry is expected to continue to expand as more Americans travel for pleasure and business. The U.S. Department of Labor predicts that employment of travel agents will grow more slowly than the average for all occupations over the next several years.

Certain factors may hinder growth for travel agents. Most airlines and other travel suppliers now offer consumers the option of making their own travel arrangements through online reservation services, readily accessible through the Internet. With this as an option, travelers are becoming less dependent upon agents to make travel arrangements for them. The American Society of Travel Agents reports that approximately 21 million consumers were booking their travel arrangements exclusively online as of June 2002. Additionally, airlines have reduced the flat commission they pay travel agencies. In March 2002, Delta Air Lines eliminated the commission (except for a select group of agents that bring the airline significant business) it paid to travel agents altogether. This may potentially reduce an agency's income, thereby making it less profitable and less able to hire new travel agents. Since these innovations are recent, their full effect on travel agents has not yet been determined.

FOR MORE INFORMATION

Visit the ASTA website to read the online pamphlet, Becoming a Travel Agent.

American Society of Travel Agents (ASTA)
1101 King Street, Suite 200
Alexandria, VA 22314
Tel: 703-739-2782
Email: askasta@astahq.com
http://www.astanet.com

For information regarding the travel industry and certification, contact:
Institute of Certified Travel Agents
148 Linden Street
PO Box 812059
Wellesley, MA 02482
Tel: 800-542-4282
Email: info@icta.com
http://www.icta.com

For information on travel careers in the U.S. government, contact:
Society of Government Travel Professionals
6935 Wisconsin Avenue, Suite 200
Bethesda, MD 20815
Tel: 301-654-8595
Email: govtvlmkt@aol.com
http://www.government-travel.org

For general information on the travel industry, contact:
Travel Industry Association of America
1100 New York Avenue, NW, Suite 450
Washington, DC 20005-3934
Tel: 202-408-8422
http://www.tia.org

WEATHER FORECASTERS

QUICK FACTS

School Subjects Computer science Earth science Physics Speech	**Certification or Licensing** Recommended
	Outlook Decline
Personal Skills Communication/ideas Technical/scientific	**DOT** 025
	GOE 02.01.01
Work Environment Primarily indoors Primarily one location	**NOC** 2114
Minimum Education Level Bachelor's degree	**O*NET-SOC** N/A
Salary Range $16,000 to $43,800 to $1,000,000+	

OVERVIEW

Weather forecasters compile and analyze weather information and pre-pare reports for daily and nightly TV or radio newscasts. Forecasters, also known as *meteorologists* and *weathercasters,* create graphics, write scripts, and explain weather maps to audiences. They also provide special reports during extreme weather conditions. To predict future weather patterns and to develop increased accuracy in weather study and forecasting, forecasters may conduct research on such subjects as atmospheric electricity, clouds, precipitation, hurricanes, and data collected from weather satellites. Other areas of research used to fore-cast weather can include ocean currents and temperature.

HISTORY

Meteorology—the science that deals with the atmosphere and weather—is an observational science, involving the study of such factors as air pressure, climate, and wind velocity. Basic weather instruments were invented hundreds of years ago. Galileo (1564–1642) invented the thermometer in 1593, and Evangelista Torricelli (1608–47) invented the barometer in 1643. Simultaneous comparison and study of weather in different areas was impossible until the telegraph was invented. Observations of the upper atmosphere from balloons and airplanes started after World War I. Not until World War II, however, was great financial support given to the development of meteorology. During this war, a very clear-cut relationship was developed between the effectiveness of new weapons and the atmosphere.

More accurate instruments for measuring and observing weather conditions, new systems of communication, and the development of satellites, radar, and high-speed computers to process and analyze weather data have helped weather forecasters and the general public to get a better understanding of the atmosphere.

THE JOB

El Niño. F5-rated tornadoes storming down tornado alley. Heat waves and ice storms. Flood-induced fires in North Dakota. Hurricanes Andrew, Hugo, and Betsy. These are just a few of the extreme weather systems that became "national celebrities" while the citizens of the threatened cities suffered. These people looked to TV and radio weather forecasters to advise them of upcoming storms, how to prepare for them, and how to recover from them. But besides broadcasting during extreme weather events, weather forecasters are on radio and TV broadcasts many times every day. On one day, people may rely on their local forecaster to help them prepare for a midnight tornado, on another day they may simply want to know whether to leave the house with an umbrella.

Some weather forecasters are reporters with broadcasting degrees, but over half of TV and radio weather forecasters have degrees in meteorology. Colleges across the country offer courses and degrees in meteorology for people who want to work for broadcast stations, weather services, research centers, flight centers, universities, and other places that study and record the weather. With a good background in the atmospheric sciences, broadcast weather forecasters can make informed predictions about the weather and can clearly explain these predictions to the public. The people of Myrtle Beach, South Carolina, look to Ed Piotrowski of WPDE-TV for the daily weather news as well as information on extreme weather conditions such as approaching hurricanes. As chief meteorologist for WPDE,

Piotrowski is responsible for delivering the forecast for radio and four television evening newscasts. "I also manage a staff and several interns," he notes.

Preparing the forecast means interpreting a great deal of data from a variety of different sources. The data may come from various weather stations around the world. Even the weather conditions swirling over the oceans can affect the weather of states far inland, so local weather forecasters keep track of the weather affecting distant cities. In addition, weather stations and ships at sea record atmospheric measurements, information that is then transmitted to other weather stations for analysis. This information makes its way to the National Weather Service in Washington, D.C., where scientists develop predictions to send to regional centers across the country. The tools used by meteorologists include weather balloons, instrumented aircraft, radar, satellites, and computers. Instrumented aircraft are high-performance airplanes used to observe many kinds of weather. Radar is used to detect rain or snow as well as other weather. Doppler radar can measure wind speed and direction. It has become the best tool for predicting severe weather. Satellites use advanced remote sensing to measure temperature, wind, and other characteristics of the atmosphere at many levels. Scientists can observe the entire surface of the earth with satellites. The introduction of computers has forever changed the research and forecasting of weather. The fastest computers are used in atmospheric research and for large-scale weather forecasting. Computers are used to produce simulations of upcoming weather.

At Piotrowski's station, the weather center receives information from the National Center for Environmental Prediction, the Storm Prediction Center, and the Severe Storms Forecast Center, as well as the National Weather Service. He explains, "All the data collected is put into many computer programs with various scientific formulas. These programs eventually put out weather scenarios for several different times in the future. Our [the forecaster's] job is to interpret these and make our forecast accordingly."

Broadcast weather forecasters may also prepare maps and graphics to aid the viewers. Broadcasting the information means reading and explaining the weather forecast to viewers and listeners. The broadcast weather forecaster must be able to concentrate on several different tasks at once. For example, when Piotrowski broadcasts to the TV audience he is actually standing in front of a plain blue wall (called a "chromakey") that shows graphics only to the viewers. In order for Piotrowski to see the map, he must watch the station's monitor. He then points to areas on the blue wall based on what he sees in the monitor; to the audience, it looks as though he is pointing to places on the map. While talking about the forecast, Piotrowski may have to listen to time cues (the amount of time left for the presentation) from the newscast producer through a hearing device placed in his ear. Throughout all this activity, the broadcast weather forecaster must stay focused and calm.

Many people look to TV and radio news for weather information to help them plan events and vacations. Farmers are often able to protect their crops by following weather forecasts and advisories. The weather forecast is a staple element of most TV and radio newscasts. Some cable and radio stations broadcast weather reports 24 hours a day; most local network affiliates broadcast reports during morning, noon, and evening newscasts, as well as provide extended weather coverage during storms and other extreme conditions. Piotrowski realizes that his responsibilities are vitally important during hurricanes. He explains, "We need to interpret the data to give people the scenario we think will play out in our area upon landfall. It could be the difference between life and death."

In addition to broadcasting weather reports, radio and TV weather forecasters often visit schools and community centers to speak on weather safety. They are also frequently involved in broadcast station promotions, taking part in community events.

REQUIREMENTS
High School
While you are in high school, you can prepare for a career as a broadcast weather forecaster by taking a number of different classes. Concentrate on the sciences—earth science, biology, chemistry, and physics—to give you an understanding of the environment and how different elements interact. Geography and mathematics courses will also be useful to you. To familiarize yourself with computers and gain experience working with graphics programs, take computer classes. Computers will be an essential tool that you'll use throughout your career. Take plenty of English and speech classes. As a broadcaster, you will need to have excellent writing and speaking skills. If your school offers any media courses in which you learn how to broadcast a radio or television show, be sure to take these classes.

Postsecondary Training
Although a degree in meteorology or atmospheric science isn't required to enter the profession, it is necessary for advancement. The

American Meteorological Society (AMS) publishes a listing of schools offering degree programs in atmospheric and related sciences. Check your local library for a copy or purchase one from the AMS (see contact information at end of article). These programs typically include such courses as atmospheric measurements, thermodynamics and chemistry, radar, cloud dynamics, and physical climatology. While in college, you should also continue to take English, speech, and communications classes to hone your communication skills and computer classes to keep up to date with this technology. It is also important, during your college years, to complete an internship as a student weather forecaster with a TV or radio station. Your college and organizations such as the AMS can help you locate an internship. Although it may not pay much—if anything—this position will allow you to make contacts with professionals and give you hands-on experience.

Certification or Licensing

The AMS and the National Weather Association (NWA) each offer certification to broadcast meteorologists. To qualify for the AMS Seal of Approval, you must meet educational requirements and demonstrate scientific competence and effective communication skills. You must submit taped samples of your work for review by an evaluation board. Requirements for the NWA Seal of Approval are similar, but you must also have a certain amount of on-air experience and pass a written exam. Although the AMS and the NWA seals are not required for broadcast weather forecasters to work in this business, you will have an advantage when looking for a job if you hold these seals. Some TV and radio stations note that their forecaster has a seal of approval in their advertisements.

Other Requirements

As a broadcast weather forecaster, you must be able to work well under pressure in order to meet deadlines for programming or plot severe weather systems. You must be able to communicate complex theories and events in a manner that is easy for the audience to understand. And, naturally, you must have an interest in weather and the environment. "Don't go into TV weather just to be on TV," Ed Piotrowski advises. "You must have a passion for the weather to do a fantastic job."

EXPLORING

There are several ways you can explore different aspects of this career while you are still in school. Consider joining a science club

that is involved in environmental activities. Ask a teacher or guidance counselor to schedule a trip to a local television station so
you can see first-hand what this work environment is like. It is
also a good idea to volunteer to work at your school's radio or TV
station. You'll learn the basics of putting on a program and might
even get on the air yourself. If your school doesn't have one of
these stations, join the newspaper staff to get some experience
working with the media. In addition, pay attention to the weathercasters on your local news and on The Weather Channel (http://
www.weatherchannel.com) to become familiar with how to deliver your forecasts.

Each year, the National Weather Service (NWS) accepts a limited
number of student volunteers, mostly college students but also a few
high school students. Local offices of the NWS also allow the public
to come in for tours by appointment. Your guidance counselor may
be able to help you with this.

Also, contact your local radio and TV stations and ask for a tour.
Tell them you are interested in broadcast meteorology and ask to
meet the weather forecasting staff. You may be able to arrange for an
informational interview with the weather forecaster, during which
you might ask that person about his or her education, experiences,
the best part of the work, and any other questions you might have.

EMPLOYERS

Most broadcast weather forecasters work for network television
affiliates and local radio stations. Because evening national newscasts do not have weather forecasts, there are fewer network opportunities for broadcast meteorologists. National cable networks, such
as The Weather Channel and 24-hour news channels, hire weather
forecasters and may offer internships.

Those who have degrees in meteorology or atmospheric science
can work for a variety of other services as well—the United States
government is the largest employer of meteorologists in the country.
Meteorologists work for the NWS, the military, the Department of
Agriculture, and other agencies.

STARTING OUT

Your college's placement office is a good resource to use when you
are looking for your first job. Many people also find their first positions either through connections they have made while interning or
through the internship itself. Ed Piotrowski's first full-time job was
with the TV station where he interned. "I was very fortunate," he

says. "I showed great initiative and the weekend job opened up right around the time I graduated."

Local ads and job listings on the Internet are other sources you should check out. The AMS and the NWA send members job listings and also post openings on their websites.

ADVANCEMENT

Someone forecasting for a network affiliate in a smaller region may want to move to a larger city and a larger audience. "Many weather people strive to get to the big cities to make the big money," Ed Piotrowski says, "but getting to the big markets can be hard and difficult to stay in."

In many cases, meteorologists work up within one station. Fulltime broadcast meteorologists generally start forecasting for the weekend news or the morning news, then move up to the evening news. A meteorologist may then become *chief meteorologist,* in charge of a newscast's weather center and staff. With each advancement comes more responsibility and a larger salary.

EARNINGS

In the newsroom, weather forecasters generally make more than sportscasters but less than lead anchors. The salary for weather forecasters varies greatly according to experience, region, and media. Those working in television typically earn more than those working in radio. According to a salary survey by the Radio-Television News Directors Association, weathercasters earned salaries that ranged from $16,000 to $1,000,000 in 2001, with a median of $43,800. Radio weather forecasters in small markets may make less than that amount.

According to the U.S. Department of Labor, the median income for meteorologists in nonsupervisory, supervisory, and managerial positions employed by the federal government was $68,100 in 2001.

WORK ENVIRONMENT

The atmosphere at a radio or TV station can be exciting, fun, and sometimes tense—especially during times of emergency. Forecasters' schedules depend on the times they are scheduled to be on the air. Those working morning shows, for example, may have to be at the station by 4 A.M. to prepare for the broadcast. The weather forecaster may also make public appearances, giving talks to schools or clubs. This gives the forecaster the opportunity to meet a lot of people and attend events; however, it also makes for busy and varied days. In addition, they have to be prepared to work odd or long hours during times of weather emergencies.

Weather forecasters work with a great deal of specialized equipment, such as computers and radar, as well as the equipment of the broadcast trade, such as the chromakey, hearing devices, and microphones. The weather forecaster is part of a team (along with such professionals as newscasters, producers, and technicians) who work to put the broadcast on the air.

OUTLOOK

The U.S. Department of Labor predicts that employment for all atmospheric scientists will increase about as fast as the average over the next several years. However, the Labor Department also predicts that employment for television and radio announcers will decline throughout the same time period. Usually, meteorologists are able to find work in the field upon graduation, though they may have to be flexible about the area of meteorology and region of the country in which they work. Positions for broadcast meteorologists, as with any positions in broadcast news, are in high demand. The number of news departments and news staffs is expected to increase at a steady rate, but the growing number of graduates looking for work in news departments will keep the field very competitive.

Currently about half of TV and radio weather forecasters do not hold meteorology degrees; with increased competition for work, forecasters without extensive backgrounds in the atmospheric sciences may find it difficult to get jobs. New tools and computer programs for the compilation and analyses of data are constantly being developed by research scientists. To find good positions, future broadcast meteorologists will need a lot of technical expertise in addition to their understanding of weather.

A national fascination with weather may lead to more outlets for broadcast meteorologists. Look for more cable weather information channels like The Weather Channel to develop. Weather disasters are requiring more coverage by news departments. In addition to forecasting, broadcast meteorologists will be involved in reporting about the after-effects of storms and other extreme conditions. Many people look to the Internet for global and regional weather information, so look for broadcast and Internet weather resources to merge. Broadcast meteorologists are becoming more actively involved in developing and maintaining pages on the World Wide Web.

FOR MORE INFORMATION

This organization has information on meteorology careers, student membership, and education. For more information, contact:
American Meteorological Society
45 Beacon Street
Boston, MA 02108-3693
Tel: 617-227-2425
Email: amsinfo@ametsoc.org
http://www.ametsoc.org/AMS

For weather and employment information and links to other weather-related sites, check out the following website:
National Oceanic and Atmospheric Administration
14th Street and Constitution Avenue, NW, Room 6217
Washington, DC 20230
Tel: 202-482-6090
Email: answers@noaa.gov
http://www.noaa.gov

To read selected sections of the monthly NWA Newsletter or find out about local chapters, check out the following website:
National Weather Association (NWA)
1697 Capri Way
Charlottesville, VA 22911-3534
Tel: 434-296-9966
Email: NatWeaAsoc@aol.com
http://www.nwas.org

To learn more about the weather, take a look at the NWS website:
National Weather Service (NWS)
1325 East-West Highway
Silver Spring, MD 20910
Tel: 301-713-0258
http://www.nws.noaa.gov

This Web site, presented by the University of Illinois, provides an overview of meteorology for high school and undergraduate students.
WW2010
http://ww2010.atmos.uiuc.edu

WRITERS

QUICK FACTS

School Subjects English Journalism	**Certification or Licensing** None available
Personal Skills Communication/ideas Helping/teaching	**Outlook** Faster than the average
	DOT 131
Work Environment Primarily indoors Primarily one location	**GOE** 01.01.02
Minimum Education Level Bachelor's degree	**NOC** 5121
Salary Range $20,570 to $42,450 to $83,180+	**O*NET-SOC** 27-3042.00, 27-3043.01, 27-3043.02, 27-3043.03, 27-3043.04

OVERVIEW

Writers are involved with expressing, editing, promoting, and interpreting ideas and facts in written form for books, magazines, trade journals, newspapers, technical studies and reports, company newsletters, radio and television broadcasts, and advertisements.

Writers develop fiction and nonfiction ideas for plays, novels, poems, and other related works; report, analyze, and interpret facts, events, and personalities; review art, music, drama, and other artistic presentations; and persuade the general public to choose or favor certain goods, services, and personalities. There are approximately 183,000 salaried writers, authors, and technical writers employed in the United States.

HISTORY

The skill of writing has existed for thousands of years. Papyrus fragments with writing by ancient Egyptians date from about 3000

B.C., and archaeological findings show that the Chinese had developed books by about 1300 B.C. A number of technical obstacles had to be overcome before printing and the profession of writing evolved. Books of the Middle Ages were copied by hand on parchment. The ornate style that marked these books helped ensure their rarity. Also, few people were able to read. Religious fervor prohibited the reproduction of secular literature.

Two factors helped create the publishing industry: the invention of the printing press by Johan Gutenberg (ca. 1397–1468) in the middle of the 15th century and the liberalism of the Protestant Reformation, which helped encourage a wider range of publications, greater literacy, and the creation of a number of works of literary merit. The first authors worked directly with printers.

The modern publishing age began in the 18th century. Printing became mechanized, and the novel, magazine, and newspaper developed. The first newspaper in the American colonies appeared in the early 18th century, but it was Benjamin Franklin (1706–1790) who, as editor and writer, made the *Pennsylvania Gazette* one of the most influential by setting a high standard for his fellow American journalists. Franklin also published the first magazine in the colonies, *The American Magazine,* in 1741.

Advances in the printing trades, photoengraving, retailing, and the availability of capital produced a boom in newspapers and magazines in the 19th century. Further mechanization in the printing field, such as the use of the Linotype machine, high-speed rotary presses, and special color reproduction processes, set the stage for still further growth in the book, newspaper, and magazine industry.

In addition to the print media, the broadcasting industry has contributed to the development of the professional writer. Film, radio, and television are sources of entertainment, information, and education that provide employment for thousands of writers.

THE JOB

Writers work in the field of communications. Specifically, they deal with the written word, whether it is destined for the printed page, broadcast, computer screen, or live theater. The nature of their work is as varied as the materials they produce: books, magazines, trade journals, newspapers, technical reports, company newsletters and other publications, advertisements, speeches, scripts for motion picture and stage productions, and scripts for radio and television broadcast. Writers develop ideas and write for all media.

Prose writers for newspapers, magazines, and books share many of the same duties. First they come up with an idea for an article or book from their own interests or are assigned a topic by an editor. The topic is of relevance to the particular publication; for example, a writer for a magazine on parenting may be assigned an article on car seat safety. Then writers begin gathering as much information as possible about the subject through library research, interviews, the Internet, observation, and other methods. They keep extensive notes from which they will draw material for their project. Once the material has been organized and arranged in logical sequence, writers prepare a written outline. The process of developing a piece of writing is exciting, although it can also involve detailed and solitary work. After researching an idea, a writer might discover that a different perspective or related topic would be more effective, entertaining, or marketable.

When working on assignment, writers submit their outlines to an editor or other company representative for approval. Then they write a first draft of the manuscript, trying to put the material into words that will have the desired effect on their audience. They often rewrite or polish sections of the material as they proceed, always searching for just the right way of imparting information or expressing an idea or opinion. A manuscript may be reviewed, corrected, and revised numerous times before a final copy is submitted. Even after that, an editor may request additional changes.

Writers for newspapers, magazines, or books often specialize in their subject matter. Some writers might have an educational background that allows them to give critical interpretations or analyses. For example, a health or science writer for a newspaper typically has a degree in biology and can interpret new ideas in the field for the average reader.

Columnists or *commentators* analyze news and social issues. They write about events from the standpoint of their own experience or opinion. *Critics* review literary, musical, or artistic works and performances. *Editorial writers* write on topics of public interest, and their comments, consistent with the viewpoints and policies of their employers, are intended to stimulate or mold public opinion. *Newswriters* work for newspapers, radio, or TV news departments, writing news stories from notes supplied by reporters or wire services.

Corporate writers and writers for nonprofit organizations have a wide variety of responsibilities. These writers may work in such places as a large insurance corporation or for a small nonprofit religious group, where they may be required to write news releases, annual reports, speeches for the company head, or public relations materials. Typically they are assigned a topic with length requirements for a given project. They may receive raw research materials, such as statistics, and they are expected to conduct additional research, including personal interviews. These writers must be able to write quickly and accurately on short deadlines, while also working with people whose primary job is not in the communications field. The written work is submitted to a supervisor and often a legal department for approval; rewrites are a normal part of this job.

Copywriters write copy that is primarily designed to sell goods and services. Their work appears as advertisements in newspapers, magazines, and other publications or as commercials on radio and television broadcasts. Sales and marketing representatives first provide information on the product and help determine the style and length of the copy. The copywriters conduct additional research and interviews; to formulate an effective approach, they study advertising trends and review surveys of consumer preferences. Armed with this information, copywriters write a draft that is submitted to the account executive and the client for approval. The copy is often returned for correction and revision until everyone involved is satisfied. Copywriters, like corporate writers, may also write articles, bulletins, news releases, sales letters, speeches, and other related informative and promotional material. Many copywriters are employed in advertising agencies. They also may work for public relations firms or in communications departments of large companies.

Technical writers can be divided into two main groups: those who convert technical information into material for the general public, and those who convey technical information between professionals. Technical writers in the first group may prepare service manuals or handbooks, instruction or repair booklets, or sales literature or brochures; those in the second group may write grant proposals, research reports, contract specifications, or research abstracts.

Screenwriters prepare scripts for motion pictures or television. They select or are assigned a subject, conduct research, write and submit a plot outline and narrative synopsis (treatment), and confer with the producer and/or director about possible revisions. Screenwriters may adapt books or plays for film and television dramatizations. They often collaborate with other screenwriters and may specialize in a particular type of script or writing.

Playwrights do similar writing for the stage. They write dialogue and describe action for plays that may be tragedies, comedies, or dramas, with themes sometimes adapted from fictional, historical, or narrative sources. Playwrights combine the elements of action, conflict, purpose, and resolution to depict events from real or imaginary life. They often make revisions even while the play is in rehearsal.

Continuity writers prepare the material read by radio and television announcers to introduce or connect various parts of their programs.

Novelists and *short story writers* create stories that may be published in books, magazines, or literary journals. They take incidents from their own lives, from news events, or from their imaginations and create characters, settings, actions, and resolutions. *Poets* create narrative, dramatic, or lyric poetry for books, magazines, or other publications, as well as for special events such as commemorations. These writers may work with literary agents or editors who help guide them through the writing process, which includes research of the subject matter and an understanding of the intended audience. Many universities and colleges offer graduate degrees in creative writing. In these programs, students work intensively with published writers to learn the art of storytelling.

Writers can be employed either as in-house staff or as freelancers. Pay varies according to experience and the position, but freelancers must provide their own office space and equipment such as computers and fax machines. Freelancers also are responsible for keeping tax records, sending out invoices, negotiating contracts, and providing their own health insurance.

Trade Magazines for Communications Majors

Advertising Age
  http://www.adage.com

Broadcast Engineering
  http://www.broadcastengineering.com

Broadcasting and Cable
  http://www.broadcastingcable.com

Communicator
  http://www.rtnda.org/communicator/current.shtml

TelevisionWeek
  http://www.tvweek.com

(continues)

Trade Magazines for Communications Majors
(continued)

Industry Standard (online only)
http://www.thestandard.com

Media Central
http://www.mediacentral.com

Multichannel News
http://www.multichannel.com

Public Relations Strategist
http://www.prsa.org/_Publications

Publishers Weekly
http://www.publishersweekly.com

Radio Business Report
http://www.rbr.com

Radio Ink
http://www.radioink.com

Radio & Records
http://www.rronline.com

Radio World
http://www.rwonline.com

Street & Smith's SportsBusiness Journal
http://www.sportsbusinessjournal.com

TV Technology
http://www.tvtechnology.com

REQUIREMENTS
High School

While in high school, build a broad educational foundation by taking courses in English, literature, foreign languages, general science, social studies, computer science, and typing. The ability to type is almost a requisite for all positions in the communications field, as is familiarity with computers.

Postsecondary Training

Competition for writing jobs almost always demands the background of a college education. Many employers prefer you have a broad liberal arts background or majors in English, literature, history, philosophy, or one of the social sciences. Other employers desire communications or journalism training in college. Occasionally a master's degree in a specialized writing field may be required. A number of schools offer courses in journalism, and some of them offer courses or majors in book publishing, publication management, and newspaper and magazine writing.

In addition to formal course work, most employers look for practical writing experience. If you have served on high school or college newspapers, yearbooks, or literary magazines, you will make a better candidate, as well as if you have worked for small community newspapers or radio stations, even in an unpaid position. Many book publishers, magazines, newspapers, and radio and television stations have summer internship programs that provide valuable training if you want to learn about the publishing and broadcasting businesses. Interns do many simple tasks, such as running errands and answering phones, but some may be asked to perform research, conduct interviews, or even write some minor pieces.

Writers who specialize in technical fields may need degrees, concentrated course work, or experience in specific subject areas. This applies frequently to engineering, business, or one of the sciences. Also, technical communications is a degree now offered at many universities and colleges.

If you wish to enter positions with the federal government, you will have to take a civil service examination and meet certain specified requirements, according to the type and level of position.

Other Requirements

To be a writer, you should be creative and able to express ideas clearly, have a broad general knowledge, be skilled in research techniques, and be computer literate. Other assets include curiosity, persistence, initiative, resourcefulness, and an accurate memory. For some jobs—on a newspaper, for example, where the activity is hectic and deadlines are short—the ability to concentrate and produce under pressure is essential.

EXPLORING

As a high school or college student, you can test your interest and aptitude in the field of writing by serving as a reporter or writer on school newspapers, yearbooks, and literary magazines. Various writing courses and workshops will offer you the opportunity to sharpen your writing skills.

Small community newspapers and local radio stations often welcome contributions from outside sources, although they may not have the resources to pay for them. Jobs in bookstores, magazine shops, and even newsstands will offer you a chance to become familiar with various publications.

You can also obtain information on writing as a career by visiting local newspapers, publishers, or radio and television stations and interviewing some of the writers who work there. Career conferences and other guidance programs frequently include speakers on the entire field of communications from local or national organizations.

EMPLOYERS

There are approximately 126,000 writers and authors, and 57,000 technical writers currently employed in the United States. Nearly a fourth of salaried writers and editors work for newspapers, magazines, and book publishers, according to the *Occupational Outlook Handbook*. Writers are also employed by advertising agencies and public relations firms, in radio and television broadcasting, and for journals and newsletters published by business and nonprofit organizations, such as professional associations, labor unions, and religious organizations. Other employers are government agencies and film production companies.

STARTING OUT

A fair amount of experience is required to gain a high-level position in the field. Most writers start out in entry-level positions. These jobs may be listed with college placement offices, or they may be obtained by applying directly to the employment departments of the individual publishers or broadcasting companies. Graduates who previously served internships with these companies often have the advantage of knowing someone who can give them a personal recommendation. Want ads in newspapers and trade journals are another source for jobs. Because of the competition for positions, however, few vacancies are listed with public or private employment agencies.

Employers in the communications field usually are interested in samples of published writing. These are often assembled in an organized portfolio or scrapbook. Bylined or signed articles are more credible (and, as a result, more useful) than stories whose source is not identified.

Beginning positions as a junior writer usually involve library research, preparation of rough drafts for part or all of a report, cataloging, and other related writing tasks. These are generally carried on under the supervision of a senior writer.

Some technical writers have entered the field after working in public relations departments or as technicians or research assistants, then transferring to technical writing as openings occur. Many firms now hire writers directly upon application or recommendation of college professors and placement offices.

ADVANCEMENT

Most writers find their first jobs as editorial or production assistants. Advancement may be more rapid in small companies, where beginners learn by doing a little bit of everything and may be given writing tasks immediately. In large firms, duties are usually more compartmentalized. Assistants in entry-level positions are assigned such tasks as research, fact checking, and copyrighting, but it generally takes much longer to advance to full-scale writing duties.

Promotion into more responsible positions may come with the assignment of more important articles and stories to write, or it may be the result of moving to another company. Mobility among employees in this field is common. An assistant in one publishing house may switch to an executive position in another. Or a writer may switch to a related field as a type of advancement.

A technical writer can be promoted to positions of responsibility by moving from such jobs as writer to technical editor to project leader or documentation manager. Opportunities in specialized positions also are possible.

Freelance or self-employed writers earn advancement in the form of larger fees as they gain exposure and establish their reputations.

EARNINGS

In 2001, median annual earnings for salaried writers and authors were $42,450 a year, according to the Bureau of Labor Statistics. The lowest 10 percent earned less than $20,570, while the highest 10 percent earned $83,180 or more. In book publishing, some specialties pay better than others. Technical writers earned a median salary of $49,370 in 2001.

In addition to their salaries, many writers earn some income from freelance work. Part-time freelancers may earn from $5,000 to $15,000 a year. Freelance earnings vary widely. Full-time established freelance writers may earn up to $75,000 a year.

WORK ENVIRONMENT

Working conditions vary for writers. Although their workweek usually runs 35 to 40 hours, many writers work overtime. A publication that is issued frequently has more deadlines closer together, creating greater pressures to meet them. The work is especially hectic on newspapers and at broadcasting companies, which operate seven days a week. Writers often work nights and weekends to meet deadlines or to cover a late-developing story.

Most writers work independently, but they often must cooperate with artists, photographers, rewriters, and advertising people who may have widely differing ideas of how the materials should be prepared and presented.

Physical surroundings range from comfortable private offices to noisy, crowded newsrooms filled with other workers typing and talking on the telephone. Some writers must confine their research to the library or telephone interviews, but others may travel to other cities or countries or to local sites, such as theaters, ballparks, airports, factories, or other offices.

The work is arduous, but most writers are seldom bored. Some jobs, such as that of the foreign correspondent, require travel. The most difficult element is the continual pressure of deadlines. People who are the most content as writers enjoy and work well with deadline pressure.

OUTLOOK

The employment of writers is expected to increase faster than the average rate of all occupations over the next several years, according to the U.S. Department of Labor. The demand for writers by newspapers, periodicals, book publishers, and nonprofit organizations is expected to increase. The growth of online publishing on company Web sites and other online services will also demand many talented writers; those with computer skills will be at an advantage as a result. Advertising and public relations will also provide job opportunities.

The major book and magazine publishers, broadcasting companies, advertising agencies, public relations firms, and the federal government account for the concentration of writers in large cities such as New York, Chicago, Los Angeles, Boston, Philadelphia, San Francisco, and Washington, D.C. Opportunities with small newspapers, corporations, and professional, religious, business, technical, and trade publications can be found throughout the country.

People entering this field should realize that the competition for jobs is extremely keen. Beginners may especially have difficulty finding employment. Of the thousands who graduate each year with degrees in English, journalism, communications, and the liberal arts, intending to establish a career as a writer, many turn to other occupations when they find that applicants far outnumber the job openings available. College students would do well to keep this in mind and prepare for an unrelated alternate career in the event they are unable to obtain a position as writer; another benefit of this approach is that, at the same time, they will become qualified as writers in a specialized field. The practicality of preparing for alternate careers is borne out by the fact that opportunities are best in firms that prepare business and trade publications and in technical writing.

Potential writers who end up working in a different field may be able to earn some income as freelancers, selling articles, stories, books, and possibly TV and movie scripts, but it is usually difficult for anyone to be self-supporting entirely on independent writing.

FOR MORE INFORMATION

For information on writing and editing careers in the field of communications, contact:

National Association of Science Writers
PO Box 890
Hedgesville, WV 25427
Tel: 304-754-5077
http://www.nasw.org

This organization offers student memberships for those interested in opinion writing.

National Conference of Editorial Writers
3899 North Front Street
Harrisburg, PA 17110
Tel: 717-703-3015
Email: ncew@pa-news.org
http://www.ncew.org

bad break: a break in the flow of text that is visually unappealing or misleading

baselines: the lines at the bottom of a text box in print design that appear in the electronic display of a page but do not print

blueprints or "blues": made from the negatives that are to be used in final printing, these are photographic prints of books that editors scan to check content accuracy.

broadband: the high-speed transmission of data, voice, and video signals over a single medium; cable's broadband provides viewers with access to interactive television, digital networks, and other advanced services.

broadside: also referred to as **landscape,** a broadside page in a book is one that can be read normally when the book is turned 90 degrees.

call letters: used for a broadcast station's identification, call letters usually have geographical or format significance.

color separations: used in the color printing process, these allow publishers and other print media professionals to print separate plates for each color page to achieve the best possible color

copyfitting: the process of estimating space and photo measurements, deleting or adding text, graphics, or photos so that a specified space is filled and is visually appealing

copyright ownership: the rights to reproduce and distribute a publication, whether it is a literary, dramatic, artistic, musical, or other work; the U.S. Copyright Office is a government agency.

digital television (DTV): different from regular analog television, DTV broadcasters send their signals to viewers digitally, which results in much higher quality audio and video

double truck: a feature story in a newspaper that spans two pages that face each other

dummy: an unprinted sample of a book, newspaper, or magazine page that is prepared as a guide for the typesetter or production worker in charge of space restrictions

Electronic News Gathering (ENG): a combination of methods of collecting newsworthy information, including the use of video and audio equipment

Emergency Alert System (EAS): the broadcast system that alerts the public to emergency situations; implemented by the Federal Communications Commission in 1994, replacing the Emergency Broadcast System

end matter: also referred to as **back matter,** the section at the end of a book that contains notes, indexes, and bibliographic information

Federal Communications Commission (FCC): established by the Communications Act of 1934, this is a government agency in charge of regulating communications via radio, television, wire, satellite, and cable

folio: page numbers of a book, newspaper, magazine, or other publication

format: in broadcasting media, refers to the type of music program, such as country or rap; in print media, refers to the style and general appearance of a publication, such as newsletter or book.

freelancer: an independent writer or editor who does work for a company on a contract basis

front matter: also referred to as **preliminaries,** this section is the first in a book and usually contains title page, copyright information, acknowledgements, and other information

gutter: the two inner margins of a book page, or the space between columns in a newspaper

house style: a compilation of style requirements to be used universally by a publishing house

ISBN: International Standard Book Number, which is printed in a book's front matter and is a way to quickly reference the publisher and title

kerning: adjusting space between words and letters so text fits better on a page

layout: the design of a book, magazine, or newspaper page; includes all fonts, type sizes, and spacing measurements that are specified by the designer or editor.

libel: injury to reputation in the written form

markup: process of putting editorial corrections and directions on a story, script, or other piece of writing

obscenities, profanities, and vulgarities: terms or phrases that are not to be used on-air or in stories because they are potentially offensive

pica: a measurement of space on a page (book, newspaper, or other) that equals 12 points

plagiarism: the act of stealing or copying existing information and presenting it as one's own original ideas

point: the basic unit of measurement for a designer; approximately 1/72 of an inch.

press conference: also referred to as a **news conference,** this is a gathering in which a specific news topic is made public and explained to the media

press release: document that is made public for the purpose of informing the media and the general public; often used to introduce new products and to announce upcoming events.

press run: the number of copies printed (applies to newspapers, magazines, books, etc.)

proofreaders' marks: instructions in the form of symbols that tell editors what corrections to make to text

proofs: a print copy of a work to be published

pull quote: quoted sentence or phrase taken from the text of an article and presented in larger, more pronounced type style, used to emphasize a point or to fill space

Radio Data System (RDS): function of a radio receiver that provides the listener with an alpha-numerical display of information about a broadcast (including the program name, the musical genre, and additional information)

recto: the right-hand page of a book; text traditionally starts on a recto page

rules: lines on software programs that guide designers in the placement of copy, but which do not show up when the work is printed

sans serif: also referred to as **Gothic type,** this font has no tails or extra curves in the style of lettering

satellite radio: a fairly new form of radio access that is made possible by satellites placed in orbit more than 22,000 miles above the Earth; signals are bounced off the satellites to radio receivers on the ground, which unscramble the digital messages into clear audio information for hundreds of stations.

serif: typefaces, such as **Roman type,** that are more decorative and include tails and curves in their lettering

signature: sheets of a book that are folded and ready to be sewn, usually 32 pages, but can also be 16, 8, or even four pages

spine: the part of a book that is visible when it is shelved; the spine is also referred to as the **backbone** and usually contains title, author's name, and publisher's name

stop set: commercial break in a broadcast

typeface: the style of lettering, such as Times Roman or Courier New

V-Chip: an electronic device built into most new televisions that allows parents to block television programs that they don't want their children to see

verso: the left-hand page in a book

widows and orphans: widows are short paragraph-ending lines that appear at the top of a column, and orphans are short-paragraph ending lines that appear at the bottom of a column; both occur when paragraphs are poorly spaced, are not visually appealing, and constitute poor design.

Sources: *AP Stylebook, Chicago Manual of Style,* and the *Dictionary of Literary Terms and Literary Theory*

The following books provide additional information on communications careers, college admissions, graduate programs, resumes, and job interviews.

Bowerman, Peter. *The Well-Fed Writer: Financial Self-Sufficiency as a Freelance Writer in Six Months or Less.* Atlanta: Fanove, 2000.

Field, Shelly. *Career Opportunities in Advertising and Public Relations.* New York: Facts On File, 2002.

Fry, Ronald. *101 Great Answers to the Toughest Interview Questions.* Franklin Lakes, N.J.: Career Press, 2000.

Guide to College Majors: Everything You Need to Know to Choose the Right Major. New York: Princeton Review, 2002.

Hedrick, Tom, Mike McKenzie, and Joe Castiglione. *The Art of Sportscasting: How to Build a Successful Career.* South Bend, Ind.: Diamond Communications, 2000.

Jerrard, Richard, and Margot Jerrard. *The Grad School Handbook: An Insider's Guide to Getting in and Succeeding.* New York: Perigee, 1998.

Johnston, Susan M. *The Career Adventure: Your Guide to Personal Assessment, Career Exploration, and Decision Making.* 3rd ed. Upper Saddle Rive, N.J.: Prentice Hall, 2001.

McKinney, Anne, ed. *Real Resumes for Media, Newspaper, Broadcasting and Public Affairs Jobs.* Fayetteville, N.C.: PREP, 2002.

Reed, Maxine K., and Robert R. Reed. *Career Opportunities in Television, Cable, and Video.* 4th ed. New York: Facts On File, 1999.

Rubinstein, Ellen. *Scoring a Great Internship (Students Helping Students).* New York: Natavi Guides, 2002.

Tullier, L. Michelle. *Networking for Everyone.* Indianapolis, Ind.: Jist Works, 1998.

Wagner, Lilya. *Careers in Fundraising.* Hoboken, N.J.: Wiley, 2001.

Weaver, Dan, and Jason Siegel. *Peterson's Breaking into Television: Proven Advice for Veterans and Interns.* Princeton, N.J.: Peterson's Guides, 1998.

Wendleton, Kate, and Wendy Alfus Rothman. *Targeting the Job You Want.* 3rd ed. Franklin Lakes, N.J.: Career Press, 2000.

Page numbers in **bold** denote major treatment of a topic.

A

advertising account executives 49–55
advancement 53
categories 50–51
earnings 53
employers 52
exploration 52
high school/postsecondary training 51
overview/history 49–50
requirements 51–52
work environment/outlook 53–54
Advertising Age 8
advertising workers 56–67
advancement 63–64
categories 57–60
earnings 64–65
employers 62–63
exploration 62
high school/postsecondary training 60–61
overview/history 56–57
requirements 60–62
work environment/outlook 65–66
Agency for Healthcare Research and Quality (AHCPR) 245
American Advertising Federation (AAF) 54, 66, 180
American Association of Advertising Agencies (AAAA) 54–55, 66–67, 180
American Association of Fundraising Counsel (AAFRC) 140
American Association of Political Consultants (AAPC) 202
American Association of University Administrators (AAUA) 94
American Association of University Professors (AAUP) 263
American Cinema Editors (ACE) 318
American College Testing (ACT) program 11
American Federation of Teachers (AFT) 263
American Job Fairs 30
American League of Lobbyists 161
American Marketing Association (AMA) 55, 67
American Medical Writers Association (AMWA) 254
American Meteorological Society (AMS) 354
American Society of Association Executives (ASAE) 161
American Society of Journalists and Authors (ASJA) 8, 100, 132
American Society of Newspaper Editors (ASNE) 194
American Society of Travel Agents (ASTA) 344
announcers 68–78
advancement 75
categories 69–70, 72
earnings 75–76
employers 74
exploration 74
high school/postsecondary training 72–73
overview/history 68–69
requirements 72–74
work environment/outlook 76–77
Armed Services Vocational Aptitude Battery (ASVAB) 12
Art Directors Club (ADC) 67
Ask the Interview Coach 45
assessment tests 11–12
Association for Authors' Representatives (AAR) 153
Association for Education in Journalism and Mass Communication (AEJMC) 100, 132, 235
Association of American Publishers 85
Association of Executive Search Consultants (AESC) 125
Association of Fundraising Professionals (AFP) 140
Association of Local Television Stations 77

B

book editors 79–86
  advancement 84
  categories 80–82
  earnings 84–85
  employers 83
  exploration 83
  high school/postsecondary
    training 82
  overview/history 79–80
  requirements 82–83
  work environment/outlook
    84, 85
Broadcast Education Association
  (BEA) 77, 108, 219, 224, 274, 333
broadcasting, advances 71
broadcast television companies
  (top 10) 305

C

cable companies (top 10) 330
campus visits 19–20
Canadian Public Relations
  Society, Inc. (CPRS) 187, 211
Certified Fundraising Executive
  (CFRE) International 141
Chronicle of Philanthropy, the 141
CineMedia 310
college
  contact 19
  degree, need 3
  fairs 18–19
  freshman, entries 15–16
  recruiters 18
  selection 16
college administrators 87–94
  advancement 92
  categories 88–89
  earnings 92–93
  employers 91
  exploration 91, 92
  high school/postsecondary training
    89–90
  overview/history 87–88
  requirements 89–90
  work environment/outlook 93
College and University Professional
  Association for Human Resources
  (CUPAHR) 94

College Board 20
columnists 95–100
  advancement 98
  categories 96
  earnings 98–99
  employers 98
  exploration 97–98
  high school/postsecondary training
    97
  overview/history 95–96
  requirements 97
  work environment/outlook 99–100
communications
  courses 6
  curriculum 7
  definition 7
  degree, usage 33
  exploration 23–24
  field, careers 13
  graduates, advice 17, 26
  job market 13
  program, expectations 12
communications major 7
  advice 13, 29
  course suggestions 21–22
  jobs 28
  personal/professional qualities 12,
    28–29
  trade magazines 359–360
Communications Roundtable 9, 24
connections, usage 27
corporate recruiters 30
Council of Public Relations Firms 9
cover letter 37–38

D

Direct Marketing Educational
  Foundation (DMA) 67
Directors Guild of America (DGA) 310,
  327
disc jockeys 101–109
  advancement 106
  categories 102, 104
  earnings 106–107
  employers 105–106
  exploration 105
  high school/postsecondary training
    104
  overview/history 101–102

requirements 104–105
work environment/outlook 107–108
Dow Jones Newspaper Fund 24, 194, 235

E

earnings 8
event planners 110–118
  advancement 116
  categories 111–113
  certification/licensing 114
  earnings 116
  employers 115
  exploration 114–115
  high school/postsecondary training 113–114
  overview/history 110–111
  requirements 113–114
  work environment/outlook 116–117
executive recruiters 119–125
  advancement 123
  categories 120–121
  certification/licensing 122
  earnings 123–124
  exploration 122–123
  high school/postsecondary training 121–122
  overview/history 119–120
  requirements 121–122
  work environment/outlook 124

F

Federal Communications Commission (FCC) 219, 274
foreign correspondents 126–133
  advancement 131
  categories 127–128
  earnings 131
  employers 130
  exploration 130
  high school/postsecondary training 128
  overview/history 126–127
  requirements 128–129
  work environment/outlook 131–132
fund-raisers 134–141
  advancement 139
  categories 135–137
  certification/licensing 137
  earnings 139
  employers 138
  exploration 138
  high school/postsecondary training 137
  overview/history 134–135
  requirements 137–138
  work environment/outlook 139–140

G

global public relations firms (top 10) 207
graduate school 45–46
Graduate School Guide 46
Graduate Schools and Programs (Peterson's) 46
Graphic Artists Guild (GAG) 67
Graduate School Directory of Communications Studies 46
guidance counselors 16

H

Health Advocacy Program 148
health advocates 142–148
  advancement 147
  categories 143–144
  earnings 147
  employers 146
  exploration 145–146
  high school/postsecondary training 144–145
  overview/history 142–143
  requirements 144–145
  work environment/outlook 147–148
high school
  course suggestion 10
Hollywood Reporter 328

I

information interviewing 31–32
  tutorial 32
Institute of Certified Travel Agents (ICTA) 344
Institute of Political Journalism 327

International Alliance of Theatrical
Stage Employees, Moving Picture
Technicians, Artists and Allied Crafts
of the United States and Canada
(IATSE) 318
International Association for
Exposition Management (IAEM) 117
International Association of Assembly
Managers (IAAM) 117
International Association of Business
Communicators 186–187, 211
International Radio and Television
Society (IRTS) 310
Internet surfing 40–41
internships 27
    participation 17, 25, 43–44
interview
    homework 41
    prescription 41–43
    punctuality 42
    questions 42

J

Job Fair, Inc. 31
jobs
    exploration 14–15
    fairs 30
    market, expectations 29
    online application 40–41
    search, acceleration 34
    training 27
    usage 45
JobWeb Guide to Resumes and
Interviews 40

K

Kennedy Information 125
Kuder Career Planning System 11

L

literary agents 149–161
    advancement 152
    categories 150
    earnings 152
    employers 151
    exploration 151
    high school/postsecondary training
    150–151

    overview/history 149–150
    requirements 150–151
    work environment/outlook 152–153
lobbyists 154–161
    advancement 160
    categories 155–157
    certification/licensing 158
    earnings 160
    employers 159
    exploration 158–159
    high school/postsecondary training
    157–158
    overview/history 154–155
    requirements 157–158
    work environment/outlook 160–161

M

magazine companies (top 10) 165
magazine editors 162–168
    advancement 166
    categories 163–164
    earnings 167
    employers 166
    exploration 166
    high school/postsecondary training
    164–165
    overview/history 162–163
    requirements 164–166
    work environment/outlook 167–168
Magazine Publishers of America 168
media companies (top 25) 129
media, diversity 173–174
media planning/buyers 169–180
    advancement 177
    categories 170–172
    earnings 177–178
    employers 176
    exploration 175–176
    high school/postsecondary training
    174–175
    overview/history 169–170
    requirements 174–175
    work environment/outlook 178–179
media relations specialists 181–187
    advancement 185
    categories 182–183
    certification/licensing 184
    earnings 185–186
    employers 185
    exploration 184

high school/postsecondary training
183–184
overview/history 181–182
requirements 183–184
work environment/outlook 186
Meeting Professionals International
(MPI) 118
minor, inclusion 22
Monster Interview Center 45
Myers-Briggs Type Indicator 11

N

National Academy of Television Arts
and Sciences (NATAS) 318
National Association of Broadcast
Employees and Technicians (NABET)
77, 109, 219
National Association of Broadcasters
(NAB) 77, 100, 108, 132–133, 202, 219,
224–225, 274, 334
National Association of Executive
Recruiters (NAER) 125
National Association of Farm
Broadcasters (NAFB) 78
National Association of Science
Writers, Inc. (NASW) 255, 300, 365
National Cable Television Association
(NCTA) 78, 334
National Communication Association
(NATCOM) 263
National Conference of Editorial
Writers (NCEW) 365
National Council for Accreditation of
Teacher Education (NCATE) 263
National Education Association (NEA)
263
National Institutes of Health (NIH)
245
National Newspaper Publishers
Association (NNPA) 194
National Oceanic and Atmospheric
Administration (NOAA) 354
National Weather Association (NWA)
354
National Weather Service (NWS) 354
networking 34–35
news director
advice 44
duties 43
personal/professional qualities 44

Newspaper Association of America
(NAA) 235, 288
newspaper companies (top 10) 229
newspaper editors 188–195
advancement 192–193
categories 189–190
earnings 193
employers 192
exploration 192
high school/postsecondary training
191
overview/history 188–189
requirements 191
work environment/outlook 193–194
Newspaper Guild, The 288

P

Pew Research Center for the People
and the Press 203
press secretaries 196–203
advancement 201
categories 197–198
earnings 201
employers 200
exploration 199–200
high school/postsecondary training
198–199
overview/history 196–197
requirements 198–199
work environment/outlook
201–202
Princeton Review 20
Producers Guild of America 327
Professional Convention Management
Association (PCMA) 118
Public Relations Society of America
(PRSA) 187, 211, 279
public relations specialists 204–211
advancement 209
categories 205–206
certification/licensing 208
earnings 209–210
employers 208–209
exploration 208
high school/postsecondary training
206–208
overview/history 204–205
requirements 206–208
work environment/outlook
210–211

Publishers Marketing Association
(PMA) 85
Publishers Weekly 153

R

radio markets (top 50) 103
radio producers 212–219
  advancement 217
  categories 213–215
  earnings 217
  employers 216–217
  exploration 216
  high school/postsecondary training
    215–216
  overview/history 212–213
  requirements 215–216
  work environment/outlook 218
radio program directors 220–225
  advancement 223
  categories 221
  earnings 223
  employers 222–223
  exploration 222
  high school/postsecondary training
    221–222
  overview/history 220
  requirements 221–222
  work environment/outlook
    223–224
Radio-Television News Directors
  Association (RTNDA) 78, 109, 219,
  225, 274, 310, 328, 334
reporter
  duties 17, 25
  employment outlook 17, 26
  personal/professional qualities 17,
    25–26
reporters 226–235
  advancement 232
  categories 227–229
  earnings 233
  employers 232
  exploration 231–232
  high school/postsecondary training
    230–231
  overview/history 226–227
  requirements 230–231
  work environment/outlook
    233–235

research assistants 236–245
  advancement 242
  categories 237–239
  earnings 242–243
  employers 241
  exploration 240–241
  high school/postsecondary training
    239–240
  overview/history 236–237
  requirements 239–240
  work environment/outlook 243–245
resume
  advice 38–39
  content 35–36
  creation 35–38
  editing 36
  format 36
  versions, creation 36–37
Resume Place, Inc. 40

S

Scholastic Aptitude Test (SAT) 11
science/medical writers 246–255
  advancement 253
  categories 247–249
  certification/licensing 250
  earnings 253
  employers 251–252
  exploration 251
  high school/postsecondary require-
    ments 249–250
  overview/history 246–247
  requirements 249–251
  work environment/outlook 253–254
situational interview 44–45
Small Publishers Association of North
  American (SPAN) 86
Society for Healthcare Consumer
  Advocacy (SHCA) 148
Society for Technical Communications
  (STC) 9, 255, 300
Society of Government Travel
  Professionals 345
Society of Professional Journalists (SPJ)
  100, 133, 195
speech teachers 256–263
  advancement 261
  categories 257–258
  certification/licensing 259

earnings 261–262
employers 260
exploration 260
high school/postsecondary training
258–259
overview/history 256–257
requirements 258–260
work environment/outlook 262–263
**sports broadcasters/announcers
264–274**
advancement 272
categories 266–268
earnings 272–273
employers 271
exploration 270–271
high school/postsecondary training
268, 270
overview/history 264–266
requirements 268, 270
work environment/outlook 273–274
sports publicists 275–279
advancement 278
categories 276–277
certification/licensing 277
earnings 279
employers 278
exploration 278
high school/postsecondary training
277
overview/history 275–276
requirements 277
work environment/outlook 279
sportswriters 280–288
advancement 286–287
categories 281–283
earnings 287
employers 285
exploration 284–285
high school/postsecondary training
283–284
overview/history 280–281
requirements 283–284
work environment/outlook 287–288

T
technical writers/editors 289–300
advancement 297–298
categories 291–294
earnings 298

employers 296
exploration 296
high school/postsecondary training
294–295
overview/history 289–291
requirements 294–295
work environment/outlook 298–300
television directors 301–310
advancement 308
categories 303–304
earnings 308
employers 307
exploration 307
high school/postsecondary training
305–306
overview/history 301–303
requirements 305–307
work environment/outlook
308–309
television editors 311–318
advancement 316
categories 312–313
earnings 316–317
employers 315
exploration 315
high school/postsecondary training
313–314
overview/history 311–312
requirements 313–314
work environment/outlook
317–318
television markets (top 50) 269
television producers 319–328
advancement 325
categories 320–322
earnings 325–326
employers 324–325
exploration 324
high school/postsecondary training
322–323
overview/history 319–320
requirements 322–324
work environment/outlook
326–327
television program directors 329–334
advancement 332
categories 330–331
earnings 332–333
employers 332
exploration 331–332

television program directors *(continued)*
   high school/postsecondary training
      331
   overview/history 329
   requirements 331
   work environment/outlook 333
travel agents 335–345
   advancement 342
   categories 336–338
   certification/licensing 339–340
   earnings 342–343
   employers 341
   exploration 340–341
   high school/postsecondary training
      338–339
   overview/history 335–336
   requirements 338–340
   work environment/outlook 343–344
Travel Industry Association of America
   (TIA) 345

U

University of Pennsylvania, School for
   Arts and Sciences 245
U.S. Census Bureau 245
U.S. House of Representatives 202
U.S. Senate 202

W

weather forecasters 346–354
   advancement 352
   categories 347–349
   certification/licensing 350
   earnings 352
   employers 351
   exploration 350–351
   high school/postsecondary training
      349–350
   overview/history 346–347
   requirements 349–350
   work environment/outlook 352–353
workforce, preparation 26–28
work, location 8
writers 355–365
   advancement 363
   categories 356–359
   earnings 363
   employers 362
   exploration 361–362
   high school/postsecondary training
      360–361
   overview/history 355–356
   requirements 360–361
   work environment/outlook 364–365
Writers Write 9
WW2010 354